Marietta Holley

My opinions and Betsy Bobbet's

Marietta Holley

**My opinions and Betsy Bobbet's**

ISBN/EAN: 9783337267223

Printed in Europe, USA, Canada, Australia, Japan

Cover: Foto ©ninafisch / pixelio.de

More available books at **www.hansebooks.com**

MR. DIBBET TELLS NEWS

# MY OPINIONS

## AND

# BETSEY BOBBET'S.

### DESIGNED AS
### A BEACON LIGHT,
TO GUIDE WOMEN TO LIFE LIBERTY AND THE PURSUIT OF HAPPINESS,
BUT WHICH MAY BE READ BY
MEMBERS OF THE STERNER SECT,
WITHOUT INJURY TO THEMSELVES
OR THE BOOK.

---

BY

JOSIAH ALLEN'S WIFE.

---

*"Who will read the Book, Samantha, when it is rote?"*

---

PUBLISHED BY SUBSCRIPTION ONLY,

---

HARTFORD, CONN.:
AMERICAN PUBLISHING COMPANY.
W. E. BLISS & CO., TOLEDO, OHIO.   F. G. GILMAN & CO., CHICAGO, ILL.
NETTLETON & CO., CINCINNATI, OHIO.
1873.

# This Book is Dedicated

To my own Lawful Pardner,

## JOSIAH.

Whom (although I have been his Consort

for a little upwards of 14 years)

I still love with a

## CAST-IRON DEVOTEDNESS.

# PREFACE.

Which is to be read, if it haint askin' too much of the kind hearted reader.

In the first days of our married life, I strained nearly every nerve to help my companion Josiah along and take care of his children by his former consort, the subject of black African slavery also wearin' on me, and a mortgage of 200 and 50 dollars on the farm. But as we prospered and the mortgage was cleared, and the children were off to school, the black African also bein' liberated about the same time of the mortgage, then my mind bein' free from these cares—the great subject of Wimmen's Rites kept a goarin' me, and a voice kept a sayin' inside of me,

"Josiah Allen's wife, write a book givin' your views on the great subject of Wimmen's Rites." But I hung back in spirit from the idea and says I, to myself, I never went to school much and don't know nothin' about grammer, and I never could spell worth a cent."

But still that deep voice kept a 'swaiden me— "Josiah Allen's wife, write a book."

Says I, "I cant write a book, I don't know no underground dungeons, I haint acquainted with no haunted houses, I never see a hero suspended over a abyss by his gallusses, I never beheld a heroine swoon away, I never see a Injun tommy hawked, nor a ghost; I never had any of these advantages; I cant write a book."

But still it kept a sayin' inside of my mind, "Josiah Allen's wife write a book about your life, as it passes in front of you and Josiah, daily, and your views on Wimmen's Rite's. The great publick wheel is a rollin' on slowly, drawin' the Femail Race into liberty: Josiah Allen's wife, put your shoulder blades to the wheel."

And so that almost hauntin' voice inside of me kept a 'swaidin me, and finally I spoke out in a loud clear voice and answered it—

" I *will* put my shoulder blades to the wheel?"

I well remember the time I said it, for it skairt Josiah almost to death. It was night and we was both settin' by the fire relapsted into silence and he—not knowin the conversation goin' on inside of my mind, thought I was crazy, and jumped up as if he was shot, and says he, in tremblin' tones,

" What is the matter Samantha?"

Says I, " Josiah I am goin' to write a book."

This skairt him worse than ever—I could see, by his ghastly countenance—and he started off on the run for the camfire bottle.

Says I, in firm but gentle axcents, " camfire cant stop me Josiah, the book will be wrote."

He see by my pale but calm countenance, that I was not delirious any, and (by experience) he knows that when my mind is made up, I have got a firm and almost cast iron resolution. He said no more, but he sot down and sithed hevily; finally he spoke out in a despairin' tone, he is pretty close (but honest),

"Who will read the book Samantha? Remember if you write it you have got to stand the brunt of it yourself—I haint no money to hire folks with to read it." And again he sithed two or three times. And he hadn't much more than got through sithein' when he asked me again in a tone of almost agony—

"Who will read the book Samantha after you write it?"

The same question was fillin' me with agonizin' apprehension, but I concealed it and answered with almost marble calm,

"I don't know Josiah, but I am determined to put my shoulder blades to the wheel and write it."

Josiah didn't say no more then, but it wore on him—for that night in the ded of night he spoke out in his sleep in a kind of a wild way,

"Who will read the book?"

I hunched him with my elbo' to wake him up, and he muttered—"I wont pay out one cent of my money to hire any body to read it."

I pitied him, for I was afraid it would end in the Night Mair, and I waked him up, and promised him then and there, that I never would ask him to pay out one cent to hire any body to read it. He has perfect confidence in me and he brightened up and haint never said a word sense against the idea, and that is the way this book come to be wrote.

# WHAT IS IN THE BOOK.

### MARRIED TO JOSIAH ALLEN.

Livin' up to one Idee—Love at First Sight—A Marriage of Love—Why did I Love Josiah?—A Becon that has never gone out—Men can't stand Flattery—My Present feelin's towards Josiah—Objections to Widowers—Comparin' Wives—Josiah not encouraged in it—Rule for Domestic Happiness ...... 17—20

### JOSIAH AND THE CHILDREN.

A hard row for Step-Mothers—Thomas Jefferson and Tirzah Ann—Thomas J. on Foreordination—Tirzah Ann's sentiments—A Hefty Angel—Makin' excuses at table—How to make Bad Cake taste good—Our Farm on the Canal—Plenty of Garden Sass—4 Tons to the acre ............................ 21—25

### AN UNMARRIED FEMALE.

Betsey Bobbet introduced—While there is Life there is Hope of getting married—Betsey's personal appearance—Betsey's Opinions and Views of a Woman's Speah—Betsey writes Poetry—A Specimen of it—Owed to Josiah—Josiah makes a Confession and gets Rebuked—Betsey Bobbet visits me unexpectedly—Gushin's of a Tender Soul—The Editah with Twins—Weddin' Affinities........................... 26—37

### HAVIN' MY PICTURE TOOK.

Down to Jonesville—In Mr. Gansey's Aunty Room—Preparin' for a Picture—The Editer of the Augur—Daughters of Bachus and Venus—Haunts of the Graces—"Logical Reveries"—A Poem—My Picture Took .......................... 38—45

### OUR SURPRISE PARTIES.

My opinions of Surprises—I am persuaded to go—A Surprise Party Surprised—Not wanted just then—An Upset in the snow—A Peaceful Evening at home—Josiah and I enjoying ourselves Doctorin'—Our Happiness interrupted—Surprised by a Party of 50—Fearful excitement of Josiah—The Enemy retire—The Editer surprised—Betsey writes a Poem upon it...... 45—57

## WHAT IS IN THE BOOK.

### A DAY OF TROUBLES.

Sugerin' Time—Woman's work—Man's work—The Editer brings his Twins—There first doin's—The trouble begins—Betsey Bobbet arrives—I think of John Rogers and have Patience—Betsey and the twins—A Soothin' Poultice—A Argument with Betsey—I Preach and Practice—Betsey asks Advice and gets It—Betsey reads a Poem—She gets more of my Opinions—Return of the Editer—Concludes to stay to Dinner—Sees Betsey and changes his mind—Grand Tableaux by the whole company............................................. 58—6

### THE MINISTER'S BEDQULT.

Thomas J. believes in water for the Baptists—Reasons for goin' to Quiltin's—The Baptist Quiltin' Party—We dispose of all our neighbors not present—Miss Dobbin, a peacemaker—The Minister's wife discussed—Betsey Bobbet arrives—She labors under great excitement and overwhelms the party with her mysterious words—Astounding disclosures—Thomas J's story to Betsey—The story discussed—Handsome Ministers—Wimmen flingin' stuns—The Minister arrives—The mystery solved,.................................................. 69—84

### A ALLEGORY ON WIMMEN'S RIGHTS.

A Wimmen's Rights Meetin'—A Wimmen's Rights man—Idiots, Lunatics and Wimmen—The Woman sheep-stealer—Wimmen have a right to go to Prison and be Hung—Wimmen in Court—The right to go to the Hop and Cistern Poles—An anti Wimmen's Rights man—Hired Husbands—Marriage and Slavery—True Marriages—Happy Homes and Children—A Angel calling for Fire Wood,....................... 85—98

### AN AXIDENT.

Bothered by Hens—A model Pup Dog—A Fall—Very sick a-bed—"That's what's the matter"—What makes Angels—Too much of a thing—Josiah being cheerful—I use Strategim—Betsey visits me and brings her Bed-Quilt—Come to spend the day—All the Family comin'—Keepin' me quiet and Chirkin' me up—She flies in terror from my wrath—Blasted Hopes.. 99—111

### THE JONESVILLE SINGIN' QUIRE.

Worryin' about Girls and not about Boys—Wimmen's Charity for Wimmen—The Prodigal Daughter's return—What is good for a Boy is good for a Girl—A Spy in the Family—Tirzah Ann's future Marrage—Thomas J. prefers a back seat—He describes the Quire—We go up to the Rehersal—A United Quire—The Entire Orkusstree—A Artistic Duett—Josiah breaks out in Song—Betsey Remonstrates in Verse.................. 112—126

### MISS SHAKESPEARE'S EARRINGS.

Josiah gives up Singin'—Betsey feelin' lonesome, visits me—She bemoans her lone state—Betsey is willin' but the men haint—A smile or a supper—Correctin' a Husband—Woman as a runnin' vine—The Elder's Choice—The Carpet Pedler—Bound for a Trade—Bill Shakespeare's present—An affectin' story—Betsey makes a purchase—Thomas J. turns poet—Betsey shows her prize—The Minister's Wife's old Jewelry—Betsey sick at heart, goes home........................... 127—144

### A NITE OF TROUBLES.

A Serenade disturbed by Thomas J.—Musical powers of Cats—Josiah on the war-path—Another Serenade—Josiah swears—"Come, oh come with me"—Josiah shows wickedness—A "meloncholly man"—The Serenader "languishes"—An Address by Thomas J—Relics left on the field............ 145—156

### 4th OF JULY IN JONESVILLE.

The Professor's Poem—The Celebration on the field—Professor Aspire Todd—The Professor's Speech—Old Mr. Bobbet endorses the speaker—The Editer interferes—"Yes! drownd the Black Cat"—The next Speaker—An Argument Illustrated—A Wife's Devotion—Adjournment for Dinner—Toasts given—A Poem by B B—At Home Countin' the Cost—What good has it done?................................. 157—171

### SIMON SLIMPSEY'S MOURNFUL FOREBODIN'S.

Thomas J. discusses the Jews—He expresses his Opinion of Betsey's Religion—A visit from Simon Slimpsey—His appearance—A Victim of bad luck—"She'll get round me"—A Poem for Modest Wimmen, by B. B.—Slimpsey don't want to marry—Reconciled to the loss of his late Consort—Overcome by his fears for the future........................... 177—187

## WHAT IS IN THE BOOK.

### FREE LOVE LECTURES.

A Beautiful October day, good to pull Beets—Betsey gets Kissed at last—A Professor that was married some—Married Men good for some purposes—A Free Love Song—A war Cry—Professor Gusher's Visit—Peppermint recommended to the Professor for his troubles—No Yearnin' for Freedom—Value of Divorce Bills—What I would do if I Yearned—A Mean Business............................... ... 188—200

### ELDER WESLEY MINKLE'S DONATION.

Betsey visits me and brings her Tattin'—She Mourns over her neglected duties—She decides in future to work and also to prey—The Donation Party—Josiah objects to them—Quotes the 'postle Paul as an Example—How we went and what was Donated—Brother Minkley re-preaches his sermon to me—The Elder tempted—The Grab Bag—The Elder throws the tempter—A new attack of the Enemy—Grab Bags and Huzzies finally overcome—Match Makin'—The Editor arrives—He congratulates himself—Married and Saved—Betsey's disapointment and wild agony—She seeks relief in Poetry—She desires to be a ghost................................201—221

### WIMMEN'S SPEAH.

The new Preacher clung to—A Visit from Betsey—A Discussion on Wimmen's Speah—Female Delicacy as shown in Waltzin' with Pirates mebbe—Wimmen as boards—Tattin' and Paintin'—Dressin' and Flirtin'—Readin' Novels—Paul's Letters—Wimmen's talk—Itchin' ears—Betsey's new Poem on Matrimony—True Marriage—About Divorces—Clingers—Baptist Wimmen Voters—Nater will out: a hen will Scratch—Wimmen won't be driven—Betsey prefers to walk home and is accommodated ................................. 222—243

### A TOWER TO NEW YORK DISCUSSED.

Progress of affairs at Jonesville—Peace and Plenty—Betsey alive but Quiet—H. Greeley and I differ in some things—I propose a Tower—Josiah shows Jealousy—Democrats short of President Stuff—H. G. up for President—Effect of Suspense on me —Josiah consents to the Tower—Preparations—An Overskirt Important—Josiah sells the Critter ................... 244—257

WHAT IS IN THE BOOK. xiii

## GOVERNED BY PRINCIPLE.

Open preparations for the Tower—Josiah's White Hat—My Principles induce me also to wear one—Old "Hail the Day" contributes Feathers—On the Political Fence—Betsey also proposes a Tower—At the Depott—Betsey Explains—The 1st Partin' for 15 years .............................. 258—271

## MEETIN' GRANT AND COLFAX.

The Ticket Master—Folks I met with—Lack of Water Privileges—A Cigar without smoke—The Smilin' Stranger—Bad use of Eggs—Grant and Colfax—"Ulysses, how do you do"—Betsey reads a Poem to Gen'l Grant—"Let us have Peace"—Betsey overcome by Strategim................... 272—287

## AT NEW YORK, ASTERS'ES TAVERN.

A Familiar Stranger—"Will you have a bus?"—Betsey's Hopes—A Vegetable Widow—Procession on Broadway—Miss Asters'es Tavern—The Register—The Elevator—First thoughts in the Mornin'—Breakfast table—An Insult—Store Tea—I leave the Water Runnin'—Betsey Dissapointed again............................................ 288—305

## MEET DR. MARY WALKER.

Call on Miss Hooker—Engaged and what of it—At Miss Woodhull's door—Of Doubtful Gender—Miss Dr. Walker—Admittance obtained—A newly Married Man—Two Roman Noses............................................ 306—312

## INTERVIEW WITH THEODORE AND VICTORY.

Elizabeth Cady Stanton—H. W. Beecher—Isabella Beecher Hooker—Susan B. Anthony—Theodore Tilton—Victory Woodhull—Male and Female Angels—Feathers on Angel's Wings—Blind Marriages—Thoroughwert Pukes—Theodore's Opinions—He Advocates Divorces—To Marry and not to Marry both Solemn—Betsey's Prayer—Theodore yields.. 313—335

## A WIMMEN'S RIGHTS LECTURER.

A Visitor—Been on a Lecture Tower—Tyrant man—A Cure for Pantin' Hearts—A Star of Hope—Dress and Statesmanship—A Dinner and a Desert............................ 336—347

## ALEXANDER'S STORE.

Mr. Cash'es Family—Alexander don't take Butter, Eggs, Socks, or Barter—A Look at Calicos—Foreign Princes—Dolly Varden and her Acquaintances—A Dreadful Discovery—Betsey's Poetry in Market ........................ 348—356

## A HARROWIN' OPERATION.

A poor Maniac—A Affectin' Sight — A Ear for Music—Tirzah Ann a Musician—Operation of the D-David—Farewell to Mrs. Asters'es............................................ 357—364

## A VISIT TO HORACE.

First Impressions of him—No Peace for Candidates—Men all Alike—Darwin's Idees—Horace's old Letters—His Admissions—Wimmen's Influence at Washington—The Wrong Foot Forrerd—A Woman, or Patrick Oh Flanegan—The Widder Albert—Queen Bees—Paul's Opinions—Christ's Example—Nearly Overcome — Betsey's Overtures — Horace and I Part............................................. 358—396

## A SEA VOYAGE.

Left by the Cars—On the Canal Boat—Terrible Storm—Dangers Surround Us—Betsey Writes a Poem—Sings Sea Odes—The Poem—At Home................................. 397—405

## OLD FRIENDS IN NEW GARMENTS.

Betsey Bobbet Married—Poor Simon Slimpsey—Betsey at Home—Her Last Poem—The End....................... 406—420

## HOME AND JOSIAH.

Bad News—Horace Greeley dead—A Review of my Tower—Victory in Jail—Miss Aster a deception—Beecher slandered—Tilton do. do.—Doubts of Josiah—My Kitchen—I wear a bow on principle—Our supper—Josiah grows sentimental—I don't discourage him...................................... 434

# PICTURES IN THE BOOK.

|   |   | PAGE. |
|---|---|---|
| 1 | THE PLEASANT SUPPER, FULL PAGE | (Frontispiece) |
| 2 | I AND JOSIAH | 19 |
| 3 | REFRESHMENTS (TAIL PIECE) | 20 |
| 4 | TIRZAH ANN | 23 |
| 5 | BETSEY BOBBET | 27 |
| 6 | READIN' POETRY | 33 |
| 7 | LOOKING FOR A VICTIM, (TAIL PIECE) | 37 |
| 8 | PREPARIN' FOR A PICTURE | 39 |
| 9 | THE PICTURE | 45 |
| 10 | THE SURPRISE PARTY, (FULL PAGE) | 53 |
| 11 | DELICIOUS, (TAIL PIECE) | 57 |
| 12 | THE QUILTIN' PARTY (FULL PAGE) | 77 |
| 13 | SCANDALIZED, (TAIL PIECE) | 81 |
| 14 | AN ACCIDENT | 101 |
| 15 | JOSIAH BEIN' CHEERFUL | 105 |
| 16 | KEEPIN' THE SICK QUIET | 109 |
| 17 | A FULL QUIRE | 123 |
| 18 | THE EAR RING PEDLER, (FULL PAGE) | 141 |
| 19 | DISGUST, (TAIL PIECE) | 144 |
| 20 | THE SERENADERS (FULL PAGE) | 150 |
| 21 | MEWSIN', (TAIL PIECE) | 156 |
| 22 | THE FOURTH OF JULY CELEBRATION (FULL PAGE) | 162 |
| 23 | WHAT HAPPENED AT THE DINNER (FULL PAGE) | 170 |
| 24 | COUNTIN' THE COST (FULL PAGE) | 175 |
| 25 | SIMON SLIMPSEY | 182 |
| 26 | SIMON OVERWHELMED | 187 |
| 27 | PROF. GUSHER | 195 |
| 28 | LIVIN' ON GOSPEL | 204 |
| 29 | THE ENEMY ATTACKED | 210 |
| 30 | THE ELDER ON THE ALERT | 213 |
| 31 | BETSEY SEEKS RELIEF | 219 |
| 32 | A STRONG ATTACHMENT (TAIL PIECE) | 221 |
| 33 | FEMALE DELICACY | 224 |

| | |
|---|---|
| 34 No Time to Vote | 226 |
| 35 Dreadful Short of Time | 227 |
| 36 No Time to Study Laws | 229 |
| 37 A Woman's Rights (full page) | 234 |
| 38 Primary Meetings and Results, (full page) | 241 |
| 39 A Victory (tail piece) | 256 |
| 40 Visit to Jonesville (full page) | 263 |
| 41 Gone (tail piece) | 271 |
| 42 The Smilin' Stranger (full page) | 273 |
| 43 "Let us have Peace" (full page) | 281 |
| 44 On the Street | 305 |
| 45 Hard at Work, (full page) | 317 |
| 46 Betsey's Prayer | 341 |
| 47 On a Lecturin' Tower [full page] | 339 |
| 48 How Would You Like It? | 342 |
| 49 Female Statesmanship | 345 |
| 50 Don't Take Barter | 350 |
| 51 Dolly Varden | 354 |
| 52 A Harrowin' Scene | 358 |
| 53 Interview with Horace, (full page) | 369 |
| 54 Fillin' Woman's Spear under Difficulties [full page] | 395 |
| 55 At Home | 402 |
| 56 Mr. Bobbet Tells News [full page] | 407 |

# MARRIED TO JOSIAH ALLEN.

IF anybody had told me when I was first born that I would marry to a widower, I should have been mad at 'em. I lived up to this idee quite a number of years, how many, is nobody's business, that I will contend for. I laughed at the idee of love in my blindness of eye. But the first minute I sot my grey eye onto Josiah Allen I knew my fate. My heart was a pray to feelin's it had heretofore been a stranger to.

Sez I to myself " Is this love?" I couldn't answer, I was too agitated.

Josiah told me afterwards that he felt jest exactly the same, only, when his heart wildly put the question to him, " Is it love you feel for Samantha Smith?" he havin' experience in the same, answered, " Yes, it is love."

I married Josiah Allen (in mother's parlor, on the fourteenth day of June, in a bran new silk dress with a long boddis waist) from pure love. Though why I loved him, I know not. I looked at his mild face beamin' on me from above his black silk stock, which kep' his head kinder stiff, and asked myself this question, "Why do you love him?" I reckolected then, and I have recalled it to his mind several times sense in our little differences of opinion, which occur in the happiest families—that I had had offers from men, handsomer than him, with more intelect than him, with more riches than him, with less children than him. Why didn't I love these various men? I knew not. I can only repeat in the immortal and almost deathless lines of the poet, "Love will go where it is sent."

Yes, Josiah Allen was my fate, and when I laid my light silk glove in his'en (they was almost of a color, a kind of cinnemen brown) before the alter, or that is before Elder Wesley Minkley, I did it with the purest and tenderest emotions of love.

And that love has been like a Becon in our pathway ever- sense. Its pure light, though it has sputtered some, and in tryin' times such as washin' days and cleanin' house times has burnt down pretty low,—has never gone out.

When I married him the bald spot on his head wuzn't much bigger than a new silver dollar. Now the top of his head is as smooth and clean as one of my stun china dinner plates, and if any horse jocky was to try to judge of his age by lookin' at his teeth, they would be baffled, not but what he has got some teeth, but they are pretty scatterin'. But still that Beeon shines, that pure love triumphs over lost teeth and van-

I AND JOSIAH.

ished sandy hair. There haint a man on the face of the earth that looks so good to me as Josiah Allen. I don't tell him this, mind you, 14 years experience of married life has taught me caution. Josiah is as good as they'l average generally, but no man can't stand too much flattery, men are naturally vain.

As I said in the commencement of this plain and

unvarnished history, I had almost a deadly objection to widowers owin' to their habit of comparin' their second wives to their first relict, to the disadvantage of the first-named pardner. Josiah tride it with me when we was first married. But I *didn't encourage him in it.* He began on several various times, "It seems to me Samantha that Polly Ann used to fry up her meat a little cripsier," or "It seems as if Polly Ann used to make my collers a little stiffer." He stopped it before we had been married a year, for *I didn't encourage it in him.*

As I mean that this book shall be a Becon light, guidin' female wimmen, to life, liberty, and the pursuit of true happiness, I would insert right here this word of solem' warnin' to my sect situated in the tryin' place of second consorts, if the relict goes to comparin' you to his foregone consort, *don't encourage him in it.* On this short rule hangs the hope of domestick harmony.

## ABOUT JOSIAH AND THE CHILDREN.

BUT step-mothers have a pretty hard row to hoe, though I don't complain. I like children, clean children first rate, and I have tried to do my duty by hisen. I have done as well by 'em as I knew how to, and I think a sight of Thomas Jefferson and Tirzah Ann. Tirzah Ann is dreadful sentimental, that is what spiles her mostly. And Thomas Jefferson thinks he knows more than his father, that is his greatest failin'. But take 'em all through, they are *full* as good as other folks'es children, and I know it. Thomas Jefferson is dreadful big feelin', he is 17 years old, he wears a stove pipe hat, and is tryin' to raise a moustache, it is now jest about as long as the fuzz on cotton flannel and most as white. They both go to Jonesville to high school, (we hire a room for 'em to Mother Allens, and they board themselves,) but they are to home every Saturday, and then they kinder quarell all day jest as brothers and sisters will. What agravates Thomas J.

the worst is to call him "bub," and Tirzah Ann
don't call him anything else unless she forgets
herself.

He seems to think it is manly to have doubts about
religeon. I put him through the catechism, and thought
he was sound. But he seems to think it is manly to
argue about free moral agency, foreordination, and pre-
destination, and his father is jest fool enough to argue
with him. Sez he last Saturday,

"Father, if it was settled beyond question six or
seven thousand years ago that I was goin' to be lost
what good does it do for me to squirm? and if it was
settled that I was goin' to be saved, how be I goin' to
help myself?" sez he, "I believe we can't help ourselves, what was meant to happen, will happen."

Before his father had time to speak—Josiah is a slow
spoken man, Tirzah Ann spoke up—

"Bub, if it was settled six or seven thousand years
ago that I should take your new jockey club and hair
oil, and use 'em all myself, why then I shall."

"Tirzah Ann," says he "If you should touch 'em it
was foreordained from creation that you would get
dreadfully hurt." But I spoke up then for the first
time, says I,

"You see Thomas J. that come to fighting you
have moral agency enough — or immoral agency.
Now" says I, "I won't hear another word from
you, you Thomas J. are a young fool, and you Josiah

Allen are a old one, now," says I "go to the barn, for I want to mop."

Tirzah Ann as I said is dreadful sentimental, I don't know which side she took it from, though I mistrust that Josiah if he had any encouragement would act spoony. I am not the woman to encourage any kind

TIRZAH ANN.

of foolishness. I remember when we was first engaged, he called me "a little angel." I jest looked at him calmly and says I,

"I weigh two hundred and 4 pounds," and he didn't call me so again.

No! sentiment aint my style, and I abhor all kinds of shams and deceitfulness. Now to the table you don't ketch me makin' excuses. I should feel as mean as pusley if I did. Though once in a while when I have particuler company, and my cookin' turns out bad, I kinder turn the conversation on to the sufferin's of our four fathers in the Revolution, how they eat their kat ridge boxes and shoe leather. It don't do us no hurt to remember their sufferin's, and after talkin' about eatin' shoe leather most any kind of cake seems tender.

I spose that life runs along with Josiah and the children and me about as easy as it does with most men and female wimmen. We have got a farm of 75 acres of land all paid for. A comfortable story and a half yeller house—good barns, and a bran new horse barn, and health. Our door yard is large and shady with apple, and pear, and cherry trees; and Tirzah Ann has got posy beds under the winder's that look first rate. And where there haint no posy beds nor shade trees, the grass grows smooth and green, and it is a splendid place to dry clothes. On the north side of the house is our orchard, the trees grow clear up to our kitchen winder, and when the north door is open in the spring of the year, and I stand there ironin', the trees all covered with pink blows it is a pleasant sight. But a still pleasanter sight is it in the fall of the year to stand in the door and see Josiah and Thomas Jefferson pickin' up barells of the great red and yeller grafts at a dollar a bushel. Beyond the orchard down a little bit of a side hill runs the clear water of the canal. In front of the house towards the south—but divided from it by a good sized door yard and a picket fence, runs the highway, and back of the house, if I do say it that ortn't to, there is as good a garden as there is in these parts. For I set my foot down in the first ont, that I *would* have garden sass of all kinds, and strawberrys, and gooseberrys, and currant, and berry bushes, and glad enough is Josiah now to think that he heard to me. It took a little work of course, but I believe in havin' things good to eat, and so does Josiah. That man has told me more'n a hundred times sense that "of all the sass that ever was made, garden sass was the best sass." To the south of the house is our big meadow—the smell of the clover in the summer is as sweet as anything, our bees get the biggest part of their honey there, the grass looks beautiful wavin' in the sunshine, and Josiah cut from it last summer 4 tons of hay to the acre.

# AN UNMARRIED FEMALE.

I SUPPOSE we are about as happy as the most of folks, but as I was sayin, a few days ago to Betsy Bobbet a neighborin' female of ours—" Every Station house in life has its various skeletons. But we ort to try to be contented with that spear of life we are called on to handle." Betsey haint married and she don't seem to be contented. She is awful opposed to wimmens rights, she thinks it is wimmens only spear to marry, but as yet she can't find any man willin' to lay holt of that spear with her. But you can read in her daily life and on her eager willin' countenance that she fully realizes the sweet words of the poet, " while there is life there is hope."

Betsey haint handsome. Her cheek bones are high, and she bein' not much more than skin and bone they show plainer than they would if she was in good order. Her complexion (not that I blame her for it) haint good, and her eyes are little and sot way back in her head. Time has seen fit to deprive her of her hair and teeth, but her large nose he has kindly suffered her to keep, but she has got the best white ivory teeth money will buy; and two long curls fastened behind each ear, besides frizzles on the top of her head, and if she wasn't naturally bald, and if the curls was the color of her hair they would look well. She is awful sentimental, I have seen a good many that had it bad,

BETSEY BOBBET.

but of all the sentimental creeters I ever did see Betsey Bobbet is the sentimentalest, you couldn't squeeze a laugh out of her with a cheeze press.

As I said she is awful opposed to wimmin's havein' any right only the right to get married. She holds on to that right as tight as any single woman I ever see which makes it hard and wearin' on the single men round here. For take the men that are the most opposed to wimmin's havin' a right, and talk the most about its bein' her duty to cling to man like a vine to a tree, they don't want Betsey to cling to them, they *won't let* her cling to 'em. For when they would be a goin' on about how wicked it was for wimmin to vote

—and it was her only spear to marry, says I to 'em "Which had you ruther do, let Betsey Bobbet cling to you or let her vote?" and they would every one of 'em quail before that question. They would drop their heads before my keen grey eyes—and move off the subject.

But Betsey don't get discourajed. Every time I see her she says in a hopeful wishful tone, " That the deepest men of minds in the country agree with her in thinkin' that it is wimmin's duty to marry, and not to vote." And then she talks a sight about the retirin' modesty and dignity of the fair sect, and how shameful and revoltin' it would be to see wimmen throwin' 'em away, and boldly and unblushin'ly talkin' about law and justice.

Why to hear Betsey Bobbet talk about wimmins throwin' their modesty away you would think if they ever went to the political pole, they would have to take their dignity and modesty and throw 'em against the pole, and go without any all the rest of their lives.

Now I don't believe in no such stuff as that, I think a woman can be bold and unwomanly in other things besides goin' with a thick veil over her face, and a brass mounted parasol, once a year, and gently and quietly dropping a vote for a christian president, or a religeous and noble minded pathmaster.

She thinks she talks dreadful polite and proper, she

says "I was cameing" instead of "I was coming," and "I have saw" instead of "I have seen," and "papah" for paper, and "deah" for dear. I don't know much about grammer, but common sense goes a good ways. She writes the poetry for the Jonesville Augur, or "Augah," as she calls it. She used to write for the opposition paper, the Jonesville Gimlet, but the editer of the Augur, a long haired chap, who moved into Jonesville a few months ago, lost his wife soon after he come there, and sense that she has turned Dimocrat, and writes for his paper stiddy. They say that he is a dreadful big feelin' man, and I have heard—it came right straight to me—his cousin's wife's sister told it to the mother in law of one of my neighbor's brother's wife, that he didn't like Betsey's poetry at all, and all he printed it for was to plague the editer of the Gimlet, because she used to write for him. I myself wouldn't give a cent a bushel for all the poetry she can write. And it seems to me, that if I was Betsey, I wouldn't try to write so much, howsumever, I don't know what turn I should take if I was Betsey Bobbet, that is a solemn subject and one I don't love to think on.

I never shall forget the first piece of her poetry I ever see. Josiah Allen and I had both on us been married goin' on a year, and I had occasion to go to his trunk one day where he kept a lot of old papers, and the first thing I laid my hand on was these verses. Josiah went with her a few times after his wife died, a 4th of July or so and two or three camp meetin's, and the poetry seemed to be wrote about the time *we* was married. It was directed over the top of it "Owed to Josiah," just as if she were in debt to him. This was the way it read.

"OWED TO JOSIAH.

Josiah I the tale have hurn,
With rigid ear, and streaming eye,
I saw from me that you did turn,
I never knew the reason why.
  Oh Josiah,
   It seemed as if I must expiah.

Why did you, Oh why did you blow
Upon my life of snowy sleet,
The fiah of love to fiercest glow,
Then turn a damphar on the heat?
  Oh Josiah,
   It seemed as if I must expiah.

I saw thee coming down the street,
*She* by your side in bonnet bloo;
The stuns that grated 'neath thy feet
Seemed crunching on my vitals too.
  Oh Josiah,
   It seemed as if I must expiah.

I saw thee washing sheep last night,
On the bridge I stood with marble brow,
The waters raged, thou clasped it tight,
I sighed, 'should both be drownded now—'
  I thought Josiah,
   Oh happy sheep to thus expiah."

I showed the poetry to Josiah that night after he came home, and told him I had read it. He looked awful ashamed to think I had seen it, and says he with a dreadful sheepish look.

"The persecution I underwent from that female can never be told, she fairly hunted me down, I had'nt no rest for the soles of my feet. I thought one spell she would marry me in spite of all I could do, without givin' me the benefit of law or gospel." He see I looked stern, and he added with a sick lookin' smile, "I thought one spell, to use Betsey's language, "I was a gonah."

I did'nt smile—oh no, for the deep principle of my sect was reared up—I says to him in a tone cold enough to almost freeze his ears, "Josiah Allen, shet up, of all the cowardly things a man ever done, it is goin' round braggin' about wimmen' likin' em, and follerin' em up. Enny man that'l do that is little enough to crawl through a knot hole without rubbing his clothes." Says I, "I suppose you made her think the moon rose in your head, and set in your heels, I dare say you acted foolish enough round her to sicken a snipe, and if you make fun of her now to please me I let you know you have got holt of the wrong individual." Now, says I, "go to bed," and I added in still more freezing accents, "for I want to mend your pantaloons." He gathered up his shoes and stockin's and started off to bed, and we haint never passed a word on the subject sence. I believe when you disagree with your pardner, in freein' your *mind* in the first

on't, and then not be a twittin' about it afterwards.
And as for bein' jealous, I should jest as soon think of
bein' jealous of a meetin'-house as I should of Josiah.
He is a well principled man. And I guess he was'nt
fur out o' the way about Betsey Bobbet, though I
would'nt encourage him by lettin' him say a word on
the subject, for I always make it a rule to stand up for
my own sect; but when I hear her go on about the
editor of the Augur, I can believe anything about
Betsey Bobbet. She came in here one day last week,
it was about ten o'clock in the mornin'. I had got my
house slick as a pin, and my dinner under way, (I was
goin' to have a biled dinner, and a cherry puddin'
biled, with sweet sass to eat on it,) and I sot down to
finish sewin' up the breadth of my new rag carpet. I
thought I would get it done while I had'nt so much
to do, for it bein' the first of March, I knew sugarin,
would be comin' on, and then cleanin' house time, and
I wanted it to put down jest as soon as the stove was
carried out in the summer kitchen. The fire was
sparklin' away, and the painted floor a shinin' and the
dinner a bilin,' and I sot there sewin' jest as calm as a
clock, not dreamin' of no trouble, when in came Betsey Bobbet.

I met her with outward calm, and asked her to set
down and lay off her things. She sot down, but she
said she could'nt lay off her things. Says she, "I was
comin' down past, and I thought I would call and let

you see the last numbah of the Augah, there is a piece in it concernin' the tariff that stirs men's souls, I like it evah so much."

She handed me the paper, folded so I couldn't see

READING POETRY.

nothin' but a piece of poetry by Betsey Bobbet. I see what she wanted of me and so I dropped my breadths of carpetin' and took hold of it and began to read it.

"Read it audible if you please," says she, "Especially the precious remahks ovah it, it is such a feast for me to be a sitting, and heah it rehealsed by a musical voice.

Says I, "I spose I can rehearse it if it will do you any good," so I began as follers:

"It is seldom that we present to the readers of the Augur (the best paper for the fireside in Jonesville or the world) with a poem like the following. It may be by the assistance of the Augur (only twelve shillings a year in advance, wood and potatoes taken in exchange) the name of Betsey Bobbet will yet be carved on the lofty pinnacle of fame's towering pillow. We think however that she could study such writers as Sylvanus Cobb, and Tupper with profit both to herself and to them.   EDITOR OF THE AUGUR."

Here Betsey interrupted me. "The deah editah of the Augah had no need to advise me to read Tuppah, for he is indeed my most favorite authar, you have devorhed him havn't you Josiah Allen's wife.?

"Devoured who?" says I, in a tone pretty near as cold as a cold icicle.

"Mahten. Fahyneah. Tuppah, that sweet authar," says she.

"No mom," says I shortly, "I hain't devoured Martin Farquhar Tupper, nor no other man, I hain't a cannibal."

"Oh! you understand me not, I meant, devorhed his sweet, tender lines."

"I hain't devoured his tenderlines, nor nothin' relatin' to him," and I made a motion to lay the paper down, but Betsey urged me to go on, and so I read.

GUSHINGS OF A TENDAH SOUL.

| Oh let who will, | Thus said I 'ere, |
| Oh let who can, | My tendah heart was touched, |
| Be tied onto | Thus said I 'ere |
| A horrid male man. | My tendah feelings gushed. |

But oh a change
Hath swept ore me,
As billows sweep
The "deep blue sea."

A voice, a **noble form,**
One day I saw;
An arrow flew,
My heart is nearly raw.

**His** first pardner lies
**Beneath the turf,**

He is wandering now,
In sorrows briny surf.

**Two** twins, the little
**Deah** cherub creechahs,
**Now** wipe the teahs,
**From off his** classic feachahs.

Oh sweet lot, worthy
Angel arisen,
To wipe the teahs,
From eyes like hisen.

"**What think you of it?**" says she as I finished readin'.

I looked right at her most a minute with a majestic look. In spite of her false curls, and her new white **ivory** teeth, she is a humbly critter. I looked at her silently while she sot and twisted her long yeller bunnet **strings, and then I** spoke out,

"Hain't the Editor of the Augur a widower with a pair of twins?"

"Yes," says she with a happy look.

Then says I, "If the man hain't a fool, he'll think you are one."

"Oh!" says she, and she dropped her bunnet strings, and clasped **her** long bony hands together in her brown **cotton** gloves, "oh, we ahdent **soles** of genious, have feelin's, you cold, practical natures know nuthing of, and if they did not gush out in poetry we should expiah. **You may** as well try to tie up the gushing cat**arack of Niagarah** with a piece of welting cord, as to **tie up the feelings** of an ahdent sole."

"Ardent sole!" says I coldly. "Which makes the most noise, Betsey Babbet, a three inch brook or a ten footer? which is the tearer? which is the roarer? deep waters run stillest. I have no faith in feelins' that stalk round in public in mournin' weeds. I have no faith in such mourners," says I.

"Oh Josiah's wife, cold, practical female being, you know me not; we are sundered as fah apart as if you was sitting on the North pole, and I was sitting on the South pole. Uncongenial being, you know me not."

"I may not know you, Betsey Bobbet, but I do know decency, and I know that no mummy would tempt me to write such stuff as that poetry and send it to a widower, with twins."

"Oh!" says she, "what appeals to the tendah feeling heart of a single female woman more, than to see a lonely man who has lost his relict? And pity never seems so much like pity as when it is given to the deah little children of widowehs. And," says she, "I think moah than as likely as not, this soaring soul of genious did not wed his affinity, but was united to a weak women of clay."

"Mere women of clay!" says I, fixin' my spektacles upon her in a most searchin' manner, "where will you find a woman, Betsey Bobbet, that hain't more or less clay? and affinity, that is the meanest word I ever heard; no married woman has any right to hear it. I'll excuse you, bein' a female, but if a man had said it to me, I'd holler to Josiah. There is a time for everything, and the time to hunt affinity is before you are married; married folks hain't no right to hunt it," says I sternly.

"We kindred souls soah above such petty feelings, we soah fah above them."

"I hain't much of a soarer," says I, "and I don't pretend to be, and to tell you the truth," says I, "I am glad I hain't."

"The Editah of the Augah," says she, and she grasped the paper offen the stand and folded it up, and presented it at me like a spear, "the Editah of this paper is a kindred soul, he appreciates me, he undahstands me, and will not our names in the pages of this very papah go down to posterety togathah?"

Then says I, drove out of all patience with her, "I wish you was there now, both of you, I wish," says I, lookin' fixedly on her, "I wish you was both of you in posterity now."

## HAVING MY PICTURE TOOK.

THE very next Saturday after I had this conversation with Betsey, I went down to Jonesville to have my picture took, Tirzah Ann bein' to home so she could get dinner for the menfolks. As for me I don't set a great deal of store by pictures, but Josiah insisted and the children insisted, and I went. Tirzah Ann wanted me to have my hair curled, but there I was firm. I give in on the handkerchief pin, but on the curl business, there I was rock.

Mr. Gansey the man that takes pictures was in another room takin' some, so I walked round the aunty room, as they call it, lookin' at the pictures that hang up on the wall, and at the people that come in to have theirs took. Some of 'em was fixed up dreadful; it seemed to me as if they tried to look so that nobody wouldn't know whose pictures they was, after they was took. Some of 'em would take off their bunnets and gaze in the lookin'-glass at themselves and

AUNTY ROOM PREPARATIONS. 39

try to look smilin', and get an expression onto their faces that they never owned.

In one corner of the room was a bewrow, with a lookin'-glass and hair brushes onto it, and before it stood a little man dreadful dressed up, with long black hair streamin' down over his coat coller, engaged in pour-

PREPARING FOR A PICTURE.

ing a vial of oil onto his head, and brushing his **hair**

with one of the brushes. I knew him in a minute, for I had seen him come into the meetin' house. Afterwards when I was jest standin' before the picture of a dreadful harmless lookin' man— he looked meek enough to make excuses to his shadder for goin' before it, and I was jest sayin' to myself, "There is a man who would fry pancakes without complainin'," I heard a voice behind me sayin',

"So the navish villian stalks round yet in decent society."

I turned round imegiately and see the little man, who had got through fixin' his hair to have his pictur took, standin' before me.

"Who do you mean?" says I calmly. "Who is stalkin' round?"

"The Editor of the Gimlet," says he, "whose vile image defiles the walls of this temple of art, the haunt of Aglia, Thalia, and Euphrosine."

"Who?" says I glancin' keenly at him over my specks, "the haunt of who?"

Says he "The daughters of Bachus and Venus."

Says I "I don't know anything about Miss Bachus, nor the Venus girls," and says I with spirit, "if they are any low creeters I don't thank you for speakin' of 'em to me, nor Josiah won't neether. This room belongs to Jeremiah Gansey, and he has got a wife, a likely woman, that belongs to the same meetin' house and the same class that I do, and he haint no business to have other girls hauntin' his rooms. If there is anything wrong goin' on I shall tell Sister Gansey."

Says he "Woman you mistake, I meant the Graces."

"Graces!" says I scornfully, "what do I care for their graces. Sister Gansey had graces enough when he married her," says I. "That is jest the way, a man will marry a woman jest as pretty as a new blown rose, and then when she fades herself out, till she looks more like a dead dandyline than a livin' creeter, cookin' *his* vittles, washin' *his* dishes, and takin' care of *his* children; then he'l go to havin' other girls hauntin' him, there haint no gospel in it," says I.

I looked him keenly in the face all the time I spoke, for I thought he was kinder' upholdin' Sister Gansey's husband, and I wanted my words to apaul him, but I suppose he made a mistake, and thought I was admirin' of him I looked so earnest at him, for he spoke up and says he,

"I see by your stiddy glance that you have discovered who I be. Yes Madam, you see before you the Editor of the Augur, but don't be nervous, don't let it affect you more than you can help, I am a mortal like yourself."

I looked at him with my most majestic look, and he continued.

"The masses who devoured my great work "Logical Reveries on the Beauties' of Slavery, are naturally anxious to see me. I don't wonder at it, not at all."

3

I was austerely silent and withdrawed to a winder and set down. But he followed me and continued on.

"That tract as you are doubtless aware, was written just before the war, and a weaker minded man might have been appalled by the bloodshed that followed its publication. But no! I said calmly, it was written on principle, and if it did bring ruin and bloodshed on the country, principle would in the end prevail. The war turned out different from what I hoped, chains broke that I could have wept to see break—but still I hung on to principle. Might I ask you Madam, exactly what your emotions were when you read 'Logical Reveries' for the first time? I suppose no President's message was ever devoured as that was."

"I never see nor heard of your 'Logical Reveries,'" says I coldly. "And thank fortune nobody can accuse me of ever touchin' a President's message—unless they belie me."

He rolled up his eyes toward the ciclin' and sithed hevily, and then says he, "Is it possible that in this enlightened community there is still such ignorance amongst the masses. I have got a copy in my pocket, I never go without one. And I will read it to you and it may be pleasant for you to tell your children and grandchildren in the future, that the author of "Logical Reveries on the Beauties of Slavery" told you with his own lips, how the great work came to be written. A poem was sent me intended as a satire on the beautiful and time hallowed system of slavery, it was a weak senseless mass of twaddle, but if the author could have foreseen the mighty consequences that flowed from it, he might well have trembled, for senseless as it was it roused the lion in me, and I replied. I divided my great work into two parts, first, that slavery was right, because the constitution didn't say it was wrong, and then I viewed the subject in a Bible and moral light, but the last bein' of less importance, of course I didn't enlarge on it, but on the first I come out strong, there I shone. I will read you a little of the poem that was sent me, that you may understand the witherin' allusions I make concernin' it. I won't read more than is necessary for that purpose, for you may get sleepy listenin' to it, but you will wake up enough when I begin to read the "Logical Reveries," I guess there couldn't anybody sleep on them. The poem I speak of commenced in the following weak illogical way.

### SLAVERY.

So held my eyes I could not see
The rightousness of slavery,
So blind was I, I could not see
The ripe fruit hang on wisdom's tree;
But groping round its roots did range,
Murmuring ever, strange, oh strange

That one handful of dust should dare
Enslave another God had made,

From his own home and kindred tear,
And scourge, and fetter, steal and trade.
If 'twas because they were less wise
Than our wise race, why not arise,
And with pretext of buying teas,
Lay in full cargoes of Chinese.
Let Fee Fo Fum, and Eng, and Chen,
Grow wise by contact with wise men;
If weakness made the traffic right,
Why not arise in manhoods might,
And bind old grandmothers with gyves,
And weakly children, and sick wives.

If twas the dark hue of their face,
Then why not free our noble race
Forever from all homely men?
With manly zeal, and outstretched hand,
Pass like a whirlwind o'er the land.
Let squint eyed, pug-nosed women be
Only a thing of memory.
Though some mistakes would happen then,
For many bond servants there are,
Fair faced, blue eyed, with silken hair.
How sweet, how pleasant to be sold
For notes in hand, or solid gold,
To benefit a brother
Both children of one father,
With each a different mother.
One mother fair and richly clothed,
One worn with toil and vain despair
Down sunken to a life she loathed;
Both children with proud saxon blood,
In one breast mixed with tropic flame,
One, heir to rank and broad estates
And one, without even a name

Jest as he arrived to this crysis in the poem, Mr. Gansey came out into the aunty room, and told me he was ready to take my picture. The Editer seein' he was obleeged to stop readin' told me, he would come down to our house a visitin' in sugarin' time, and finish readin' the poetry to me.  I ketched holt of my principles to stiddy 'em, for I see they was a totterin' and says to him with outward calmness,

"If you come fetch the twins."

He said he would.  I then told Mr. Gansey I was ready for the picture.  I believe there haint nothin' that will take the expression out of anybody's eyes, like havin' poetry read for a hour and a half, unless it is to have your head screwed back into a pair of tongs, and be told to look at nothin' and wink at it as much as you are a mind to. Under both of these circumstances, it didn't suprise me a mite that one of my eyes was took blind.

THE PICTURE.

But as Mr. Gansey said as he looked admirin'ly on it, with the exception of that one blind eye, it was a perfect and strikin' picture.  I paid him his dollar and started off home, and I hope now that Josiah and the children will be satisfied.

# OUR SURPRIZE PARTIES.

ABOUT one week after this picture eppysode, there was a surprise party appointed. They had been havin' 'em all winter, and the children had been crazy to have me go to 'em—everybody went, old and young, but I held back. Says I: "I don't approve of 'em, and I won't go."

But finally they got their father on their side; says he: "It won't hurt you Samantha, to go for once."

Says I: "Josiah, the place for old folks is to home; and I don't believe in surprise parties anyway, I think they are perfect nuisances. It stands to reason if you want to see your friends, you can invite 'em, and if anybody is too poor to bake a cake or two, and a pan of cookies, they are too poor to go into company at all." Says I: "I haint proud, nor never was called so, but I don't want Tom, Dick and Harry, that I never spoke to in my life, feel as if they was free to break into my house at any time they please." Says I: "it would make me feel perfectly wild, to think there was a whole drove of people, liable to rush in here at any minute, and I won't rush into other people's housen."

"It would be fun, mother," says Thomas J.; "I should love to see you and Deacon Gowdey or old Bobbet, playin' wink 'em slyly."

'Let 'em wink at me if they dare to," says I sternly; "let me catch 'em at it. I don't believe in surprise parties," and I went on in about as cold a tone as they make. "Have you forgot how Mrs. Gowdey had her parlor lamp smashed to bits, and a set of stun china? Have you forgot how four or five stranger men got drunk to Peedicks'es, and had to be carried up stairs and laid out on her spare bed? Have you forgot how Celestine Wilkins fell with her baby in her arms, as she was catchin' old Gowdey, and cracked the little innocent creeters nose? Have you forgot how Betsey Bobbet lost out her teeth a runnin' after the editor of the Augur, and he stepped on 'em and smashed 'em all to bits? Have you forgot these coincidences?" Says I: "I don't believe in surprise parties."

"No more do I," says Josiah; "but the children feel so about our goin', sposen we go, for once! No livin' woman could do better for children than you have by mine, Samantha, but I don't suppose you feel exactly as I do about pleasin' 'em, it haint natteral you should."

Here he knew he had got me. If ever a woman

wanted to do her duty by another woman's children, it is Samantha Allen, whose maiden name was Smith. Josiah knew jest how to start me; men are deep. I went to the very next party, which was to be held two miles beyond Jonesville; they had had 'em so fast, they had used up all the nearer places. They had heard of this family, who had a big house, and the women had been to the same meetin' house with Betsey Bobbet two or three times, and she had met her in a store a year before, and had been introduced to her, so she said she felt perfectly free to go. And as she was the leader it was decided on. They went in two big loads, but Josiah and I went in a cutter alone.

We got started ahead of the loads, and when we got to the house we see it was lit up real pleasant, and a little single cutter stood by the gate. We went up to the door and knocked, and a motherly lookin' woman with a bunch of catnip in her hand, came to the door.

" Good evenin'," says I, but she seemed to be a little deaf, and didn't answer, and I see, as we stepped in, through a door partly open, a room full of women.

" Good many have got here," says I a little louder.

" Yes, a very good doctor," says she.

"What in the world!"—I begun to say in wild amaze.

" No, it is a boy."

I turned right round, and laid holt of Josiah; says

I, "Start this minute, Josiah Allen, for the door." I laid holt of him, and got him to the door, and we never spoke another word till we was in the sleigh, and turned round towards home; then says I,

"Mebby you'll hear to *me*, another time, Josiah.

"I wish you wouldn't be so agravatin'," says he.

Jest then we met the first load, where Tirzah Ann and Thomas Jefferson was, and we told 'em to "turn round, for they couldn't have us, they had other company." So they turned round. We had got most back to Jonesville, when we met the other load; they had tipped over in the snow, and as we drove out most to the fence to get by 'em, Josiah told 'em the same we had the other load.

Says Betsey Bobbet, risin' up out of the snow with a buffalo skin on her back, which made her look wild,

"Did they say we *must not* come?"

"No, they didn't say jest that," says Josiah. "But they don't want you."

"Wall then, my deah boys and girls," says she, scramblin' into the sleigh. "Let us proceed onwards, if they did not say we *should not* come."

Her load went on, for her brother, Shakespeare Bobbet, was the driver. How they got along I haint never enquired, and they don't seem over free to talk about it. But they kep' on havin' 'em, most every night. Betsey Bobbet as I said was the leader, and she led 'em once into a house where they had the small pox, and once where they was makin' preparations for a funeral. Somehow Tirzah and Thomas Jefferson seemed to be sick of 'em, and as for Josiah, though he didn't say much, I knew he felt the more.

This coinsidense took place on Tuesday night, and the next week a Monday I had had a awful day's work a washin', and we had been up all night the night before with Josiah, who had the new ralegy in his back. We hadn't one of us slept a wink the night before, and Thomas Jefferson and Tirzah Ann had gone to bed early. It had been a lowery day, and I couldn't hang out my calico clothes, and so many of 'em was hung round the kitchen on lines and clothes bars, and nails, that Josiah and I looked as if we was a settin' in a wet calico tent. And what made it look still more melancholy and sad, I found when I went to light the lamp, that the kerosene was all gone, and bein' out of candles, I made for the first time what they call a "slut," which is a button tied up in a rag, and put in a saucer of lard; you set fire to the rag, and it makes a light that is better than no light at all, jest as a slut is better than no woman at all; I suppose in that way it derived its name. But it haint a dazzlin' light, nothin' like so gay and festive as gas.

I, beat out with work and watchin', thought I would soak my feet before I went to bed, and so I put some water into the mop pail, and sot by the stove with my feet in it. The thought had come to me after I got my night-cap on. Josiah sot behind the stove, rubbin some linament onto his back; he had jest spoke to me, and says he,

"I believe this linament makes, my back feel easier, Samantha, I hope I shall get a little rest to-night."

Says I, "I hope so too, Josiah." And jest as I said the words, without any warning the door opened, and in come what seemed to me at the time to be a hundred and 50 men, wimmen, and children, headed by Betsey Bobbet.

Josiah, so wild with horror and amazement that he forgot for the time bein' his lameness, leaped from his chair, and tore so wildly at his shirt that he tore two pieces right out of the red flannel, and they shone on each shoulder of his white shirt like red stars; he then backed up against the wall between the back door and the wood box. I rose up and stood in the mop pail, too wild with amaze to get out of it, for the same reason heedin' not my night-cap.

"We have come to suprize you," says Betsey Bobbet, sweetly.

I looked at 'em in speechless horror, and my tongue clove to the roof of my mouth; no word did I speak, but I glared at 'em with looks which I suppose filled 'em with awe and dread, for Betsey Bobbet spoke again in plaintive accents,

"Will you not let us suprize you?"

Then I found voice, and "No! no!" says I wildly. "I won't be suprized! you sha'n't suprize us to-night! We won't be suprized! Speak, Josiah," says I, appealin' to him in my extremity. "Speak! tell her! will we be suprized to-night?"

"No! no!" says he in firm, decided, warlike tones, as he stood backed up against the wall, holdin' his clothes on—with his red flannel epaulettes on his shoulders like a officer, "no, we won't be suprized!"

"You see, deah friends," says she to the crowd, "she will not let us suprize her, we will go." But she turned at the door, and says she in reproachful accents, "May be it is right and propah to serve a old friend and neighbah in this way—I have known you a long time, Josiah Allen's wife."

"I have known you plenty long enough," says I, steppin' out of the pail, and shettin' the door pretty hard after 'em.

Josiah came from behind the stove pushin' a chair in front of him, and says he,

"Darn suprize parties, and darn—"

"Don't swear, Josiah, I should think you was bad enough off without swearin'-"

"I *will* darn Betsey Bobbet, Samantha. Oh, my back!" he groaned, settin' down slowly, "I can't set down nor stand up."

"You jumped up lively enough, when they come in," says I.

THE SURPRISE PARTY.

"Throw that in my face, will you? What could I du? And there is a pin stickin' into my shoulder, do get it out, Samantha, it has been there all the time, only I haint sensed it till now."

"Wall," says I in a kinder, soothin tone, drawin' it out of his shoulder, where it must have hurt awfully, only he hadn't felt it in his greater troubles—" Less be thankful that we are as well off as we be. Betsey might have insisted on stopin'. I will rub your shoulders with the linament, and I guess you will feel better; do you suppose they will be mad?"

"I don't know, nor I don't care, but I hope so," says he.

And truly his wish come to pass, for Betsey was real mad; the rest didn't seem to mind it. But she was real short to me for three days. Which shows it makes a difference with her who does the same thing, for they went that night right from here to the Editor of the Augur's. And it come straight to me from Celestine Wilkins, who was there, that he turned 'em out doors, and shet the door in their faces.

The way it was, his hired girl had left him that very day, and one of the twins was took sick with wind colic. He had jest got the sick baby to sleep, and laid it in the cradle, and had gin the little well one some playthings, and set her down on the carpet, and he was washin' the supper dishes, with his shirt sleeves rolled up, and a pink bib-apron on that belonged

to his late wife. They said he had jest finished, and
was wringin' out his dishcloth, when he heard a awful
screamin' from the well twin, and he rushed out with
his dishcloth hangin' over his arm, and found that she
had swallowed a side-thimble; he ketched her up, and
spatted her back, and the thimble flew out half way
across the floor. She screamed, and held her breath,
and the sick one waked up, and sot up in the cradle
and screamed fearfully, and jest then the door bust
open, and in come the suprize party headed by Betsey
Bobbet. They said that he, half crazy as he was, told
Betsey that "if she didn't head 'em off that minute,
he would prosecute the whole of 'em." Some of 'em
was mad about it, he acted so threat'nin', but Betsey
wasn't, for in the next week's Augur these verses
came out:

### IT IS SWEET TO FORGIVE.

> It is sweet to be—it is sweet to live,
> But sweetch the sweet word "forgive;"
> If harsh, loud words should spoken be,
> Say "Soul be calm they come from he—
> When he was wild with toil and grief,
> When colic could not find relief;
> Such woe and cares should have sufficed,
> Then, he should not have been surprized.
>
> When twins are well, and the world looks bright,
> To be surprized, is sweet and right,
> But when twins are sick, and the world looks sad,
> To be surprized is hard and bad,
> And when side thimbles swallowed be,

## A SELF-SACRIFICIN' FEMALE.

How can the world look sweet to he—
Who owns the twin—faih babe, heaven bless it,
Who hath no own motheh to caress it.

Its own motheh hath sweetly gone above,
Oh how much it needs a motheh's love.
My own heart runs o'er with tenderness,
But its deah father tries to do his best,
But housework, men can't perfectly understand,
Oh! how he needs a helping hand.
Ah! when twins are sick and hired girls have flown,
It is sad for a deah man to be alone.

# A DAY OF TROUBLE.

SUGERIN' time come pretty late this year, and I told Josiah, that I didn't believe I should have a better time through the whole year, to visit his folks, and mother Smith, than I should now before we begun to make sugar, for I knew no sooner had I got that out of the way, than it would be time to clean house, and make soap. And then when the dairy work come on, I knew I never should get off. So I went. But never shall I forget the day I got back. I had been gone a week, and the childern bein' both off to school, Josiah got along alone. I have always said, and I say still, that I had jest as lives have a roarin' lion do my housework, as a man. Every thing that could be bottom side up in the house, was.

I had a fortnights washin' to do, the house to clean up, churnin' to do, and bakin'; for Josiah had eat up everything slick and clean, the buttery shelves looked like the dessert of Sarah. Then I had a batch of maple sugar to do off, for the trees begun to run after

I went away and Josiah had syruped off—and some preserves to make, for his folks had gin me some pound sweets, and they was a spilein'. So it seemed as if everything come that day, besides my common housework—and well doth the poet say—"That a woman never gets her work done up," for she don't.

Now when a man ploughs a field, or runs up a line of figgers, or writes a serming, or kills a beef critter, there it is done—no more to be done over. But sposen a woman washes up her dishes clean as a fiddle, no sooner does she wash 'em up once, than she has to, right over and over agin, three times three hundred and 65 times every year. And the same with the rest of her work, blackin' stoves, and fillin' lamps, and washin' and moppin' floors, and the same with cookin'. Why jest the idee of paradin' out the table and teakettle 3 times 3 hundred and 65 times every year is enough to make a woman sweat. And then to think of all the cookin' utensils and ingredients—why if it wuzzn't for principle, no woman could stand the idee, let alone the labor, for it haint so much the mussle she has to lay out, as the strain on her mind.

Now last Monday, no sooner did I get my hands into the suds holt of one of Josiah's dirty shirts, than the sugar would mount up in the kettle and sozzle over on the top of the furnace in the summer kitchen —or else the preserves would swell up and drizzle over the side of the pan on to the stove—or else the puddin' I was a bakin' for dinner would show signs of scorchin', and jest as I was in the heat of the warfare, as you may say, who should drive up but the Editor of the Agur. He was a goin' on further, to engage a hired girl he had hearn of, and on his way back, he was goin' to stop and read that poetry, and eat some maple sugar; and he wanted to leave the twins till he come back.

Says he, "They won't be any trouble to you, will they?" I thought of the martyrs, and with a appearance of outward composure, I answered him in a sort of blind way; but I won't deny that I had to keep a sayin', John Rogers! John Rogers' over to myself all the time I was ondoin' of 'em, or I should have said somethin' I was sorry for afterwards. The poetry woried me the most, I won't deny.

After the father drove off, the first dive the biggest twin made was at the clock, he crep' up to that, and broke off the pendulum, so it haint been since, while I was a hangin' thier cloaks in the bedroom. And while I was a puttin' thier little oversocks under the stove to dry, the littlest one clim' up and sot down in a pail of maple syrup, and while I was a wringin' him out, the biggest one dove under the bed, at Josiah's tin trunk where he keeps a lot of old papers, and come a creepin' out, drawin' it after him like a handsled. There was a gography in it, and a Fox'es book of martyrs, and a lot of other such light reading' and

## BETSEY AND THE TWINS. 61

I let the twins have 'em to recreate themselves on, and it kep 'em still most a minute.

I hadn't much more'n got my eye offen that Fox'es book of Martyrs—when there appeared before 'em a still more mournful sight, it was Betsey Bobbet come to spend the day.

I murmured dreamily to myself "John Rogers"— But that didn't do, I had to say to myself with firmness—"Josiah Allen's wife, haint you ashamed of yourself, what are your sufferin's to John Roger'ses? Think of the agony of that man—think of his 9 children follerin' him, and the one at the breast, what are your sufferin's compared to his'en?" Then with a brow of calm I advanced to meet her. I see she had got over bein' mad about the surprise party, for she smiled on me once or twice, and as she looked at the twins, she smiled 2 times on each of 'em, which made 4 and says she in tender tones,

"You deah little motherless things." Then she tried to kiss 'em. But the biggest one gripped her by her false hair, which was flax, and I should think by a careless estimate, that he pulled out about enough to make half a knot of thread. The little one didn't do much harm, only I think he loosened her teeth a little, he hit her pretty near the mouth, and I thought as she arose she slipped 'em back in thier place. But she only said,

"Sweet! sweet little things, how ardent and impulsive they are, so like thier deah Pa."

She took out her work, and says she, "I have come to spend the day. I saw thier deah Pa bringin' the deah little twins in heah, and I thought maybe I could comfort the precious little motherless things some, if I should come over heah. If there is any object upon the earth, Josiah Allen's wife, that appeals to a feelin' heart, it is the sweet little children of widowers. I cannot remember the time when I did not want to comfort them, and thier deah Pa's. I have always felt that it was woman's highest speah, her only mission to soothe, to cling, to smile, to coo. I have always felt it, and for yeah's back it has been a growin' on me. I feel that you do not feel as I do in this matter, you do not feel that it is woman's greatest privilege, her crowning blessing, to soothe lacerations, to be a sort of a poultice to the noble, manly breast when it is torn with the cares of life."

This was too much, in the agitated frame of mind I then was.

"Am I a poultice Betsey Bobbet, do I look like one?—am I in the condition to be one?" I cried turnin' my face, red and drippin' with prespiration towards her, and then attacked one of Josiah's shirt sleeves agin. "What has my sect done" says I, as I wildly rubbed his shirt sleeves, "That they have got to be lacerator soothers, when they have got everything else under the sun to do?" Here I stirred down the preserves that was a runnin' over, and turned a pail full of syrup into the sugar kettle. "Everybody says that men are stronger than women, and why should they be treated as if they was glass china, liable to break all to pieces if they haint handled careful. And if they have got to be soothed," says I in an agitated tone, caused by my emotions (and by pumpin' 6 pails of water to fill up the biler), "Why don't they get men to sooth'em? They have as much agin time as wimmen have; evenin's they don't have anything else to do, they might jest as well be a soothin' each other as to be a hangin' round grocery stores, or settin' by the fire whittlin'."

I see I was frightenin' her by my delerious tone and I continued more mildly, as I stirred down the strugglin' sugar with one hand—removed a cake from the oven with the other—watched my apple preserves with a eagle vision, and listened intently to the voice of the twins, who was playin' in the woodhouse.

"I had jest as soon soothe lacerations as not, Betsey, if I hadn't everything else to do. I had jest as lives set down and smile at Josiah by the hour, but who would fry him nut cakes? I could smoothe down his bald head affectionately, but who would do off this batch of sugar? I could coo at him day in and day out, but who would skim milk—wash pans—get vittles—wash and iron—and patch and scour—and darn and fry—and make and mend—and bake and bile while I was a cooin', tell me?" says I.

Betsey spoke not, but quailed, and I continued—

"Women haint any stronger than men, naturally; thier backs and thier nerves haint made of any stouter timber; their hearts are jest as liable to ache as men's are; so with thier heads; and after doin' a hard day's work when she is jest ready to drop down, a little smilin' and cooin' would do a woman jest as much good as a man. Not what," I repeated in the firm tone of principle " Not but what I am willin' to coo, if I only had time."

A pause enshued durin' which I bent over the washtub and rubbed with all my might on Josiah's shirt sleeve. I had got one sleeve so I could see streaks of white in it, (Josiah is awful hard on his shirt sleeves), and I lifted up my face and continued in still more reesonable tones, as I took out my rice puddin' and cleaned out the bottom of the oven, (the pudden had run over and was a scorchin' on), and scraped the oven bottom with a knife,

" Now Josiah Allen will go out into that lot," says I, glanceein' out of the north window " and plough right straight along, furrow after furrow, no sweat of mind about it at all; his mind is in that free calm state that he could write poetry."

" Speaking of poetry, reminds me," said Betsey, and I see her hand go into her pocket; I knew what was a comin', and I went on hurriedly, wavin' off what I knew must be, as long as I could. " Now, I, a workin' jest as hard as he accordin' to my strength, and havin' to look 40 ways to once, and 40 different strains on my mind, now tell me candidly, Betsey Bobbet, which is in the best condition for cooin', Josiah Allen or me? but it haint expected of him," says I in agitated tones, "I am expected to do all the smilin' and cooin' there is done, though you know," says I sternly, "that I haint no time for it."

"In this poem, Josiah Allen's wife, is embodied my views, which are widely different from yours."

I see it was vain to struggle against fate, she had the poetry in her hand. I rescued the twins from beneath a half a bushel of beans they had pulled over onto themselves—took off my preserves which had burnt to the pan while I was a rescuin', and calmly listened to her, while I picked up the beans with one hand, and held off the twins with the other.

"There is one thing I want to ask your advice about, Josiah Allen's wife. This poem is for the Jonesville Augah. You know I used always to write for the opposition papah, the Jonesville Gimlet, but as I said the othah day, since the Editah of the Augah lost his wife I feel that duty is a drawing of me that way. Now do you think that it would be any more pleasing and comforting to that deah Editah to have me sign my name Bettie Bobbet—or Betsey, as I always have?" And loosin' herself in thought she murmured dreamily to the twins, who was a pullin' each other's hair on the floor at her feet—

"Sweet little mothahless things, you couldn't tell me, could you, deahs, how your deah Pa would feel about it?"

Here the twins laid holt of each other so I had to part 'em, and as I did so I said to Betsey, "If you haint a fool you will hang on to the Betsey. You can't find a woman nowadays that answers to her true name. I expect," says I in a tone of cold and almost witherin' sarcasm, "that these old ears will yet hear some young minister preach about Johnnie the Baptist, and Minnie Magdalen. Hang on to the Betsey; as for the Bobbet," says I, lookin' pityingly on her, "that will hang on for itself."

I was too well bread to interrupt her further, and I pared my potatoes, pounded my beefsteak, and ground my coffee for dinner, and listened. This commenced also as if she had been havin' a account with Love, and had come out in his debt.

### OWED TO LOVE.

Ah, when my deah future companion's heart with grief is rife,
With his bosom's smart, with the cares of life,
Ah, what higher, sweeter, bliss could be,
Than to be a soothing poultice unto he?

And if he have any companions lost—if they from earth have risen,
Ah, I could weep tears of joy—for the deah bliss of wiping away hisen;
Or if he (should happen to) have any twins, or othah blessed little ties,
Ah, *how willingly* on the altah of duty, B. Bobbet, herself would sacrifice.

I would (all the rest of) life to the cold winds fling,
And live for love—and live to cling.
Fame, victuals, away! away! our food shall be,
His smile on me—my sweet smile on he.

There was pretty near twenty verses of 'em, and as she finished she said to me—

"What think you of my poem, Josiah Allen's wife?"

"Says I, fixin' my sharp grey eyes upon her keenly, "I have had more experience with men than you have, Betsey;" I see a dark shadow settlin' on her eye-brow, and I hastened to apologise—"you haint to blame for it, Betsey—we all know you haint to blame."

She grew calm, and I proceeded, "How long do you suppose you could board a man on clear smiles, Betsey—you jest try it for a few meals and you'd find out. I have lived with Josiah Allen 14 years, and I ought to know somethin' of the natur of man, which is about alike in all of 'em, and I say, and I contend for it, that you might jest as well try to cling to a bear as to a hungry man. After dinner, sentiment would have a chance, and you might smile on him. But then," says I thoughtfully, "there is the dishes to wash."

Jest at that minute the Editor of the Augur stopped at the gate, and Betsey, catchin' up a twin on each arm, stood up to the winder, smilin'.

He jumped out, and took a great roll of poetry out from under the buggy seat—I sithed as I see it. But fate was better to me than I deserved. For Josiah was jest leadin' the horse into the horse barn, when

4

the Editor happened to look up and see Betsey. Josiah says he swore—says he "the d——!" I won't say what it was, for I belong to the meetin' house, but it wasn't the Deity though it begun with a D. He jumped into the buggy agin, and says Josiah,

"You had better stay to dinner, my wife is gettin' a awful good one—and the sugar is most done."

Josiah says he groaned, but he only said—

"Fetch out the twins."

Says Josiah, "You had better stay to dinner—you haint got no women folks to your house—and I know what it is to live on pancakes," and wantin' to have a little fun with him, says he, "Betsey Bobbet is here."

Josiah says he swore agin, and agin says he, "fetch out the twins." And he looked so kind o' wild and fearful towards the door, that Josiah started off on the run.

Betsey was determined to carry one of the twins out, but jest at the door he tore every mite of hair offen her head, and she, bein' bald naturally, dropped him. And Josiah carried 'em out, one on each arm, and he drove off with 'em fast. Betsey wouldn't stay to dinner all I could do and say, she acted mad. But one sweet thought filled me with such joyful emotion that I smiled as I thought of it—I shouldn't have to listen to any more poetry that day.

# THE MINISTER'S BEDQUILT.

The Baptists in our neighborhood have been piecen' up a bedquilt for their minister. He has preached considerable, and held a Sunday school to our school-house, and I wasn't goin' to have any bedquilts done for him without havin' my hand in it to help it along. I despise the idee of folks bein' so sot on their own meetin' housen. Thier is enough worldly things for neighbors to fight about, such as hens, and the school-marm, without takin' what little religion they have got and go to peltin' each other with it.

Sposen Baptists do love water better'n they do dry land? What of it? If my Baptist brethren feel any better to baptise thierselves in the Atlantic ocian, it haint none of my business. Somehow Josiah seems to be more sot onto his own meetin' house than I do. Thomas Jefferson said when we was a arguin' about it the mornin' of the quiltin', says he, "The more water the better," says he, "it would do some of the brethren good to put 'em asoak and let 'em lay over night."

I shet him up pretty quick, for I will not countenance such light talk—but Josiah laughed, he encourages that boy in it, all I can do and say.

I always make a pint of goin' to quiltins any way, whether I go on Methodist principle (as in this case) or not, for you can't be backbited to your face, that is a moral certainty. I know women jest like a book, for I have been one quite a spell. I always stand up for my own sect, still I know sartin effects foller sartin causes. Such as two bricks bein' sot up side by side, if one tumbles over on to the other, the other can't stand up, it haint natur. If a toper holds a glass of liquor to his mouth he can't help swallowin' it, it haint nater. If a young man goes out slay-ridin' with a pretty girl, and the buffalo robe slips off, he can't help holdin' it round her, it haint nater. And quiltin' jest sets women to slanderin' as easy and beautiful as any thing you ever see. I was the first one there, for reasons I have named; I always go early.

I hadn't been there long before Mrs. Deacon Dobbins came, and then the Widder Tubbs, and then Squire Edwards'es wife and Maggie Snow, and then the Dagget girls. (We call 'em *girls*, though it would be jest as proper to call mutton, lamb.)

Miss Wilkins' baby had the mumps, and the Peedicks and Gowdey's had unexpected company. But with Miss Jones where the quiltin' was held, and her girls Mary Ann and Alzina, we made as many as could get round the quilt handy.

The quilt was made of different kinds of calico; all the women round had pieced up a block or two, and we took up a collection to get the battin' and linin' and the cloth to set it together with, which was turkey red, and come to quilt it, it looked well. We quilted it herrin' bone, with a runnin' vine round the border.

After the pathmaster was demorilized, the schoolteacher tore to pieces, the party to Peedicks scandalized, Sophronia Gowdey's charieter broke down—and her mother's new bunnet pronounced a perfect fright, and twenty years too young for her—and Miss Wilkins' baby voted a unquestionable idiot, and the rest of the unrepresented neighborhood dealt with, Lucinda Dagget spoke up and says she—

"I hope the minister will like the bedquilt." (Lucinda is the one that studies mathematics to harden her mind, and has the Roman nose.)

"It haint no ways likely he will," says her sister Ophelia; (she is the one that frizzles her hair on top and wears spectacles.) "It haint no ways likely he will—for he is a cold man, a stun statute."

Now you see I set my eyes by that minister, if he is of another persuasion. He is always doin' good to somebody, besides preachin' more like a angel than a human bein'. I can't never forget—and I don't want to—how he took holt of my hand, and how his voice trembled and the tears stood in his eyes, when we thought our Tirzah Ann was a dyin'—she was in his Sunday School class. There is some lines in your life you can't rub out, if you try to ever so hard. And I wasn't goin' to set still and hear him run down. It riled up the old Smith blood, and when that is riled, Josiah says he always feels that it is best to take his hat and leave, till it settles. I spoke right up and says I—

"Lucky for him he was made of stun before he was married, for common flesh and blood would have gin' out a hundred times, chaste round by the girls as he was." You see it was the town talk, how Ophelia Dagget acted before he was married, and she almost went into a decline, and took heaps of motherwort and fetty.

"I don't know what you mean, Miss Allen," says she, turnin' red as a red brick, "I never heard of his bein' chaste, I knew I never could bear the sight of him."

"The distant sight," says Alzina Jones.

Ophelia looked so mad at that, that I don't know but she would have pricked her with her quiltin' needle, if old Miss Dobbins hadn't spoke up. She is a fat old lady, with a double chin, "mild and lovely as Mount Vernon's sister. She always agrees with everybody. Thomas Jefferson calls her "Woolen

Apron" for he says he heard her one day say to Miss Gowdy—"I don't like woolen aprons, do you Miss Gowdy?"

"Why yes, Miss Dobbin, I do."

"Well so do I," says she. But good old soul, if we was all such peace makers as she is, we should be pretty sure of Heaven. Though Thomas Jefferson says, "if Satan should ask her to go to his house, she would go, rather than hurt his feelin's." That boy worrys me, I don't know what he is a comin' to.

As I said, she looked up mildly over her spectacles, and nodded her purple cap ribbons two or three times, and said "yes," "jest so," to both of us. And then to change the subject says she;

"Has the minister's wife got home yet?"

"I think not," says Maggie Snow. "I was to the village yesterday, and she hadn't come then."

"I suppose her mother is well off," says the Widder Tubbs, "and as long as she stays there, she saves the minister five dollars a week, I should think she would stay all summer." The widder is about as equinomical a woman as belongs to his meetin house.

"It don't look well for her to be gone so long," says Lucinda Dagget, "I am very much afraid it will make talk."

"Mebby it will save the minister five dollars a week," says Ophelia, "as extravagant as she is in dress, as many as four silk dresses she has got, and there's Baptist folks as good as she is that hain't got but one—and one certain Baptist person *full* as good as she is that hain't got any." (Ophelia's best dress is poplin.) "It wont take her long to run out the minister's salary."

"She had her silk dresses before she was married, and her folks were wealthy," says Mrs. Squire Edwards.

"As much as we have done for them, and are still doing," says Lucinda, "it seems ungrateful in her to wear such a bunnet as she wore last summer, a plain white straw, with a little bit of ribbon onto it, not a flower nor a feather, it looked so scrimped and stingy, I have thought she wore it on purpose to mortify us before the Methodists. Jest as if we couldn't afford to dress our minister's wife as well as they did theirs."

Maggie Snow's cheeks was a getting as red as fire, and her eyes began to shine, jest as they did that day she found some boys stonein' her kitten. She and the minister's wife are the greatest friends that ever was. And I see she couldn't hold in much longer. She was jest openin' her mouth to speak, when the door opened and in walked Betsey Bobbet.

"My! it seems to me you are late, Betsey, but walk right into the spare bedroom, and take off your things."

"Things! says Betsey, in a reckless tone, "who

cares for things!" And she dropped into the nearest rocking chair and commenced to rock herself violently and says she "would that I had died when I was a infant babe."

"Amen!" whispered Alzina Jones, to Maggie Snow.

Betsey didn't hear her, and again she groaned out, "Would that I had been laid in yondeh church yard, before my eyes had got open to depravity and wickedness."

"Do tell us what is the matter Betsey," says Miss Jones..

"Yes do," says Miss Deacon Dobbins.

"Matter enuff," says she, "No wondeh there is earthquakes and jars. I heard the news jest as I came out of our gate, and it made me weak as a cat, I had to stop to every house on the way down heah, to rest, and not a soul had heard of it, till I told 'em. Such a shock as it gave me, I shant get over it for a week, but it is just as I always told you, I always said the minister's wife wasn't any *too* good. It didn't surprise me not a bit."

"You can't tell me one word against Mary Morton that I'll believe," says Maggie Snow.

"You will admit that the minister went North last Tuesday, wont you."

Seven wimmin spoke up at once and said: "Yes, his mother was took sick, and telegraphed for him."

4*

"So he said," said Betsey Bobbet, "so he said, but I believe it is for good."

"Oh dear," shrieked Ophelia Dagget, "I shall faint away, ketch hold of me, somebody."

"Ketch hold of yourself," says I coolly, and then says I to Betsey, "I don't believe he has run away no more than I believe that I am the next President of the United States."

"Well, if he is not, he will wish he had, his wife come home this morning on the cars.

Four wimmens said "Did she," two said, "Do tell," and three opened their mouths and looked at her speechlesss. Amongst these last was Miss Deacon Dobbins. But I spoke out in a collected manner, "What of it?"

Says she, "I believe the poor, deah man mistrusted it all out and run away from trouble and disgrace brought upon him by that female, his wife."

"How dare you speak the word disgrace in connection with Mary Morton?" says Maggie Snow.

"How dare I?" says Betsey. "Ask Thomas Jefferson Allen, as it happened, I got it from his own mouth, it did not come through two or three."

"Got what?" says I, and I continued in pretty cold tones, "If you can speak the English language, Betsey Bobbet, and have got sense enough to tell a straight story, tell it and be done with it," says I. "Thomas Jefferson has been to Jonesville ever sense mornin'."

THE QUILTIN' PARTY

"Yes," says she, "and he was coming home, jest as I started for heah, and he stopped by our gate, and says he, 'Betsey, I have got something to tell you. I want to tell it to somebody that can keep it, it ought to be kept,' says he; and then he went on and told; says he,—'The minister's wife has got home, and she didn't come alone neither.'"

"Says I, what do you mean? He looked as mysterious as a white ghost, and says he, 'I mean what I say.' Says he, 'I was in the men's room at the depot this morning, and I heard the minister's wife in the next room talking to some body she called Hugh, you know her husband's name is Charles. I heard her tell this Hugh that she loved him, loved him better than the whole world;' and then he made me promise not to tell, but he said he heerd not only one kiss, but fourteen or fifteen."

"Now," says Betsey, "what do you think of that female?"

"Good Heavens!" cried Ophelia Dagget, "am I deceived? is this a phantagory of the brain? have I got ears? have I got ears?" says she wildly, glaring at me.

"You can feel and see," says I pretty short.

"Will he live with the wretched creature?" continued Ophelia, "no he will get a divorcement from her, such a tender hearted man too, as he is, if ever a man wanted a comforter in a tryin' time, he is the man, and to-morrow I will go and comfort him."

"Methinks you will find him first," says Betsey Bobbet. "And after he is found, methinks there is a certain person he would be as glad to see as he would another certain person."

"There is some mistake," says Maggie Snow. "Thomas Jefferson is always joking," and her face blushed up kinder red as she spoke about Thomas J.

I don't make no matches, nor break none, but I watch things pretty keen, if I don't say much.

"It was a male man," says Lucinda Dagget, "else why did she call him Hugh? You have all heerd Elder Morton say that his wife hadn't a relative on earth, except a mother and a maiden aunt. It couldn't have been her mother, and it couldn't have been the maiden aunt, for her name was Martha instead of Hugh; besides," she continued, (she had so hardened her mind with mathematics that she could grapple the hardest fact, and floor it, so to speak,) "besides, the maiden aunt died six months ago, that settles the matter conclusively, it was not the maiden aunt."

"I have thought something was on the Elders mind, for quite a spell, I have spoke to sister Gowdy about it a number of times," then she kinder rolled up her eyes just as she does in conference meetin's, and says she, "it is an awful dispensation, but I hope he'll turn it into a means of grace, I hope his spiritual strength will be renewed, but I have borryed a good deal of trouble about his bein' so handsome, I have noticed handsome ministers don't turn out well, they most always have somethin' happen to 'em, sooner or later, but I hope he'll be led."

"I never thought that Miss Morton was any too good."

"Neither did I," said Lucinda Dagget.

"She has turned out jest as I always thought she would," says Ophelia, "and I think jest as much of her, as I do of them that stand up for her." Maggie Snow spoke up then, jest as clear as a bell her voice sounded. She hain't afraid of anybody, for she is Lawyer Snow's only child, and has been to Boston to school. Says she "Aunt Allen," she is a little related to me on her mother's side. "Aunt Allen, why is it as a general rule, the worst folks are the ones to suspect other people of bein' bad."

Says I, "Maggy, they draw their pictures from memery, they think, 'now if *I* had that opportunity to do wrong, I should certainly improve it—and so of course *they* did.' And they want to pull down other folks'es reputations, for they feel as if their own goodness is in a totterin' condition, and if it falls, they want somethin' for it to fall on, so as to come down easier like."

Maggy Snow laughed, and so did Squire Edwards' wife, and the Jones'es—but Betsey Bobbet, and the Dagget girls looked black as Erobius. And says Betsey Bobbet to me, "I shouldn't think, Josiah Allen's wife, that *you* would countenance such conduct."

"I will first know that there is wrong conduct," says I—"Miss Morton's face is just as innocent as a baby's, and I hain't a goin' to mistrust any evil out of them pretty brown eyes, till I am obleeged to."

"Well, you will have to believe it," says Ophelia Dagget—and there shall be somethin' done about it as sure as my name is Ophelia Dagget."

"Let him that is without sin amongst you cast the first stone," says Miss Squire Edwards—a better Baptist women never lived than she is.

"Yes," says I in almost piercen' tones, "which of us is good enough to go into the stun business? Even 'pposin' it was true, which I never will believe on earth, which of us could stun her on gospel grounds? —who will you find that is free from all kind of sin"? and as I spoke, remorseful thoughts almost knocked against my heart, how I had scolded Josiah the night before for goin' in his stockin feet.

"I never see a female women yet that I thought was perfect, and yet how willin' they are to go to handlin' these stuns—why wimmen fling enough stuns at each other every day, to make a stun wall that would reach from pole to pole."

Just at this minute the hired girl come in, and said supper was on the table, and we all went out to eat it. Miss Jones said there wasn't anything on the table fit to eat, and she was afraid we couldn't make out—but it was a splendid supper, fit for the Zaar of Rushy.

We hadn't moren' got up from the supper table, and got back into the parlor, when we heard a knock onto the front door, and Miss Jones went and opened it, and who of all the live world should walk in but the minister! The faces of the wimmen as he entered would have been a study for Michael Angelico, or any of them old painters. Miss Jones was that flustrated that she asked him the first thing to take his bunnet off, and then she bethought herself, and says she, 'How's your Ma?' before she had sat him a chair or anything. But he looked as pleasant and composed as ever, though his eyes kinder laughed. And he thanked her and told her he left his mother the day before a good deal better, and then he turned to Maggy Snow, and says he,"

"I have come after you Miss Maggy, my wife come home this mornin' and was so anxious to see you that I told her as I had business past your house this afternoon, I would call for you as I went home, and your mother told me you were here. I think I know why she wants to see you so very much now. She is so proud of our boy, she can't wait till ——"

"Your boy," gasped nine wimmen to once.

"Yes," says he smilin' more pleasant than I ever seen him. "I know you will wish me joy, we have a nice little boy, little Hugh, for my wife has named him already for her father, he is a fine healthy little fellow almost two months old."

It wouldn't have done no good for Michael Angelico or Mr. Ruben, to have been there then, nor none of the rest of them we read about, for if they had their palates'es and easels'es all ready, they never could have done justice to the faces of the Dagget girls, and Betsey Bobbet. And as for Miss Deacon Dobbins, her spectacles fell off unnoticed and she opened her mouth so wide, it was very doubtful to me if she could ever shut it again. Maggy Snow's face shone like a Cherubim, and as for me, I can truly say I was happy enough to sing the Te Deus.

# A ALLEGORY ON WIMMEN'S RIGHTS.

ABOUT a couple of weeks after the quiltin', Thomas Jefferson said to Josiah, one Saturday mornin',

"Father, can I have the old mare to go to Jonesville to-night?"

"What do you want to go to Jonesville for?" said his father, "you come from there last night."

"There is goin' to be a lecture on wimmin's rights; can I have her, father?"

"I s'pose so," says Josiah, kinder short, and after Thomas J. went out, Josiah went on—

"Wimmin's rights, wimmin's rights, I wonder how many more fools are goin' a caperin' round the country preachin' 'em up—I am sick of wimmin's rights, I don't believe in 'em."

This riled up the old Smith blood, and says I to him with a glance that went clear through to the back side of his head—

"I know you don't, Josiah Allen—I can tell a man

that is for wimmin's rights as fur as I can see 'em. There is a free, easy swing to thier walk—a noble look to thier faces—thier big hearts and soles love liberty and justice, and bein' free themselves they want everybody else to be free. These men haint jealous of a woman's influence—haint afraid that she won't pay him proper respect if she haint obleeged to—and they needn't be afraid, for these are the very men that wimmin look up to, and worship,—and always will. A good, noble, true man is the best job old natur ever turned off her hands, or ever will—a man, that would wipe off a baby's tears as soft as a woman could, or "die with his face to the foe."

"They are most always big, noble-sized men, too," says I, with another look at Josiah that pierced him like a arrow; (Josiah don't weigh quite one hundred by the steelyards.)

"I don't know as I am to blame, Samantha, for not bein' a very hefty man."

"You can let your sole grow, Josiah Allen, by thinkin' big, noble-sized thoughts, and I believe if you did, you would weigh more by the steelyards."

"Wall, I don't care, Samantha, I stick to it, that I am sick of wimmin's rights; if wimmin would take care of the rights they have got now, they would do better than they do do."

Now I love to see folks use reason if they have got any—and I won't stand no importations cast on to my sect—and so I says to him in a tone of cold and almost freezin' dignity—

"What do you mean, Josiah?"

"I mean that women hain't no business a votin'; they had better let the laws alone, and tend to thier housework.  The law loves wimmin and protects 'em."

"If the law loves wimmin so well, why don't he give her as much wages as men get for doin' the same work?  Why don't he give her half as much, Josiah Allen?"

Josiah waved off my question, seemin'ly not noticin' of it—and continued with the doggy obstinacy of his sect—

"Wimmin haint no business with the laws of the country."

"If they haint no business with the law, the law haint no business with them," says I warmly.  "Of the three classes that haint no business with the law—lunatics, idiots, and wimmin—the lunatics and idiots have the best time of it," says I, with a great rush of ideas into my brain that almost lifted up the border of my head-dress.  "Let a idiot kill a man; 'What of it?' says the law; let a luny steal a sheep; again the law murmurs in a calm and gentle tone, 'What of it? they haint no business with the law and the law haint no business with them.'  But let one of the third class, let a woman steal a sheep, does the law soothe her in these comfortin' tones? No, it thunders to her, in awful accents, 'You haint no business with the law, but the law has a good deal of business with you, vile female, start for State's prison; you haint nothin' at all to do with the law, only to pay all the taxes it tells you to—embrace a license bill that is ruinin' your husband—give up your innocent little children to a wicked father if it tells you to—and a few other little things, such as bein' dragged off to prison by it—chained up for life, and hung, and et cetery.'"

Josiah sot motionless—and in a rapped eloquence I went on in the allegory way.

"'Methought I once heard the words,' sighs the female, 'True government consists in the consent of the governed;' did I dream them, or did the voice of a luny pour them into my ear?'

"'Haint I told you,' frowns the law on her, 'that that don't mean wimmin—have I got to explain to your weakened female comprehension again, the great fundymental truth, that wimmin haint included and mingled in the law books and statutes of the country only in a condemnin' and punishin' sense, as it were. Though I feel it to be bendin' down my powerful manly dignity to elucidate the subject further, I will consent to remind you of the consolin' fact, that though you wimmin are, from the tender softness of your natures, and the illogical weakness of your minds, unfit from ever havin' any voice in makin' the laws that govern you; you have the right, and nobody can ever deprive you of it, to be punished in a future world jest as hard as a man of the strongest intellect, and to be hung in this world jest as dead as a dead man; and what more can you ask for, you unreasonable female woman you?'

"Then groans the woman as the great fundymental truth rushes upon her—

"'I can be hung by the political rope, but I can't help twist it.'

"'Jest so,' says the law, 'that rope takes noble and manly fingers, and fingers of principle to twist it, and not the weak unprincipled grasp of lunatics, idiots, and wimmin.'

"'Alas!' sithes the woman to herself, 'would that I had the sweet rights of my wild and foolish companions, the idiots and lunys. But,' says she, venturing with a beating heart, the timid and bashful inquiry, 'are the laws always just, that I should obey them thus implicitly? There is old Creshus, he stole two millions, and the law cleared him triumphantly. Several men have killed various other men, and the law insistin' they was out of their heads, (had got out of 'em for the occasion, and got into 'em agin the minute they was cleared,) let 'em off with sound necks. And I, a poor woman, have only stole a sheep, a small-sized sheep too, that my offspring might not perish with hunger—is it right to liberate in a triumphin' way the two million stealer and the man murderer, and inkarcerate the poor sheep stealer? and my children was *so* hungry, and it was such a small sheep,' says the woman in pleadin' accents.

"'Idiots! lunatics! and wimmin! are they goin' to speak t' thunders the law. 'Can I believe my noble right ear? can I bein' blindfolded trust my seventeen senses? I'll have you understand that it haint no woman's business whether the laws are just or unjust, all you have got to do is jest to obey 'em, so start off for prison, my young woman.'

"'But my house-work,' pleads the woman; 'woman's place is home: it is her duty to remain at all hazards within its holy and protectin' precincts; how can I leave its sacred retirement to moulder in State's prison?'

"'House-work!' and the law fairly yells the words, he is so filled with contempt at the idee. 'Housework! jest as if house-work is goin' to stand in the way of the noble administration of the law. I admit the recklessness and immorality of her leavin' that holy haven, long enough to vote—but I guess she can leave her house-work long enough to be condemned, and hung, and so forth.'

"'But I have got a infant,' says the woman, 'of tender days, how can I go?'

"'That is nothing to the case,' says the law in stern

tones. 'The peculiar conditions of motherhood only unfits a female woman from ridin' to town with her husband, in a covered carriage, once a year, and layin' her vote on a pole. I'll have you understand it is no hindrance to her at all in a cold and naked cell, or in a public court room crowded with men.'

"'But the indelikacy, the outrage to my womanly nature?' says the woman.

"'Not another word out of your head, young woman,' says the law, 'or I'll fine you for contempt. I guess the law knows what is indelikacy, and what haint; where modesty comes in, and where it don't; now start for prison bareheaded, for I levy on your bunnet for contempt of me.'

"As the young woman totters along to prison, is it any wonder that she sithes to herself, but in a low tone, that the law might not hear her, and deprive her also of her shoes for her contemptas thoughts—

"'Would that I were a idiot; alas! is it not possible that I may become even now a luny?—then I should be respected.'"

As I finished my allegory and looked down from the side of the house, where my eyes had been fastened in the rapped eloquence of thought, I see Josiah with a contented countenance, readin' the almanac, and I said to him in a voice before which he quailed—

"Josiah Allen, you haint heard a word I've said, you know you haint."

"Yes I have," says he, shettin' up the almanac; "I heard you say wimmin ought to vote, and I say she hadn't. I shall always say that she is too fraguile, too delikate, it would be too hard for her to go to the pole."

"There is one pole you are willin' enough I should go to, Josiah Allen," and I stopped allegorin', and spoke with witherin' dignity and self respect—"and that is the hop pole." (Josiah has sot out a new hop yard, and he proudly brags to the neighbors that I am the fastest picker in the yard.) "You are willin' enough I should handle them poles!" He looked smit and conscience struck, but still true to the inherient principles of his sect, and thier doggy obstinacy, he murmured—

"If wimmin know when they are well off, they will let poles and 'lection boxes alone, it is too wearin for the fair sect."

"Josiah Allen," says I, "you think that for a woman to stand up straight on her feet, under a blazin' sun, and lift both her arms above her head, and pick seven bushels of hops, mingled with worms and spiders, into a gigantic box, day in, and day out, is awful healthy, so strengthenin' and stimulatin' to wimmin, but when it comes to droppin' a little slip of clean paper into a small seven by nine box, once a year in a shady room, you are afraid it is goin' to break down a woman's constitution to once."

He was speechless, and clung to Ayer'es almanac mechanically (as it were) and I continued—

"There is another pole you are willin' enough for me to handle, and that is our cistern pole. If you should spend some of the breath you waste—in pityin' the poor wimmin that have got to vote—in lyin' a pump, you would raise 25 cents in my estimation, Josiah Allen. You have let me pull on that old cistern pole thirteen years, and get a ten quart pail of water on to the end of it, and I guess the political pole wouldn't draw much harder than that does."

"I guess I will get one, Samantha, when I sell the old critter. I have been a calculatin' to every year, but things will kinder run along."

"I am aware of that," says I in a tone of dignity cold as a lump of cold ice. "I am aware of that. You may go into any neighborhood you please, and if there is a family in it, where the wife has to set up leeches, make soap, cut her own kindlin' wood, build fires in winter, set up stove-pipes, drownd kittens, hang out clothes lines, cord beds, cut up pork, skin calves, and hatchel flax with a baby lashed to her side—I haint afraid to bet you a ten cent bill, that that womans husband thinks that wimmin are too feeble and delicate to go the pole."

Josiah was speechless for pretty near half a minute, and when he did speak it was words calculated to draw my attention from contemplatin' that side of the subject. It was for reasons, I have too much respect for my husband to even hint at—odious to him, as odious

4x

could be—he wanted me to forget it, and in the gentle and sheepish manner men can so readily assume when they are talkin' to females he said, as he gently fingered Ayer's almanac, and looked pensively at the dyin' female revivin' at a view of the bottle—

"We men think too much of you wimmin to want you to lose your sweet, dignified, retirin' modesty that is your chieftest charm. How long would dignity and modesty stand firm before the wild Urena of public life? You are made to be happy wives, to be guarded by the stronger sect, from the cold blast and the torrid zone. To have a fence built around you by manly strength, to keep out the cares and troubles of life. Why, if I was one of the fair sect, I would have a husband to fence me in, if I had to hire one."

He meant this last, about hirin' a husband, as a joke, for he smiled feebly as he said it, and in other and happier times stern duty would have compelled me to laugh at it—but not now, oh no, my breast was heavin' with too many different sized emotions.

"You would hire one, would you? a woman don't lose her dignity and modesty a racin' round tryin' to get married, does she? Oh no," says I, as sarcastic as sarcastic could be, and then I added sternly, "If it ever does come in fashion to hire husbands by the year, I know of one that could be rented cheap, if his wife had the proceeds and avails in a pecuniary sense."

He looked almost mortified, but still he murmur'd

as if mechanically. "It is wimmen's place to marry and not to vote."

"Josiah Allen," says I, "Anybody would think to hear you talk that a woman couldn't do but just one of the two things any way—marry or vote, and had got to take her choice of the two at the pint of the bayonet. And anybody would think to hear you go on, that if a women could live in any other way, she wouldn't be married, and you couldn't get her to." Says I, looking at him shrewdly, "if marryin' is such a dreadful nice thing for wimmen I don't see what you are afraid of. You men act kinder guilty about it, and I don't wonder at it, for take a bad husband, and thier haint no kind of slavery to be compared to wife slavery. It is jest as natural for a mean, cowardly man to want to abuse and tyranize over them that they can, them that are dependent on 'em, as for a noble and generous man to want to protect them that are weak and in their power. Figurin' accordin' to the closest rule of arithmetic, there are at least one-third mean, dissopated, drunken men in the world, and they most all have wives, and let them tread on these wives ever so hard, if they only tread accordin' to law, she can't escape. And suppose she tries to escape, blood-hounds haint half so bitter as public opinion on a women that parts with her husband, chains and handcuffs haint to be compared to her pride, and her **love for her** children, and so she keeps still, and suffers agony enough to make four first class martyrs. Field slaves have a few hours for rest at night, and a hope, to kinder boy them up, of gettin' a better master. But the wife slave has no hope of a change of masters, and let him be ever so degraded and brutal is at his mercy day and night. Men seem to be awful afraid that wimmen wont be so fierce for marryin' anybody, for a home and a support, if they can support themselves independent, and be jest as respectable in the eyes of the world. But" says I,

"In them days when men and wimmen are both independent—free and equal, they will marry in the only true way—from love and not from necessity. They will marry because God will join their two hearts and hands so you cant get 'em apart no how. But to hear you talk Josiah Allen, anybody would think that there wouldn't another woman marry on earth, if they could get rid of it, and support themselves without it." And then I added, fixin' my keen grey eyes upon his'en. "You act guilty about it Josiah Allen." "But" says I, "just so long as the sun shines down upon the earth and the earth answers back to it, blowin' all out full of beauty—Jest so long as the moon looks down lovin'ly upon old ocien makin' her heart beat the faster, jest so long will the hearts and souls God made for each other, answer to each other's call. God's laws can't be repealed, Josiah Allen, they wasn't made in Washington, D. C."

I hardly ever see a man quail more than he did, and

to tell the truth, I guess I never had been quite so eloquent in all the 14 years we had lived together—I felt so eloquent that I couldn't stop myself and I went on.

"When did you ever see a couple that hated each other, or didn't care for each other, but what their children, was either jest as mean as pusley—or else wilted and unhappy lookin' like a potato sprout in a dark suller? What that potato sprout wants is sunshine, Josiah Allen. What them children wants is love. The fact is love is what makes a home—I don't care whether its walls are white, stone, marble or bass wood. If there haint a face to the winder a waitin' for you, when you have been off to the store, what good does all your things do you, though you have traded off ten pounds of butter?" A lot of folks may get together in a big splendid house, and be called by the same name, and eat and sleep under the same roof till they die, and call it home, but if love don't board with 'em, give me an umbrella and a stump. But the children of these marriages that I speak of, when they see such perfect harmony of mind and heart in their father and mother, when they have been brought up in such a warm, bright, happy home—they can't no more help growin' up sweet, and noble, and happy, than your wheat can help growin' up straight and green when the warm rain and the sunshine falls on it. These children, Josiah Allen, are the future men and wimmens who are goin' to put their shoulder blades to the wheel and roll this world straight into millenium." Says Josiah,

"Wimmen are too good to vote with us men, wimmen haint much more nor less than angels any way."

When you have been soarin' in eloquence, it is always hard to be brought down sudden—it hurts you to light—and this speech sickened me, and says I, in a tone so cold that he shivered imperceptibly.

"Josiah Allen, there is one angel that would be glad to have a little wood got for her to get dinner with," "there is one angel that cut every stick of wood she burnt yesterday, that same angel doin' a big washin' at the same time," and says I, repeatin' the words, as I glanced at the beef over the cold and chilly stove, "I should like a handful of wood Josiah Allen."

"I would get you some this minute Samantha," says he gettin' up and takin' down his plantin' bag, "but you know jest how hurried I be with my spring's work, can't you pick up a little for this forenoon? you haint got much to do have you?"

"Oh no!" says I in a lofty tone of irony, "Nothin' at all, only a big ironin', ten pies and six loaves of bread to bake, a cheese curd to run up, 3 hens to scald, churnin' and moppin' and dinner to get. Jest a easy mornin's work for a angel."

"Wall then, I guess you'll get along, and to-morrow I'll try to get you some."

I said no more, but with lofty emotions surgin' in my breast, I took my axe and started for the wood-pile.

# A AXIDENT.

I have been sick enough with a axident. Josiah had got his plantin' all done, and the garden seeds was comin' up nice as a pin, I will have a good garden. But the hens bothered me most to death, and kep' me a chasin' out after 'em all the time. No sooner would I get 'em off the peas, then they would be on the mush mellons, and then the cowcumbers would take it and then the string beans, and there I was rushin' out doors bareheaded all times of day. It was worse for me than all my house work, and so I told Josiah.

One day I went out full sail after 'em, and I fell kerslap over a rail that lay in the grass, and turned my ancle jint, and I was laid up bed sick for two weeks. It makes me out of patience to think of it, for we might have a dog that is worth somethin' if it wasn't for Josiah, but as it is, if he haint to the house I have to do all the chasin' there is done, for I might as well get the door step started on to the cattle, or hens, as to get our dog off of it, to go on to any thing.

And he is big as a young eliphant too, eats as much

as a cow, and of all the lazy critters I ever did see, he is the .cap sheaf. Why, when Josiah sets him on to the hens, he has to take him by the collar and kinder draws him along, all the way. And as for cows and calves, he seems to be afraid of 'em, somethin' kinder constitutionel Josiah says. I tell him he might better bark 'em off himself, especially as he is a first rate hand at it, you can't tell him from a dog when he sets out.

One mornin' I says to him, "Josiah Allen, what's the use of your keepin' that pup?"

Says he "Samantha, he is a good feller, if I will kinder run ahead of him, and keep between him and the cows, he will go on to them first rate, he seems to want encouragement."

"Encouragement!" says I, "I should think as much."

I didn't say no more, and that very day the axident happened. Josiah heard me holler, and he come runnin' from the barn—and a scairter man I never see. He took me right up, and was carryin' of me in. I was in awful agony—and the first words I remember sayin' was these, in a faint voice."

"I wonder if you'll keep that pup now?"

Says he firmly, yet with pity, and with pale and anxious face.

"Mebby you didn't encourage him enough."

Says I deliriously, "Did you expect I was goin' to

carry him in my arms and throw him at the hens? I tried every other way."

"Wall, wall!" says he, kinder soothin'ly, "Do keep

THE AXIDENT.

still, how do you expect I'm goin' to carry you if you tonse round so."

He laid me down on the lounge in the settin' room, and I never got off of it, for two weeks. Fever set in —I had been kinder unwell for quite a spell, but I wouldn't give up. I would keep 'round to work. But this axident seemed to be the last hump on the camels back, I had to give in, and Tirzah Ann had to come home from school to do the work.

When the news got out that I was sick, lots of folks came to see me. And every one wanted me to take some different kinds of patented medicine, or herb drink—why my stomach would have been drounded out, a perfect wreck—if I had took half. And then every one would name my descase some new name. Why I told Josiah at the end of the week, that accordin' to their tell, I had got every desease under the sun, unless it was the horse distemper.

One mornin' Miss Gowdey came in, and asked me in a melancholy way, if I had ever had the kind pox. I told her I had.

"Well," says she, "I mistrust you have got the very oh Lord."

It was a Saturday mornin' and Thomas Jefferson was to home, and he spoke up and said "that was a good desease, and he hoped it would prevail; he knew quite a number that he thought it would do 'em good to have it."

She looked real shocked, but knew it was some of Thomas J's. fun. There was one woman that would come in, in a calm, quiet way about 2 times a week, and say in a mild, collected tone,

"You have got the tizick."

Says I, "the pain is in my foot mostly."

"I can't help that," says she gently, but firmly, "There is tizick with it. And I think that is what ailed Josiah when he was sick."

"Why," says I, "that was the newraligy, the doctors said."

"Doctors are liable to mistakes," says she in the same firm but modest accents, "I have always thought it was the tizick. There are more folks that are tiziky than you think for, in this world. I am a master hand for knowin' it when I see it." She would then in an affectionate manner advise me to doctor for the tizick, and then she would gently depart.

There are 2 kinds of wimmen that go to see the sick. There's them low voiced, still footed wimmen, that walks right in, and lays their hands on your hot foreheads so soothin' like, that the pain gets ashamed of itself and sneaks off. I call 'em God's angels. Spozen they haint got wings, I don't care, I contend for it they are servin' the Lord jest as much as if they was a standin' up in a row, all feathered out, with a palm tree in one hand and a harp in the other.

So I told old Gowdey one cold winter day—(he is awful stingy, he has got a big wood lot—yet lets lots of poor families most freeze round him, in the winter time. He will pray for 'em by the hour, but it don't seem to warm 'em up much)—he says to me,

"Oh! if I was only a angel! if I only had holt of the palm tree up yonder that is waitin' for me."

Says I, coolly, "if it is used right, I think good body maple goes a good ways toward makin' a angel."

As I say, I have had these angels in my room—some kinder slimmish ones, some, that would go nigh on to 2 hundred by the stellyards, I don't care if they went 3 hundred quick, I should call 'em angels jest the same.

Then there is them wimmen that go to have a good time of it, they get kinder sick of stayin' to home, and nothin' happenin'. And so they take thier work, and flock in to visit the afflicted. I should think I had pretty near 25 a day of 'em, and each one started 25 different subjects. Wild, crazy subjects, most of 'em, such as fires, runaway matches, and whirlwinds; earthquakes, neighborhood fightin', and butter that wouldn't come; great tidal waves, railroad axidents, balky horses, and overskirts; man slaughter, politix, schism, and frizzled hair.

I believe it would have drawed more sweat from a able bodied man to have laid still and heard it, than to mow a five acre lot in dog days. And there my head was takin' on, and achin' as if it would come off all the time.

If I could have had one thing at a time, I could have stood it better. I shouldn't have minded a earthquake so much, if I could have give my full attention to it, but I must have conflegrations at the same time on my mind, and hens that wouldn't set, and drunken men, and crazy wimmin, and jumpin' sheep, and female suffragin' and calico cut biasin', and the Rushen war, and politix. It did seem some of the time, that my head must split open, and I guess the doctor got scairt about me, for one mornin' after he went away, Josiah came into the room, and I see that he looked awful sober and gloomy, but the minute he ketched my eye, he began to snicker and laugh. I didn't say nothin' at first, and shet my eyes, but when I opened 'em agin, there he was a standin' lookin' down on me with the same mournful, agonized expression onto his features; not a word did he speak, but when he see me a lookin' at him, he bust out laughin' agin, and then says I—

"What is the matter, Josiah Allen?"

Says he, "I'm a bein' cheerful, Samantha!"

BEIN' CHEERFUL.

Says I in the faint accents of weakness, "You are bein' a natural born idiot, and do you stop it."

Says he, "I won't stop it, Samantha, I *will* be cheerful;" and he giggled.

Says I, "Won't you go out, and let me rest a little, Josiah Allen?"

"No!" says he firmly, I will stand by you, and I will be cheerful," and he snickered the loudest he had yet, but at the same time his countenance was so awfully gloomy and anxious lookin' that it filled me with a strange awe as he continued—

"The doctor told me that you must be kep' perfectly quiet, and I must be cheerful before you, and while I have the spirit of a man I *will* be cheerful," and with a despairin' countenance, he giggled and snickered.

I knew what a case he was to do his duty, and I groaned out, "There haint no use a tryin' to stop him."

"No," says he, "there haint no use a arguin' with me—I shall do my duty." And he bust out into a awful laugh that almost choked him.

I knew there wouldn't be no rest for me, while he stood there performin' like a circus, and so says I in a strategim way—

"It seems to me as if I should like a little lemonade, Josiah, but the lemons are all gone."

Says he, "I will harness up the old mare and start for Jonesville this minute, and get you some."

But after he got out in the kitchen, and his hat on, he stuck his head into the door, and with a mournful countenance, snickered.

After he fairly sot sail for Jonesville, now, thinks I to myself, I will have a good nap, and rest my head while he is gone, and I had jest got settled down, and was thinkin' sweetly how slow the old mare was, when I heerd a noise in the kitchen. And Tirzah Ann come in, and says she—

"Betsey Bobbet has come; I told her I guessed you was a goin' to sleep, and she hadn't better come in but she acted so mad about it, that I don't know what to do."

Before I could find time to tell her to lock the door, and put a chair against it, Betsey come right in, and says she—

"Josiah Allen's wife, how do you feel this mornin'?" and she added sweetly, "You see I have come."

"I feel dreadful bad and feverish, this mornin'," says I, groanin' in spite of myself. For my head felt the worst it had, everything looked big, and sick to the stomach to me, kinder waverin' and floatin' round like.

"Yes, I know jest how you feel, Josiah Allen's wife, for I have felt jest so, only a great deal worse—why, talkin' about fevahs, Josiah Allen's wife, I have had such a fevah that the sweat stood in great drops all ovah me."

She took her things off, and laid 'em on the table, and she had a bag hangin' on her arm pretty near as big as a flour sack, and she laid that down in one chair and took another one herself, and then she continued,

"I have come down to spend the entiah day with you, Josiah Allen's wife. We heerd that you was sick, and we thought we would all come doun and spend the day with you. We have got relations from a distance visitin' us,—relations on fathah's side—and they are all a comin'. Mothah is comin' and Aunt Betsey, and cousin Annah Mariah and her two children. But we don't want you to make any fuss for us at all—only cousin Annah Mariah was sayin' yesterday that she did want an old-fashioned boiled dinnah, before she went back to New York. Mothah was goin' to boil one yesterday, but you know jest how it scents up a house, and in *my* situation, not knowin' *when* I shall receive interestin' calls, I *do* want to keep up a agreeable atmospheah. I told Annah Mariah *you* had all kinds of garden sauce. We don't want you to make any difference for us—not in the least—but boiled dinnahs, with a boiled puddin' and sugar sauce, are perfectly beautiful."

I groaned in a low tone, but Betsey was so engaged a talkin', that she didn't heed it, but went on in a high, excited tone—

"I come on a little ahead, for I wanted to get a pattern for a bedquilt, if you have got one to suit me. I am goin' to piece up a bedquilt out of small pieces of calico I have been savin' for yeahs. And I brought the whole bag of calicoes along, for Mothah and cousin Annah Mariah said they would assist me in piecin' up to-day, aftah I get them cut out. You know I may want bedquilts suddenly. A great many young girls are bein' snatched away this spring. I think it becomes us all to be prepared. Aunt Betsey would help me too, but she is in a dreadful hurry with a rag carpet. She is goin' to bring down a basket full of red and yellow rags that mothah gave her, to tear up today. She said that it was not very pretty work to carry visatin', but I told her you was sick and would not mind it. I guess," she continued, takin' up her bag, "I will pour these calicoes all out upon the table, and then I will look at your bedquilts and patterns." And she poured out about half a bushel of crazy look-

KEEPIN' THE SICK QUIET.

in' pieces of calico on the table, no two pieces of a size or color.

I groaned loudly, in spite of myself, and shut my eyes. She heard the groan, and see the agony on to my eye brow, and says she,

"The doctor said to our house this morning, that you must be kept perfectly quiet—and I tell you Josiah Allen's wife, that you *must not* get excited. We talked it over this morning, we said we were all going to put in together, that you should keep perfectly quiet, and not get excited in your mind. And now what would you advise me to do? Would you have a sunflower bedquilt, or a blazing stah? Take it right to yourself Josiah Allen's wife, what would you do about it? But do not excite yourself any. Blazing stah's look more showy, but then sun-floweh's are easier to quilt. Quilt once around every piece, and it is enough, and looks well on the other side, I am going to line it with otteh coloh—white looks betteh, but if two little children jest of an age, should happen to be a playing on it, it would keep clean longeh."

Agin I groaned, and says Betsey, "I do wish you would take my advice Josiah Allen's wife, and keep perfectly quiet in your mind. I should think you would," says she reproachfully. "When I have told you, how much betteh it would be for you. I guess," says she, "that you need chirking up a little. I must enliven you, and make you look happier before I go on with my bedquilt, and before we begin to look at your patterns and bedquilts, I will read a little to you, I calculated too, if you was low spirited; I came prepared." And takin' a paper out of her pocket she says,

"I will now proceed to read to you one of the longest, most noble and eloquent editorials that has eveh come out in the pages of the Augah, written by its noble and eloquent Editah. It is six columns in length, and is concerning our relations with Spain."

This was too much—too much—and I sprung up on my couch, and cried wildly,

"Let the Editor of the Augur and his relations go to Spain! And do you go to Spain with your relations!" says I, "and do you start this minute!"

Betsey was appalled, and turned to flee, and I cried out agin,

"Do you take your bedquilt with you."

She gathered up her calicoes, and fled. And I sunk back, shed one or two briny tears of relief, and then sunk into a sweet and refreshin' sleep. And from that hour I gained on it. But in the next week's Augur, these and 10 more verses like 'em come out.

### BLASTED HOPES.

I do not mind my cold rebuffs
To be turned out with bedquilt stuffs;
Philosophy would ease my smart,
Would say, "Oh peace, sad female heart·"
But Oh, this is the woe to me,
She would not listen unto he.

If it had been *my* soaring muse,
That she in wild scorn did refuse,
I could like marble statute rise,
And face her wrath with tearless eyes;
T'would not have been such a blow to me,
But, she would not listen unto *he*.

# THE JONESVILLE SINGIN' QUIRE.

Thomas Jefferson is a good boy. His teacher to the Jonesville Academy told me the other day, says he,

"Thomas J. is full of fun, but I don't believe he has a single bad habit; and I don't believe he knows any more about bad things, than Tirzah Ann, and she is a girl of a thousand."

This made my heart beat with pure and fervent emotions of joy, for I knew it was true, but I tell you I have had to work for it. I was determined from the first, that Thomas Jefferson needn't think because he was a boy he could do anything that would be considered disgraceful if he was a girl. Now some mothers will worry themselves to death about thier girls, so afraid they will get into bad company and bring disgrace onto 'em. I have said to 'em sometimes,

"Why don't you worry about your boys?"

"Oh things are winked at in a man that haint in a woman."

"Says I, "There is one woman that no man can get

to wink at 'em, and that is Samantha Allen, whose maiden name was Smith." Says I, "It is enough to make anybody's blood bile in thier vains to think how different sin is looked upon in a man and woman. I say sin is sin, and you can't make goodness out of it by parsin' it in the masculine gender, no more'n you can by parsin' it in the feminine or neutral.

And wimmin are the most to blame in this respect. I believe in givin' the D—— I won't speak the gentleman's name right out, because I belong to the Methodist Meetin' house, but you know who I mean, and I believe in givin' him his due, if you owe him anything, and I say men haint half so bad as wimmen about holdin' up male sinners and stompin' down female ones.

Wimmen are meaner than pusly about some things, and this is one of 'em. Now wimmen will go out and kill the fatted calf with thier own hands to feast the male prodigal that has been livin' on husks. But let the woman that he has been boardin' with on the same bundle of husks, ask meekly for a little mite of this veal critter, will she get it? No! She won't get so much as one of the huffs. She will be told to keep on eatin' her husks, and after she has got through with 'em to die, for after a *woman* has once cat husks, she can't never eat any other vittles. And if she asks meekly, why is her stomach so different from the male husk eater, *he* went right off from husks to fatted calves, they'll say to her 'what is sin in a woman haint sin in a man. Men are such noble creatures that they *will* be a little wild, it is expected of 'em, but after they have sowed all thier wild oats, they always settle down and make the very best of men.'

"'Can't I settle down too?' cries the poor woman. '*I* am sick of wild oats too, *I* am sick of husks—I want to live a good life, in the sight of God and man—can't I settle down too?'

"'Yes you can settle down in the grave,' they say to her—'When a woman has sinned once, that is all the place there is for her—a woman *cannot* be forgiven.' There is an old sayin' 'Go and sin no more.' But that is eighteen hundred years old—awful old fashioned.'"

And then after they have feasted the male husk eater, on this gospel veal, and fell on his neck and embraced him a few times, they will take him into thier houses and marry him to their purest and prettiest daughter, while at the same time they won't have the female husker in thier kitchen to wash for 'em at 4 cents an article.

I say it is a shame and a disgrace, for the woman to bear all the burden of sufferin' and all the burden of shame too; it is a mean, cowardly piece of business, and I should think the very stuns would go to yellin' at each other to see such injustice.

But Josiah Allen's children haint been brought **up**

in any such kind of a way. They have been brought up to think that sin of any kind is jest as bad in a man as it is in a woman. And any place of amusement that was bad for a woman to go to, was bad for a man.

Now when Thomas Jefferson was a little feller, he was bewitched to go to circuses, and Josiah said,

"Better let him go, Samantha, it haint no place for wimmin or girls, but it won't hurt a boy."

Says I, "Josiah Allen, the Lord made Thomas Jefferson with jest as pure a heart as Tirzah Ann, and no bigger eyes and ears, and if Thomas J. goes to the circus, Tirzah Ann goes too."

That stopped that. And then he was bewitched to get with other boys that smoked and chewed tobacco, and Josiah was jest that easy turn, that he would have let him go with 'em. But says I—

"Josiah Allen, if Thomas Jefferson goes with those boys, and gets to chewin' and smokin' tobacco, I shall buy Tirzah Ann a pipe."

And that stopped that.

"And about drinkin'," says I. "Thomas Jefferson, if it should ever be the will of Providence to change you into a wild bear, I will chain you up, and do the best I can by you. But if you ever do it yourself, turn yourself into a wild beast by drinkin', I will run away, for I never could stand it, never. And," I continued, "if I ever see you hangin' round bar-rooms and tavern doors, Tirzah Ann shall hang too."

Josiah argued with me, says he, "It don't look so bad for a boy as it does for a girl."

Says I, "Custom makes the difference; we are more used to seein' men. But," says I, "when liquor goes to work to make a fool and a brute of anybody it don't stop to ask about sect, it makes a wild beast and a idiot of a man or a woman, and to look down from Heaven, I guess a man looks as bad layin' dead drunk in a gutter as a woman does," says I; "things look different from up there, than what they do to us—it is a more sightly place. And you talk about *looks*, Josiah Allen. I don't go on clear looks, I go onto principle. Will the Lord say to me in the last day, 'Josiah Allen's wife, how is it with the sole of Tirzah Ann—as for Thomas Jefferson's sole, he bein' a boy it haint of no account?' No! I shall have to give an account to Him for my dealin's with both of these soles, male and female. And I should feel guilty if I brought him up to think that what was impure for a woman, was pure for a man. If man has a greater desire to do wrong—which I won't dispute," says I lookin' keenly on to Josiah, "he has greater strength to resist temptation. And so," says I in mild accents, but firm as old Plymouth Rock, "if Thomas Jefferson hangs, Tirzah Ann shall hang too."

I have brought Thomas Jefferson up to think that it was jest as bad for him to listen to a bad story or song, as for a girl, or worse, for he had more strength

to run away, and that it was a disgrace for him to talk
or listen to any stuff that he would be ashamed to have
Tirzah Ann or me hear.  I have brought him up to
think that manliness didn't consist in havin' a cigar in
his mouth, and his hat on one side, and swearin' and
slang phrases, and a knowledge of questionable amuse-
ments, but in layin' holt of every duty that come to
him, with a brave heart and a cheerful face ; in helpin'
to right the wrong, and protect the weak, and makin'
the most and the best of the mind and the soul God
had given him.  In short, I have brought him up to
think that purity and virtue are both masculine and
femanine gender, and that God's angels are not neces-
sarily all she ones.

Tirzah Ann too has come up well, though I say it,
that shouldn't, her head haint all full, runnin' over,
and frizzlin' out on top of it, with thoughts of beaux
and flirtin'.  I have brought her up to think that marriage wasn't the chief end of life, but savin' her soul.
Tirzah Ann's own grandmother on her mother's side,
used to come visatin' us and stay weeks at a time,
kinder spyin' out I spose how I done by the children,
—thank fortune, I wasn't afraid to have her spy, all
she was a mind too, I wouldn't have been afraid to
had Benedict Arnold, and Major Andre come as spys.
I did well by 'em, and she owned it, though she did
think I made Tirzah Ann's night gowns a little too
full round the neck, and Thomas Jefferson's rounda-

bouts a little too long behind. But as I was a sayin', the old lady begun to kinder train Tirzah Ann up to the prevailin' idee of its bein' her only aim in life to catch a husband, and if she would only grow up and be a real good girl she should marry.

I didn't say nothin' to the old lady, for I respect old age, but I took Josiah out one side, and says I,

"Josiah Allen, if Tirzah Ann is to be brought up to think that marriage is the chief aim of her life, Thomas J. shall be brought up to think that marriage is his chief aim." Says I, "it looks just as flat in a woman, as it does in a man."

Josiah didn't make much of any answer to me, he is an easy man. But as that was the old lady's last visit (she was took bed rid the next week, and haint walked a step sense), I haint had no more trouble on them grounds.

When Tirzah Ann gets old enough, if a good true man, a man for instance, such as I think Whitfield Minkley, our minister's oldest boy is a goin' to make, if such a man offers Tirzah Ann his love which is the greatest honor a man can do a woman, why Tirzah will, I presume, if she loves him well enough, marry him. I should give my consent, and so would Josiah. But to have all her mind sot onto that hope and expectatin' till she begins to look wild, I have discouraged it in her.

I have told her that goodness, truth, honor, vertue

and nobility come first as aims in life. Says I,

"Tirzah Ann, seek these things first, and then if a husband is added unto you, you may know it is the Lord's will, and accept him like any other dispensation of Providence, and—" I continued as dreamy thoughts of Josiah floated through my mind," make the best of him."

I feel thankful to think they have both come up as well as they have. Tirzah Ann is more of a quiet turn, but Thomas J., though his morals are sound, is dreadful full of fun, I worry some about him for he haint made no professions, I never could get him forred onto the anxious seat. He told Elder Minkley last winter that " the seats were all made of the same kind of basswood, and he could be jest as anxious out by the door, as he could on one of the front seats.

Says Elder Minkley, "My dear boy, I want you to find the Lord."

"I haint never lost him," says Thomas Jefferson.

It shocked Elder Minkley dreadfully—but it sot me to thinkin'. He was always an odd child, always askin' the curiousest questions, and I brought him up to think that the Lord was with him all the time, and see what he was doin', and mebby he was in the right of it, mebby he felt as if he hadn't never lost Him. He was always the greatest case to be out in the woods and lots, findin' everything—and sometimes I have almost thought the trash he thinks so much of, such as shells and pieces of rock and stun, and flowers and moss, are a kind of means of grace to him, and then agin I don't know. If I really thought they was I don't suppose I should have pitched 'em out of the winder so many times as I have, clutterin' up the house so.

I worry about him awfully sometimes, and then agin I lay holt of the promises. Now last Saturday night to have heard him go on, about the Jonesville quire, you'd a thought he never had a sober, solemn thought in his head. They meet to practice Saturday nights, and he had been to hear 'em. I stood his light talk as long as I could, and finally I told him to stop it, for I would not hear him go on so.

"Wall," says he, "you go yourself mother sometime, and see thier carryin's on. Why," says he, "if fightin' entitles anybody to a pension, they ought to draw 96 dollars a year, every one of 'em—you go yourself, and hear 'em rehearse if you dont believe me—" and then he begun to sing,

'Just before the battle, mother,
I am thinkin' now of you.'

"I'll be hanged if I would rehearse," says Josiah, "what makes 'em?"

"Let 'em rehearse," says I sternly, "I should think there was need enough of it."

It happened that very next night, Elder Merton preached to the red school house, and Josiah hitched up the old mare, and we went over. It was the first time I had been out sense the axident. Thomas J. and Tirzah Ann walked.

Josiah and I sot right behind the quire, and we could hear every word they said, and while Elder Merton was readin' the hymn, " How sweet for brethren to agree," old Gowdey whispered to Mr. Peedick in wrathful accents,

" I wonder if you will put us all to open shame to-night by screechin' two or three notes above us all ?"

He caught my keen grey eye fixed sternly upon him, and his tone changed in a minute to a mild, sheepish one, and he added smilin' "as it were, deah brother Peedick."

Mr. Peedick designed not to reply to him, for he was shakin, his fist at one of the younger brethrin' in the quire, and says he,

" Let me catch you pressin' the key agin to-night, you young villain, if you think it is best."

" I shall press as many keys as I am a minter for all you. You'r always findin' fault with sunthin' or other," muttered he.

Betsey Bobbet and Sophronia Gowdey was lookin' at each other all this time with looks that made ones blood run cold in thier vains.

Mr. Peedick commenced the tune, but unfortunately struck into short metre. They all commenced loud and strong, but couldn't get any further than " How sweet for bretherin." As they all come to a sudden halt there in front of that word—Mr. Gowdey—lookin' daggers at Mr. Peedick—took out his pitch fork, as if it was a pistol, and he was goin' to shoot him with it, but applyin' it to his own ear, he started off on the longest metre that had ever been in our neighborhood. After addin' the tune to the words, there was so much tune to carry, that the best calculator in tunes couldn't do it.

At that very minute when it looked dark, and gloomy indeed for the quire, an old lady, the best behaved in the quire, who had minded her own business, and chawed caraway peacefully, come out and started it to the tune of "Oh that will be joyful."

They all joined in at the top of their voice, and though they each one put in flats and sharps to suit thier own taste, they kinder hung together till they got to the chorus, and then Mr. Gowdey looked round and frowned fiercely at Shakespeare Bobbet who seemed to be flattin' most of any of 'em, and Betsey Bobbet punched Sophronia Gowdey in the side with her parasol, and told her she was "disgracin' the quire—and to sing slower," and then they all yelled

    How sweet is unitee—e
    How sweet is unitee,
    How sweet for bretheren' to agree,
    How sweet is unitee.

It seemed as if the very feather on my bunnet stood up straight, to hear 'em, it was so awful. Then they collected their strength, and drawin' long breaths, they

THE SINGING QUIRE.

yelled out the next verses like wild Indians round sufferin' whites they was murderin'. If any one had iron ears, it would have went off well, all but for one thing—there was an old man who insisted on bein' in the quire, who was too blind to see the words, and always sung by ear, and bein' a little deaf he got the words wrong, but he sung out loud and clear like a trembone,

> How sweet is onion tee—e,
> How sweet is onion tea.

Elder Merton made a awful good prayer, about trials purifyin' folks and makin' 'em better, and the same heroic patient look was on his face, when he give out the next him.

This piece begun with a long duett between the tenor and the alto, and Betsey Bobbet by open war and strategim had carried the day, and was to sing this part alone with the tenor. She knew the Editer of the Augur was the only tenor singer in the quire. She was so proud and happy thinkin' she was goin' to sing alone with him, that not rightly sensin' where she was, and what she was about, she pitched her part too low, and here was where I had my trial with Josiah.

There is no more sing to Josiah Allen than there is to a one horse wagon, and I have tried to convince him of it, but I can't, and he will probably go down to the grave thinkin' he can sing base. But thier is no sing to it, that, I will contend for with my last breath, it is nothin' more nor less than a roar. But one thing I will give him the praise of, he is a dreadful willin' man in the time of trouble, and if he takes it into his head that it is his duty to sing, you can't stop him no more than you can stop a clap of thunder, and when he does let his voice out, he lets it out strong, I can tell you. As Betsey finished the first line, I heard him say to himself.

"It is a shame for one woman to sing base alone, in a room full of men." And before I could stop him, he struck in with his awful energy, you couldn't hear Betsey's voice, nor the Editor's, no more than you could hear two flies buzzin' in a car whistle.  It was dreadful.  And as he finished the first verse, I ketched hold of his vest, I didn't stand up, by reason of bein' lame yet from the axident—and says I,

"If you sing another verse in that way, I'll part with you," says I, "what do you mean Josiah Allen?"

Says he, lookin' down on me with the persperation a pourin' down his face,

"I am a singin' base."

Says I, "Do you set down and behave yourself, she has pitched it too low, it hain't base, Josiah."

Says he, "I know better Samantha, it *is* base, I guess I know base when I hear it."

But I still held him by the vest, determined that he shouldn't start off again, if I could hender it, and jest at that minute the duett begun agin, and Sophronia Gowdey took advantage of Betsey's indignation and suprise, and took the part right out of her mouth, and struck in with the Editor of the Augur—she is kinder after him too, and she broke out with the curiousest variations you ever heard.  The warblin's and quaverin's and shakin's, she put in was the curiousest of any thing I ever heard.  And thankful was I that it took up Josiah's attention so, that he sunk down on his seat, and listened to 'em with breathless awe, and never offered to put in his note at all.

I waited till they got through singin' and then I whispered to him, and says I,

"Now do you keep still for the rest of this meetin' Josiah Allen."

Says he, "As long as I call myself a man, I will have the privilege of singin' base."

"*Sing*," says I in a tone almost cold enough to make his whiskers frosty, "I'd call it *singin'* if I was you." It worried me all through meetin' time, and thankful was I when he dropped off into a sweet sleep jest before meetin' was out. He never heard 'em sing the last time, and I had to hunch him for the benediction.

In the next week's Augur came out a lot of verses, among which were the following: they were headed

SORROWS OF THE HEART.

Written on bein' broken into, while singin' a duett with a deah friend.

BY BETSY BOBBET.

* * * * * * * *

And sweetness neveh seems so sweet,
As when his voice and mine doth meet,
I rise, I soah, earth's sorrows leaving,
I almost seem to be in heaveng.

But when we are sweetly going on,
Tis hard to be broke in upon;
To droundcd be, oh foul disgrace,
In awful roars of dreadful base.

And when another female in her vain endeavors,
To fascinate a certain noble man, puts in such quavers,
And trills and warbles with such sickish variation,
It don't raise her at all in that man's estimation.

There was 13 verses and Josiah read them all, but I wouldn't read but 7 of 'em. I don't like poetry.

## MISS SHAKESPEARE'S EARRINGS.

Them verses of Betsey's kinder worked Josiah up, I know, though he didn't say much. That line "dreadful roars of awful base" mortified him, I know, because he actually did think that he sung pretty enough for a orkusstry. I didn't say much to him about it. I don't believe in twittin' all the time, about anything, for it makes anybody feel as unpleasant as it does to set down on a paper of carpet tacks. I only said to him—

"I tried to convince you, Josiah, that you *couldn't* sing, for 14 years, and now that it has come out in poetry mebby you'll believe it. I guess you'll listen to me another time, Josiah Allen."

He says, "I wish you wouldn't be so aggravatin', Samantha."

That was all that was said on either side. But I noticed that he didn't sing any more. We went to several conference meetin's that week, and not one roar did he give. It was an awful relief to me, for I never felt safe for a minute, not knowin' when he would break out.

The next week Saturday after the poetry come out, Tirzah took it into her head that she wanted to go to Elder Morton's a visitin'; Maggie Snow was a goin' to meet her there, and I told her to go—I'd get along with the work somehow.

I had to work pretty hard, but then I got it all out of the way early, and my head combed and my dress changed, and I was jest pinnin' my linen coller over my clean gingham dress (broun and black plaid) to the lookin' glass, when lookin' up, who should I see but Betsey Bobbet comin' through the gate. She stopped a minute to Tirzah Ann's posy bed, and then she come along kinder gradually, and stopped and looked at my new tufted bedspread that I have got out a whitenin' on the grass, and then she come up the steps and come in.

Somehow I was kinder glad to see her that day. I had had first rate luck with all my bakin', every thing had turned out well, and I felt real reconciled to havin' a visit from her.

But I see she looket ruther gloomy, and after she sot down and took out her tattin' and begun to tat, she spoke up and says she—

"Josiah Allen's wife, I feel awful deprested to-day."

"What is the matter?" says I in a cheerful tone.

"I feel lonely," says she, "more lonely than I have felt for yeahs."

Again says I kindly but firmly—

"What is the matter, Betsey?"

"I had a dream last night, Josiah Allen's wife."

"What was it?" says I in a sympathizin' accent, for she did look meloncholly and sad indeed.

"I dreamed I was married, Josiah Allen's wife," says she in a heart-broken tone, and she laid her hand on my arm in her deep emotion. "I tell you it was hard after dreamin' that, to wake up again to the cold realities and cares of this life; it was *hard*," she repeated, and a tear gently flowed down her Roman nose and dropped off onto her overskirt. She knew salt water would spot otter color awfully, and so she drew her handkerchief out of her pocket, and spread it in her lap, (it was white trimmed with narrow edgein') and continued—

"Life seemed so hard and lonesome to me, that I sot up in the end of the bed and wept. I tried to get to sleep again, hopin' I would dream it ovah, but I could not."

And again two salt tears fell in about the middle of the handkerchief. I see she needed consolation, and my gratitude made me feel soft to her, and so says I in a reasurin' tone—

"To be sure husbands are handy on 4th of July's, and funeral prosessions, it looks kinder lonesome to see a woman streamin' along alone, but they are contrary creeters, Betsey, when they are a mind to be."

And then to turn the conversation and get her mind offen her trouble, says I,

"How did you like my bed spread, Betsey?"

"It is beautiful," says she sorrowfully.

"Yes," says I, "it looks well enough now its done, but it most wore my fingers out a tuftin' it—it's a sight of work."

But I saw how hard it was to draw her mind off from broodin' over her troubles, for she spoke in a mournful tone,

"How sweet it must be to weah the fingers out for a deah companion. I would be willing to weah mine clear down to the bone. I made a vow some yeahs ago," says she, kinder chirkin' up a little, and beginnin' to tat agin. "I made a vow yeahs ago that I would make my deah future companion happy, for I would neveh, neveh fail to meet him with a sweet smile as he came home to me at twilight. I felt that that was all he would requireh to make him happy. Do you think it was a rash vow, Josiah Allen's wife?"

"Oh," says I in a sort of blind way, "I guess it won't do any hurt. But, if a man couldn't have but one of the two, a smile or a supper, as he come home at night, I believe he would take the supper."

"Oh deah," says Betsey, "such cold, practical ideahs are painful to me."

"Wall," says I cheerfully but firmly, "if you ever

have the opportunity, you try both ways. You jest let your fire go out, and your house and you look like fury, and nothin' to eat, and you stand on the door smilin' like a first class idiot—and then agin you have a first rate supper on the table, stewed oysters, and warm biscuit and honey, or somethin' else first rate, and a bright fire shinin' on a clean hearth, and the tea-kettle a singin', and the tea-table all set out neat as a pink, and you goin' round in a cheerful, sensible way gettin' the supper onto the table, and you jest watch, and see which of the two ways is the most agreable to him.

Betsey still looked unconvinced, and I proceeded onwards.

"Now I never was any hand to stand and smile at Josiah for two or three hours on a stretch, it would make me feel like a natural born idiot; but I always have a bright fire, and a warm supper a waitin' for him when he comes home at night."

"Oh food! food! what is food to the deathless emotions of the soul. What does the aching young heart care for what food it eats—let my deah future companion smile on me, and that is enough."

Says I in reasonable tones, "A man *can't* smile on an empty stomach Betsey, not for any length of time. And no man can't eat soggy bread, with little chunks of salaratus in it, and clammy potatoes, and beefsteak burnt and raw in spots, and drink dishwatery tea, and muddy coffee, and smile—or they might give one or 2 sickly, deathly smiles, but they wouldn't keep it up, you depend upon it they wouldn't, and it haint in the natur' of a man to, and I say they hadn't ought to. I have seen bread Betsey Bobbet, that was enough to break down any man's affection for a woman, unless he had firm principle to back it up—and love's young dream has been drounded in thick, muddy coffee more'n once. If there haint anything pleasant in a man's home how can he keep attached to it? Nobody, man nor woman can't respect what haint respectable, or love what haint lovable. I believe in bein' cheerful Betsey; a complainin', fretful woman in the house, is worse than a cold, drizzlin' rain comin' right down all the time onto the cook stove. Of course men have to be corrected, I correct Josiah frequently, but I believe in doin' it all up at one time and then have it over with, jest like a smart dash of a thunder shower that clears up the air."

"Oh, how a female woman that is blest with a deah companion, can even speak of correcting him, is a mystery to me."

But again I spoke, and my tone was as firm and lofty as Bunker Hill monument—

"Men *have* to be corrected, Betsey, there wouldn't be no livin' with 'em unless you did."

"Well," says she, "you can entertain such views as you will, but for me, I *will* be clingin' in my nature,

I *will* be respected by men, they do so love to have wimmin clingin', that I will, until I die, carry out this belief that is so sweet to them—until I die I will nevah let go of this speah."

I didn't say nothin', for gratitude tied up my tongue, but as I rose and went up stairs to wind me a little more yarn—I thought I wouldn't bring down the swifts for so little as I wanted to wind—I thought sadly to myself, what a hard, hard time she had had, sense I had known her, a handlin' that spear. We got to talkin' about it the other day, how long she had been a handlin' of it. Says Thomas Jefferson, " She has been brandishin' it for fifty years."

Says I, " Shet up, Thomas J., she haint been born longer ago than that."

Says he—" She was born with that spear in her hand."

But as I said she has had a hard and mournful time a tryin' to make a runnin' vine of herself sense I knew her. And Josiah says she was at it, for years before I ever see her. She has tried to make a vine of herself to all kinds of trees, straight and crooked, sound and rotten, young and old. Her mind is sot the most now, on the Editer of the Augur, but she pays attention to any and every single man that comes in her way. And it seems strange to me that them that preach up this doctrine of woman's only spear, don't admire one who carrys it out to its full extent. It

6*

seems kinder ungrateful in 'em, to think that when
Betsey is so willin' to be a vine, they will not be a
tree; but they won't, they seem sot against it.

I say if men insist on makin' runnin' vines of wimmin, they ought to provide trees for 'em to run up on,
it haint nothin' more'n justice that they should, but
they won't and don't. Now ten years ago the Methodist minister before Elder Wesley Minkly came, was a
widower of some twenty odd years, and he was sorely
stricken with years and rheumatiz. But Betsey showed
plainly her willin'ness and desire to be a vine, if he
would be a tree. But he would not be a tree—he
acted real obstinate about it, considerin' his belief.
For he was awful opposed to wimmin's havin' any
rights only the right to marry. He preached a beautiful sermon about woman's holy mission, and how
awful it was in her, to have any ambition outside of
her own home. And how sweet it was to see her in
her confidin' weakness and gentleness clingin' to man's
manly strength. There wasn't a dry eye in the house
only mine. Betsey wept aloud, she was so affected
by it. And it was beautiful, I don't deny it; I always
respected clingers. But I love to see folks use reason.
And I say again, how can a woman cling when she
haint got nothin' to cling to? That day I put it fair
and square to our old minister, he went home with us
to supper, and he begun on me about wimmin's rights,
for he knew I believe in wimmin's havin a right. Says

he, "It is flyin' in the face of the Bible for a woman not to marry."

Says I, "Elder how can any lady make brick without straw or sand—*how* can a woman marry without a man is forthcomin'?" says I, "wimmen's will may be good, but there is some things she can not do, and this is one of 'em." Says I, "as our laws are at present no women can marry unless she has a man to marry to. And if the man is obstinate and hangs back what is she to do?"

He begun to look a little sheepish and tried to kinder turn off the subject on to religion.

But no steamboat ever sailed onward under the power of biled water steam, more grandly than did Samantha Allen's words under the steam of bilein principle. I fixed my eyes upon him with seemin'ly an arrow in each one of 'em, and says I—

"Which had you rather do Elder, let Betsey Bobbet vote, or cling to you? She is fairly achin' to make a runnin' vine of herself, and says I, in slow, deep, awful tones, are you willin' to be a tree?"

Again he weakly murmured somethin' on the subject of religion, but I asked him again in slower, awfuler tones.

"*Are you willin' to be a tree?*"

He turned to Josiah, and says he, "I guess I will go out to the barn and bring in my saddle bags." He had come to stay all night. And that man went to the barn smit and conscience struck, and haint opened his head to me sense about wimmin's not havin' a right.

I had jest arrived at this crysis in my thoughts, and had also got my yarn wound up—my yarn and my revery endin' up at jest the same time, when Betsey came to the foot of the stairs and called out—

"Josiah Allen's wife, a gentleman is below, and craves an audience with you."

I sot back my swifts, and went down, expectin' from the reverential tone of her voice to see a United States Governor, or a Deacon at the very least. But it wasn't either of 'em, it was a peddler. He wanted to know if I could get some dinner for him, and I thinkin' one more trial wouldn't kill me said I would. He was a loose jinted sort of a chap, with his hat sot onto one side of his head, but his eyes had a twinkle to 'em, that give the idee that he knew what he was about.

After dinner he kep' a bringin' on his goods from his cart, and praisin' 'em up, the lies that man told was enough to apaul the ablest bodied man, but Betsey swallowed every word. After I had coldly rejected all his other overtures for tradin', he brought on a strip of stair carpetin', a thin striped yarn carpet, and says he—

"Can't I sell you this beautiful carpet? it is the pure Ingrain."

"Ingrain," says I, "so be you Ingrain as much,"

"I guess I know," says he, "for I bought it of old

Ingrain himself, I give the old man 12 shillin's a yard for it, but seein' it is you, and I like your looks so much, and it seems so much like home to me here, I will let you have it for 75 cents, cheaper than dirt to walk on, or boards."

"I don't wan't it," says I, "I have got carpets enough."

"Do you want it for 50 cents?" says he follerin' me to the wood-box.

"No!" says I pretty sharp, for I don't want to say no two times, to anybody.

"Would 25 cents be any indoosement to you?" says he, follerin' me to the buttery door.

"No!" says I in my most energetic voice, and started for the suller with a plate of nutcakes.

"Would 18 pence tempt you?" says he, hollerin' down the suller way.

Then says I, comin' up out of the suller with the old Smith blood bilin' up in my veins, "Say another word to me about your old stair carpet if you dare; jest let me ketch you at it," says I; "be I goin' to have you traipse all over the house after me? be I goin' to be made crazy as a loon by you?"

"Oh, Josiah Allen's wife," says Betsey, "do not be so hasty; of course the gentleman wishes to dispose of his goods, else why should he be in the mercanteel business?"

I didn't say nothin'—gratitude still had holt of me

—but I inwardly determined that not one word would I say if he cheated her out of her eye teeth.

Addressin' his attention to Betsey, he took a pair of old fashioned ear rings out of his jacket pocket, and says he—

"I carry these in my pocket for fear I will be robbed of 'em. I hadn't ought to carry 'em at all, a single man goin' alone round the country as I do, but I have got a pistol, and let anybody tackle me for these ear rings if they dare to," says he, lookin' savage.

"Is thier intrinsick worth so large?" says Betsey.

"It haint so much thier neat value," says he, "although that is enormous, as who owned 'em informally. Whose ears do you suppose these have had hold of?"

"How can I judge," says Betsey with a winnin' smile, "nevah havin' seen them before."

"Jest so," says he, "you never was acquainted with 'em, but these very identical creeters used to belong to Miss Shakespeare. Yes, these belonged to Hamlet's mother," says he, lookin' pensively upon them. "Bill bought 'em at old Stratford."

"Bill?" says Betsey inquirin'ly.

"Yes," says he, "old Shakespeare. I have been reared with his folks so much, that I have got into the habit of callin' him Bill, jest as they do."

"Then you have been there?" says Betsey with a admirin' look.

"Oh yes, wintered there and partly summered.

But as I was sayin' William bought 'em and give 'em to his wife, when he first begun to pay attention to her. Bill bought 'em at a auction of a one-eyed man with a wooden leg, by the name of Brown. Miss Shakespeare wore 'em as long as she lived, and they was kept in the family till I bought 'em. A sister of one of his brother-in-laws was obleeged to part with 'em to get morpheen."

"I suppose you ask a large price for them?" says Betsey, examanin' 'em with a reverential look onto her countenance.

"How much! how much you remind me of a favorite sister of mine, who died when she was fifteen. She was considered by good judges to be the handsomest girl in North America. But business before pleasure. I ought to have upwards of 30 dollars a head for 'em, but seein' it is you, and it haint no ways likely I shall ever meet with another wo— young girl that I feel under bonds to sell 'em to, you may have 'em for 13 dollars and a ½."

"That is more money than I thought of expendin' to-day," says Betsey in a thoughtful tone.

"Let me tell you what I will do; I don't care seein' it is you, if I do get cheated, I am willin' to be cheated by one that looks so much like that angel sister. Give me 13 dollars and a ½, and I will throw in the pin that goes with 'em. I did want to keep that to remind me of them happy days at old Stratford," and he took the breastpin out of his pocket, and put it in her hand in a quick kind of a way. "Take 'em," says he, turnin' his eyes away, " take 'em and put 'em out of my sight, quick! or I shall repent."

"I do not want to rob you of them," says Betsey tenderly.

"Take 'em," says he in a wild kind of a way, "take 'em, and give me the money quick, before I am completely unmanned."

She handed him the money, and says he in agitated tones, "Take care of the ear rings, and heaven bless you." And he ketched up his things, and started off in a awful hurry. Betsey gazed pensively out of the winder, till he disapeared in the distance, and then she begun to brag about her ear rings, as Miss Shakespeare's relicks. Thomas Jefferson praised 'em awfully to Betsey's face, when he came home, but when I was in the buttery cuttin' cake for supper, he come and leaned over me and whispered—

> "Who bought for gold the purest brass?
> Mother, who brought this grief to pass?
> What is this maiden's name? Alas!
>     Betsey Bobbet."

And when I went down suller for the butter, he come and stood in the outside suller door, and says he,

> "How was she fooled, this lovely dame?
> How was her reason overcame?
> What was this lovely creature's name?
>     Betsey Bobbet."

THE EAR RING PEDLER.

That is jest the way he kep' at it, he would kinder happen round where I was, and every chance he would get he would have over a string of them verses, till it did seem as if I should go crazy. Finally I said to him in tones before which he quailed,

"If I hear one word more of poetry from you to-night I will complain to your father," says I wildly, " I don't believe there is another woman in the United States that suffers so much from poetry as I do! What have I done," says I still more wildly, "that I should be so tormented by it?" says I, " I won't hear another word of poetry to-night," says I, " I will stand for my rights—I will not be drove into insanity with poetry."

Betsey started for home in good season, and I told her I would go as fur as Squire Edwards'es with her. Miss Edwards was out by the gate, and of course Betsey had to stop and show the ear rings. She was jest lookin' at 'em when the minister and Maggie Snow and Tirzah Ann drove up to the gate, and wanted to know what we was lookin' at so close, and Betsey, castin' a proud and haughty look onto the girls, told him that—

"It was a paih of ear rings that had belonged to the immortal Mr. Shakespeah's wife informally."

The minute Elder Merton set his eyes on 'em, " Why," says he, " my wife sold these to a peddler to day."

" Yes," says Tirzah Ann, " these are the very ones;

she sold them for a dozen shirt buttons and a paper of pins."

"I do not believe it," says Betsey wildly.

"It is so," said the minister. "My wife's father got them for her, they proved to be brass, and so she never wore them; to-day the peddler wanted to buy old jewelry, and she brought out some broken rings, and these were in the box, and she told him he might have them in welcome, but he threw out the buttons and a paper of pins."

"I do not believe it—I cannot believe it," says Betsey gaspin' for breath.

"Well, it is the truth," says Maggie Snow (she can't bear Betsey), "and I heard him say he would get 'em off onto some fool, and make her think—"

"I am in such a hurry I must go," said Betsey, and she left without sayin' another word.

# A NIGHT OF TROUBLES.

Truly last night was a night of troubles to us. We was kept awake all the forepart of the night with cats fightin'. It does beat all how they went on, how many there was of 'em I dont know; Josiah thought there was upwards of 50. I myself made a calm estimate of between 3 and 4. But I tell you they went in strong what there was of 'em. What under heavens they found to talk about so long, and in such unearthly voices, is a mystery to me. You couldn't sleep no more than if you was in Pandemonium. And about 11, I guess it was, I heard Thomas Jefferson holler out of his chamber winder, (it was Friday night and the children was both to home,) says he—

"You have preached long enough brothers on that text, I'll put in a seventhly for you." And then I heard a brick fall. "You've protracted your meetin' here plenty long enough. You may adjourn now to somebody else's window and exhort them a spell."

And then I heard another brick fall. "Now I wonder if you'll come round on this circuit right away."

Thomas Jefferson's room is right over ourn, and I raised up in the end of the bed and hollered to him to "stop his noise." But Josiah said, "do let him be, do let him kill the old creeters, I am wore out."

Says I "Josiah I dont mind his killin' the cats, but I wont have him talkin about thier holdin' a protracted meetin' and preachin', I won't have it," says I.

"Wall," says he "do lay down, the most I care for is to get rid of the cats."

Says I, "you do have wicked streaks Josiah, and the way you let that boy go on is awful," says I, "where do you think you will go to Josiah Allen?"

Says he, "I shall go into another bed if you can't stop talkin'. I have been kept awake till midnight by them creeters, and now you want to finish the night."

Josiah is a real even tempered man, but nothin' makes him so kinder fretful as to be kept awake by cats. And it is awful, awfully mysterious too. For sometimes as you listen, you say mildly to yourself, how can a animal so small give utterance to a noise so large, large enough for a eliphant? Then sometimes agin as you listen, you will get encouraged, thinkin' that last yawl has really finished 'em and you think they are at rest, and better off than they can be here in this world, utterin' such deathly and terrific shrieks, and you know *you* are happier. So you will be real encouraged, and begin to be sleepy, when they break out agin all of a sudden, seemin' to say up in a small fine voice, "We won't go home till mornin'" drawin' out the "mornin'" in the most threatenin' and insultin' manner. And then a great hoarse grum voice will take it up " *We won't Go Home till Mornin'* " and then they will spit fiercely, and shriek out the appaulin' words both together. It is discouragin', and I couldn't deny it, so I lay down, and we both went to sleep.

I hadn't more'n got into a nap, when Josiah waked me up groanin', and says he, "them darned cats are at it agin."

"Well," says I coolly, "you needn't swear so, if they be." I listened a minute, and says I, "it haint cats,"

Says he, "it is."

Says I, "Josiah Allen, I know better, it haint cats."

"Wall what is it," says he "if it haint?"

I sot up in the end of bed, and pushed back my night cap from my left ear and listened, and says I,

"It is a akordeun."

"How come a akordeun under our winder?" says he.

"Says I, "It is Shakespeare Bobbet seranadin' Tirzah Ann, and he has got under the wrong winder."

He leaped out of bed, and started for the door.

Says I, "Josiah Allen come back here this minute," says I, "do you realize your condition? you haint dressed."

He siezed his hat from the bureau, and put it on his head, and went on. Says I, "Josiah Allen if you go to the door in that condition, I'll prosicute you; what do you mean actin' so to-night? says I, "you was young once yourself."

"I wuzzn't a confounded fool if I was young," says he.

Says I, "come back to bed Josiah Allen, do you want to get the Bobbets'es and the Dobbs'es mad at you?"

"Yes I *do*," he snapped out.

"I should think you would be ashamed Josiah swearin' and actin' as you have to-night," and says I, "you will get your death cold standin' there without any clothes on, come back to bed this minute Josiah Allen."

It haint often I set up, but when I do, I will be minded; so finally he took off his hat and come to bed, and there we had to lay and listen. Not one word could Tirzah Ann hear, for her room was clear to the other end of the house, and such a time as I had to keep Josiah in the bed. The first he played was what they call an involuntary, and I confess it did sound like a cat, before they get to spitin, and tearin' out fur, you know they will go on kinder meloncholy. He

THOMAS J. ADDRESSES THE SERENADER.

JOSIAH'S PROPOSED RAID.

went on in that way for a length of time which I cant set down with any kind of accuracy, Josiah thinks it was about 2 hours and a half, I myself don't believe it was more than a quarter of an hour. Finally he broke out singin' a tune the chorus of which was,

"Oh think of me—oh think of me."

"No danger of our not thinkin' on you," says Josiah, no danger on it."

It was a long piece and he played and sung it in a slow, and affectin' manner. He then played and sung the follerin'

"Come! oh come with me Miss Allen,
 The moon is beaming;
 Oh Tirzah; come with me,
 The stars are gleaming;
 All around is bright, with beauty teeming,
 Moonlight hours—in my opinion—
 Is the time for love.

 My skiff is by the shore,
 She's light, she's free,
 To ply the feathered oar Miss Allen,
 Would be joy to me.
 And as we glide along,
 My song shall be,
 (If you'l excuse the liberty Tirzah)
 I love but thee, I love but thee.

 Chorus—Tra la la Miss Tirzah,
     Tra la la Miss Allen,
     Tra la la, tra la la,
     My dear young maid.

He then broke out into another piece, the chorus of which was,

"Curb oh curb thy bosom's pain
 I'll come again, I'll come again."

"No you wont," says Josiah, "you wont never get away, I *will* get up Samantha."

Says I, in low but awful accents, "Josiah Allen, if you make another move, I'll part with you," says I, "it does beat all, how you keep actin' to-night; haint it as hard for me as it is for you? do you think it is any comfort for me to lay here and hear it?" says I, "that is jest the way with you men, you haint no more patience than nothin' in the world, you was young once yourself."

"Throw that in my face agin will you? what if I *wuz*! Oh do hear him go on," says he shakin' his fist. "Curb oh curb thy bosom's pain," if I was out there my young feller, I would give you a pain you couldn't curb so easy, though it might not be in your bosom."

Says I "Josiah Allen, you have showed more wickedness to-night, than I thought you had in you;" says I "would you like to have your pastur, and Deacon Dobbs, and sister Graves hear your revengeful threats? if you was layin' helpless on a sick bed would you be throwin' your arms about, and shakin' your fist in that way? it scares me to think a pardner of mine should keep actin' as you have," says I "you have fell 25 cents in my estimation to-night."

"Wall," says he, "what comfort is there in his prowlin' round here, makin' two old folks lay all night in perfect agony?"

"It haint much after midnight, and if it was," says

I, in a deep and majestic tone. "Do you calculate, Josiah Allen to go through life without any trouble? if you do you will find yourself mistaken," says I. "Do be still."

"I *wont* be still Samantha."

Just then he begun a new piece, durin' which the akordeun sounded the most meloncholly and cast down it had yet, and his voice was solemn, and affectin'. I never thought much of Shakespeare Bobbet. He is about Thomas Jefferson's age, his moustache is if possible thinner than hisen, should say whiter, only that is a impossibility. He is jest the age when he wants to be older, and when folks are willin' he should, for you dont want to call him Mr. Bobbet and to call him "bub" as you always have, he takes as a deadly insult. He thinks he is in love with Tirzah Ann, which is jest as bad as long as it lasts as if he was; jest as painful to him and to her. As I said he sung these words in a slow and affectin' manner.

> When I think of thee, thou lovely dame,
> I feel so weak and overcame,
> That tears would burst from my eye-lid,
> Did not my stern manhood forbid;
>     For Tirzah Ann,
>     I am a meloncholly man.
>
> I scorn my books, what are fur lnts
> To such a wretch; or silk cravats;
> My feelin's prey to such extents,
> Victuals are of no consequence.
>     Oh Tirzah Ann,
>     I am a meloncholly man.

## THE LAST PIECE SUNG.

As *he* waited on you from spellin' school,
My anguish spurned all curb and rule,
My manhood cried, "be calm! forbear!"
Else I should have tore out my hair;
    For Tirzah Ann,
    I was a meloncholly man.

As I walked behind, *he* little knew
What danger did his steps pursue;
I had no dagger to unsheath,
But fiercely did I grate my teeth;
    For Tirzah Ann,
    I was a meloncholly man.

I'm wastin' slow, my last year's vests
Hang loose on me; my nightly rests
Are thin as gauze, and thoughts of you,
Gashes 'em wildly through and through,
    Oh Tirzah Ann,
    I am a meloncholly man.

My heart is in such a burning state,
I feel it soon must conflagrate;
But ere I go to be a ghost,
What bliss—could'st thou tell me thou dost—
    Sweet Tirzan Ann—
    Think on this meloncholly man.

He did'nt sing but one more piece after this. I don't remember the words for it was a long piece. Josiah insists that it was as long as Milton's Paradise Lost.

Says I, "don't be a fool Josiah, you never read it."

"I have hefted the book," says he, "and know the size of it, and I know it was as long if not longer."

Says I agin, in a cool collected manner, "don't be a fool Josiah, there wasn't more than 25 or 30 verses at the outside." That was when we was talkin' it over to the breakfast table this mornin,' but I confess it did seem awful long there in the dead of the night; though I wouldn't encourage Josiah by sayin' so, he loves the last word now, and I don't know what he would be if I encouraged him in it. I can't remember the words, as I said, but the chorus of each verse was

Oh! I languish for thee, Oh! I languish for thee, wherever that I be, Oh! Oh! Oh! I am languishin' for thee, I am languishin' for thee.

As I said I never set much store by Shakespeare Bobbet, but truly everybody has their strong pints; there was quavers put in there into them "Oh's" that never can be put in agin by anybody. Even Josiah lay motionless listenin' to 'em in a kind of awe. Jest then we heard Thomas Jefferson speakin' out of the winder overhead.

"My musical young friend, haven't you languished enough for one night? Because if you have, father and mother and I, bein' kept awake by other serenaaders the forepart of the night, will love to excuse you, will thank you for your labers in our behalf, and love to bid you good evenin', Tirzah Ann bein' fast asleep in the other end of the house. But don't let me hurry you Shakespeare, my dear young friend, if you haint languished enough, you keep right on languishin'. I hope I haint hard hearted enough to deny a young man and neighbor the privilege of languishin'.

I heard a sound of footsteps under the winder, followed seemin'ly instantaneously by the rattlin' of the board fence at the extremity of the garden. Judgin' from the sound, he must have got over the ground at a rate seldom equaled and never outdone.

A button was found under the winder in the mornin,' lost off we suppose by the impassioned beats of a too ardent heart, and a too vehement pair of lungs, exercised too much by the boldness and variety of the quavers durin' the last tune. That button and a few locks of Malta fur, is all we have left to remind us of our sufferin's.

## 4th OF JULY IN JONESVILLE.

A few days before the 4th Betsey Bobbet come into oure house in the mornin' and says she,

"Have you heard the news?"

"No," says I pretty brief, for I was jest puttin' in the ingrediences to a six quart pan loaf of fruit cake, and on them occasions I want my mind cool and unruffled.

"Aspire Todd is goin' to deliver the oration," says she.

"Aspire Todd! Who's he?" says I cooly.

"Josiah Allen's wife," says she, "have you forgotten the sweet poem that thrilled us so in the Jonesville Gimblet a few weeks since?"

"I haint been thrilled by no poem," says I with an almost icy face pourin' in my melted butter.

"Then it must be that you have never seen it, I have it in my port money and I will read it to you," says she, not heedin' the dark frown gatherin' on my eyebrow, and she begun to read,

> A questioning sail sent over the Mystic Sea.
>
> BY PROF. ASPIRE TODD.
>
> So the majestic thunder-bolt of feeling,
> Out of our inner lives, our unseen beings flow,
> Vague dreams revealing.
> Oh, is it so? Alas! or no,
> How be it, Ah! how so?
>
> Is matter going to rule the deathless mind?
> What is matter? Is it indeed so?
> Oh, truths combined;
> Do the Magaloi theoi still tower to and fro?
> How do they move? How flow?
>
> Monstrous, aeriform, phantoms sublime,
> Come leer at me, and Cadmian teeth my soul gnaw,
> Through chiliasms of time;
> Transcendentaly and remorslessly gnaw;
> By what agency? Is it a law?
>
> Perish the vacuens in huge immensities;
> Hurl the broad thunderbolt of feeling free,
> The vision dies;
> So lulls the bellowing surf, upon the mystic sea,
> Is it indeed so? Alas! Oh me.

"How this sweet poem appeals to tender hearts," says Betsey as she concluded it.

"How it appeals to tender heads" says I almost coldly, measurin' out my cinnamon in a big spoon.

"Josiah Allen's wife, has not your soul never sailed on that mystical sea he so sweetly depictures?"

"Not an inch," says I firmly, "not an inch."

"Have you not never been haunted by sorrowful phantoms you would fain bury in oblivion's sea?"

"Not once," says I "not a phantom," and says I as I measured out my raisons and English currants, " if folks would work as I do, from mornin' till night and earn thier honest bread by the sweat of thier eyebrows, they wouldn't be tore so much by phantoms as they be; it is your shiftless creeters that are always bein' gored by phantoms, and havin' 'em leer at 'em," says I with my spectacles bent keenly on her, " Why don't they leer at me Betsey Bobbet?"

"Because you are intellectually blind, you cannot see."

"I see enough," says I, "I see more'n I want to a good deal of the time." In a dignified silence, I then chopped my raisons impressively and Betsey started for home.

The celebration was held in Josiah's sugar bush, and I meant to be on the ground in good season, for when I have jobs I dread, I am for takin' 'em by the forelock and grapplin' with 'em at once. But as I was bakin' my last plum puddin' and chicken pie, the folks begun to stream by, I hadn't no idee thier could be so many folks scairt up in Jonesville. I thought to myself, I wonder if they'd flock out so to a prayer-meetin.' But they kep' a comin', all kind of folks, in all kinds of vehicles, from a 6 horse team, down to peacible lookin' men and wimmen drawin' baby wagons, with two babies in most of 'em.

There was a stagin' built in most the middle of the

grove for the leadin' men of Jonesville, and some board seats all round it for the folks to set on. As Josiah owned the ground, he was invited to set upon the stagin'.

And as I glanced up at that man every little while through the day, I thought proudly to myself, there may be nobler lookin' men there, and men that would weigh more by the steelyards, but there haint a whiter shirt bosom there than Josiah Allen's.

When I got there the seats was full. Betsey Bobbet was jest ahead of me, and says she,

"Come on, Josiah Allen's wife, let us have a seat, we can obtain one, if we push and scramble enough." As I looked upon her carryin' out her doctrine, pushin' and scramblin', I thought to myself, if I didn't know to the contrary, I never should take you for a modest dignifier and retirer. And as I beheld her breathin' hard, and her elboes wildly wavin' in the air, pushin' in between native men of Jonesville and foreigners, I again methought, I don't believe you would be so sweaty and out of breath a votin' as you be now. And as I watched her labors and efforts I continued to methink sadly, how strange! how strange! that retirin' modesty and delicacy can stand so firm in some situations, and then be so quickly overthrowed in others seemin'ly not near so hard.

Betsey finally got a seat, wedged in between a large healthy Irishman and a native constable, and she

THE FOURTH OF JULY CELEBRATION.

motioned for me to come on, at the same time pokin' a respectable old gentleman in front of her, with her parasol, to make him move along. Says I,

"I may as well die one way as another, as well expier a standin' up, as in tryin' to get a seat," and I quietly leaned up against a hemlock tree and composed myself for events. A man heard my words which I spoke about 1-2 to myself, and says he,

"Take my seat, mum."

Says I "No! keep it."

Says he "I am jest comin' down with a fit, I have got to leave the ground instantly."

Says I "In them cases I will." So I sot. His tongue seemed thick, and his breath smelt of brandy, but I make no insinuations.

About noon Prof. Aspire Todd walked slowly on to the ground, arm in arm with the editor of the Gimlet, old Mr. Bobbet follerin' him closely behind. Countin' 2 eyes to a person, and the exceptions are triflin', there was 700 and fifty or sixty eyes aimed at him as he walked through the crowd. He was dressed in a new shinin' suit of black, his complexion was deathly, his hair was jest turned from white, and was combed straight back from his forward and hung down long, over his coat coller. He had a big moustache, about the color of his hair, only bearin' a little more on the sandy, and a couple of pale blue eyes with a pair of spectacles over 'em.

As he walked upon the stagin' behind the Editor of

7*

the Gimlet, the band struck up, "Hail to the chief, that in trihump advances." As soon as it stopped playin' the Editer of the Gimlet come forward and said—

"Fellow citizens of Jonesville and the adjacent and surroundin' world, I have the honor and privilege of presenting to you the orator of the day, the noble and eloquent Prof. Aspire Todd Esq.

Prof. Todd came forward and made a low bow.

"Bretheren and sisters of Jonesville" says he; "Friends and patrons of Liberty, in risin' upon this acroter, I have signified by that act, a desire and a willingness to address you. I am not here fellow and sister citizens, to outrage your feelings by triflin' remarks, I am not here male patrons of liberty to lead your noble, and you female patrons your tender footsteps into the flowery fields of useless rhetorical eloquence; I am here noble brothers and sisters of Jonesville not in a mephitical manner, and I trust not in a mentorial, but to present a few plain truths in a plain manner, for your consideration. My friends we are in one sense but tennifolious blossoms of life; or, if you will pardon the tergiversation, we are all but mincratin' tennirosters, hovering upon an illinition of mythoplasm."

"Jess so," cried old Bobbet, who was settin' on a bench right under the speaker's stand, with his fat red face lookin' up shinin' with pride and enthusiasm, (and the brandy he had took to honor the old Revolutionary heroes) "Jess so! so we be!"

Prof. Todd looked down on him in a troubled kind of a way for a minute, and then went on—

"Noble inhabitants of Jonesville and the rural districts, we are actinolitic bein's, each of our souls, like the acalphia, radiates a circle of prismatic tentacles, showing the divine irridescent essence of which composed are they."

"Jes' so," shouted old Bobbet louder than before. "Jes' so, so they did, I've always said so."

"And if we are content to moulder out our existence, like fibrous, veticulated, polypus, clingin' to the crustaceous courts of custom, if we cling not like soarin' prytanes to the phantoms that lower thier sceptres down through the murky waves of retrogression, endeavorin' to lure us upward in the scale of progressive bein'—in what degree do we differ from the accolphia?"

"Jes' so," says old Bobbet, lookin' defiantly round on the audience. "There he has got you, how can they?"

Prof. Todd stopped again, looked down on Bobbet, and put his hand to his brow in a wild kind of a way, for a minute, and then went on."

"Let us, noble brethren in the broad field of humanity, let us rise, let us prove that mind is superior to matter, let us prove ourselves superior to the acalphia—"

"Yes, less," says old Bobbet, "less prove ourselves."

"Let us shame the actinia," said the Professor.

"Yes, jes' so!" shouted old Bobbet, "less shame him!" and in his enthusiasm he got up and hollered agin, "Less shame him."

Prof. Todd stopped stone still, his face red as blood, he drinked several swallows of water, and then he whispered a few words to the Editer of the Gimlet who immegiately come forward and said—

"Although it is a scene of touchin' beauty, to see an old gentleman, and a bald-headed one, so in love with eloquence, and to give such remarkable proofs of it at his age, still as it is the request of my young friend— and I am proud to say 'my young friend' in regard to one gifted in so remarkable a degree—at his request I beg to be permitted to hint, that if the bald-headed old gentleman in the linen coat can conceal his admiration, and supress his applause, he will confer a favor on my gifted young friend, and through him indirectly to Jonesville, to America, and the great cause of humanity, throughout the length and breadth of the country."

Here he made a low bow and sot down. Prof. Todd continued his piece without any more interruption, till most the last, he wanted the public of Jonesville to "dround black care in the deep waters of oblivion, mind not her mad throes of dissolvin' bein', but let the deep waters cover her black head, and march onward."

Then the old gentleman forgot himself, and sprung up and hollered—

"Yes! dround the black cat, hold her head under! What if she is mad! don't mind her screamin'! there will be cats enough left in the world! do as he tells you to! less dround her!"

Prof. Todd finished in a few words, and set down lookin' gloomy and morbid.

The next speaker was a large, healthy lookin' man, who talked aginst wimmin's rights. He didn't bring up no new arguments, but talked as they all do who oppose 'em. About wimmin outragin' and destroyin' thier modesty, by bein' in the same street with a man once every lection day. And he talked grand about how woman's weakness arroused all the shivelry and nobility of a man's nature, and how it was his dearest and most sacred privilege and happiness, to protect her from even a summer's breeze, if it dared to blow too hard on her beloved and delicate form.

Why, before he had got half through, a stranger from another world who had never seen a woman, wouldn't have had the least idee that they was made of clay as man was, but would have thought they was made of some thin gauze, liable at any minute to blow away, and that man's only employment was to stand and watch 'em, for fear some zephyr would get the advantage of 'em. He called wimmin every pretty name he could think of, and says he, wavin' his hands in the air in a rapped eloquence, and beatin' his breast in the same he cried,

"Shall these weak, helpless angels, these seraphines, these sweet, delicate, cooin' doves—whose only mission it is to sweetly coo—these rainbows, these posys vote? Never! my bretheren, never will we put such hardships upon 'em."

As he sot down, he professed himself and all the rest of his sect ready to die at any time, and in any way wimmin should say, rather than they should vote, or have any other hardship. Betsey Bobbet wept aloud, she was so delighted with it.

Jest as they concluded thier frantic cheers over his speech, a thin, feeble lookin' woman come by where I stood, drawin' a large baby wagon with two children in it, seemin'ly a two-year-old, and a yearlin'. She also carried one in her arms who was lame. She looked so beat out and so ready to drop down, that I got up and give her my seat, and says I,

"You look ready to fall down."

"Am I too late," says she, "to hear my husband's speech?"

"Is that your husband," says I, "that is laughin' and talkin' with that pretty girl?"

"Yes," says she with a sort of troubled look.

"Well, he jest finished."

She looked ready to cry, and as I took the lame child from her breakin' arms, says I—

"This is too hard for you."

"I wouldn't mind gettin' 'em on to the ground," says she, "I haint had only three miles to bring 'em, that wouldn't be much if it wasn't for the work I had to do before I come."

"What did you have to do?" says I in pityin' accents.

"Oh, I had to fix him off, brush his clothes and black his boots, and then I did up all my work, and then I had to go out and make six length of fence—the cattle broke into the corn yesterday, and he was busy writin' his piece, and couldn't fix it—and then I had to mend his coat," glancin' at a thick coat in the wagon. "He didn't know but he should want it to wear home, he knew he was goin' to make a great effort, and thought he should sweat some, he is dreadful easy to take cold," says she with a worried look.

"Why didn't he help you along with the children?" says I, in a indignant tone.

"Oh, he said he had to make a great exertion to-day, and he wanted to have his mind free and clear; he is one of the kind that can't have their minds trammeled."

"It would do him good to be trammeled—hard!" says I, lookin' darkly on him.

"Don't speak so of him," says she beseechingly.

"Are you satisfied with his doin's?" says I, lookin' keenly at her.

"Oh yes," says she in a trustin' tone, liftin' her

care-worn, weary countenance to mine, "oh yes, you don't know how beautiful he can *talk*."

I said no more, for it is a invincible rule of my life, not to make no disturbances in families. But I give the yearlin' pretty near a pound of candy on the spot, and the glances I cast on *him* and the pretty girl he was a flirtin' with, was cold enough to freeze 'em both into a male and female glazier.

Lawyer Nugent now got up and said, " That whereas the speaking was foreclosed, or in other words finished, he motioned they should adjourn to the dinner table, as the fair committee had signified by a snowy signal that fluttered like a dove of promise above waves of emerald, or in plainer terms by a *towel*, that dinner was forthcoming; whereas he motioned that they should adjourn *sine die* to the aforesaid table."

Old Mr. Bobbet, and the Editer of the Gimlet seconded the motion at the same time. And Shakespeare Bobbet wantin' to do somethin' in a public way, got up and motioned "that they proceed to the table on the usial road", but there wasn't any other way—only to wade the creek—that didn't seem to be necessary, but nobody took no notice of it, so it was jest as well.

The dinner was good, but there was an awful crowd round the tables, and I was glad I wore my old lawn dress, for the children was thick, and so was bread and butter, and sass of all kinds, and jell tarts And I hain't no shirk. I jest plunged right into the heat of

WHAT HAPPENED AT THE DINNER

## DINNER AND TOAST.      171

the battle, as you may say, waitin' on the children, and the spots on my dress skirt would have been too much for anybody that couldn't count 40. To say nothin' about old Mr. Peedick steppin' through the back breadth, and Betsey Bobbet ketchin' holt of me, and rippin' it off the waist as much as 1-2 a yard. And then a horse started up behind the widder Tubbs, as I was bendin' down in front of her to get somethin' out of a basket, and she weighin' above 200, was precipitated onto my straw bonnet, jammin' it down almost as flat as it was before it was braided. I came off pretty well in other respects, only about two yards of the ruffin' of my black silk cape was tore by two boys who got to fightin' behind me, and bein' blind with rage tore it off, thinkin' they had got holt of each other's hair. There was a considerable number of toasts drank, I cant remember all of 'em, but among 'em was these,

"The eagle of Liberty; May her quills lengthen till the proud shadow of her wings shall sweetly rest on every land."

"The 4th of July; the star which our old four fathers tore from the ferocious mane of the howling lion of England, and set in the calm and majestic brow of *E pluribus unum.* May it gleam with brighter and brighter radience, till the lion shall hide his dazzled eyes, and cower like a stricken lamb at the feet of *E pluribus.*"

"Dr. Bombus our respected citizen; how he tenderly ushers us into a world of trial, and professionally and scientifically assists us out of it. May his troubles be as small as his morphine powders, and the circle of his joys as well rounded as his pills."

"The press of Jonesville, the Gimlet, and the Augur; May they perforate the crust of ignorance with a gigantic hole, through which blushing civilization can sweetly peer into futurity."

"The fair sect: first in war, first in peace, and first in the hearts of their countrymen. May them that love the aforesaid, flourish like a green bayberry tree, whereas may them that hate them, dwindle down as near to nothin' as the bonnets of the aforesaid."

That peice of toast was Lawer Nugent's.

Prof. Aspire Todd's was the last.

"The Lumineus Lamp of Progression, whose sciatherical shadows falling upon earthly matter, not promoting sciolism, or Siccity, may it illumine humanity as it tardigradely floats from matter's aquius wastes, to minds majestic and apyrous climes."

Shakspeare Bobbet then rose up, and says he,

"Before we leave this joyous grove I have a poem which I was requested to read to you, it is dedicated to the Goddess of Liberty, and was **transposed** by another female, who modestly desires her name not to be mentioned any further than the initials B. B."

He then read the follerin' spirited lines:

> Before all causes East or West,
> I love the Liberty cause the best,
> I love its cheerful greetings;
> No joys on earth can e'er be found,
> Like those pure pleasures that abound,
> At Jonesville Liberty meetings.
>
> To all the world I give my hand,
> My heart is with that noble band,
> The Jonesville Liberty brothers;
> May every land preserved be,
> Each clime that dotes on Liberty—
> Jonesville before all others.

The picknick never broke up till most night, I went home a little while before it broke, and if there was a beat out creeter, I was; I jest dropped my delapidated form into a rockin' chair with a red cushien and says I,

"There needn't be another word said, I will never go to another 4th as long as my name is Josiah Allen's wife."

"You haint patriotic enough Semantha says Josiah, you dont love your country."

"What good has it done the nation to have me all tore to pieces? says I, "Look at my dress, look at my bonnet and cape, any one ought to be a iron clad to stand it, look at my dishes!" says I.

"I guess the old heroes of the Revolution went through more than that," says Josiah.

"Well I haint a old hero!" says I coolly.

"Well you can honor 'em cant you?"

"Honor 'em! Josiah Allen what good has it done to old Mr. Layfayette to have my new earthern pie plates smashed to bits, and a couple of tines broke off of one of my best forks? What good has it done to old Thomas Jefferson, to have my lawn dress tore off of me by Betsey Bobbet? what benefit has it been to John Adams, or Isaac Putnam to have old Peedick step through it? what honor has it been to George Washington to have my straw bonnet flatted down tight to my head? I am sick of this talk about honorin, and liberty and duty, I am sick of it," says I "folks will make a pack horse of duty, and ride it to circus'es, and bull fights, if we had 'em. You may talk about honorin' the old heroes and goin' through all these performances to please 'em. But if they are in Heaven they can get along without heerin' the Jonesville brass band, and if they haint, they are probably where fireworks haint much of a rarity to 'em."

Josiah quailed before my lofty tone and I relapsed into a weary and delapidated silence.

COUNTIN' THE COST.

## SIMON SLIMPSEY AND HIS MOURNFUL FOREBODIN'S.

TWO or three weeks after this, Thomas Jefferson went to the school house to meetin' one Sunday night, and he broke out to the breakfast table the next mornin'—

"Mother, I am sick of the Jews," says he, "I should think the Jews had a hard enough time a wanderin' for 40 years, it seems to me if I was in minister's places I would let 'em rest a little while now, and go to preachin' to livin' sinners, when the world is full of 'em. There was two or three drunkards there last night, a thief, four hypocrites, and—"

"One little conceited creeter that thinks he knows more than his old minister," says I in a rebukin' tone.

"Yes, I noticed Shakespeare Bobbet was there," says he calmly. "But wouldn't it have been better, mother, to have preached to these livin' sinners that are goin to destruction round him, and that ought to be chased up, and punched in the side with the Gospel, than to chase round them old Jews for an hour and a half? Them old men deserve rest, and ought to have it."

Says I, "Elder Wesley Minkley used 'em as a means of grace to carry his hearers towards heaven."

Says Thomas, "I can go out in the woods alone, and lay down and look up to the sky, and get nearer to heaven, than I can by follerin' up them old dead Jews."

Says I in awful earnest tones, "Thomas Jefferson, you are gettin' into a dangerous path," says I, "don't let me hear another word of such talk; we should all be willin' to bear our crosses."

"I am willin' to bear any reasonable cross, mother, but I hate to tackle them old Jews and shoulder 'em, for there don't seem to be any need of it."

I put on about as cold a look onto my face as I could under the circumstances, (I had been fryin' buckwheat pancakes,) and Thomas J. turned to his father—

"Betsey Bobbet talked in meetin' last night after the sermon, father, she said she knew that she was religious, because she felt that she loved the brethren."

Josiah laughed, the way he encourages that boy is awful, but I spoke in almost frigid tones, as I passed him his 3d cup of coffee,

"She meant it in a scriptural sense, of course."

"I guess you'd think she meant it in a earthly sense,

if you had seen her hang on to old Slimpsey last night, she'll marry that old man yet, if he don't look out."

"Oh shaw!" says I coolly, "she is payin' attention to the Editer of the Augur."

"She'll never get him," says he; "she means to be on the safe side, and get one or the other of 'em; how stiddy she has been to meetin' sense old Slimpsey moved into the place."

"You shall not make light of her religion, Thomas Jefferson," says I, pretty severely.

"I won't, mother, I shouldn't feel right to, for it is light enough now, it don't all consist in talkin' in meetin', mother. I don't believe in folks'es usin' up all their religion Sunday nights, and then goin' without any all the rest of the week, it looks as shiftless in 'em as a three-year-old hat on a female. The religion that gets up on Sunday nights, and then sets down all the rest of the week, I don't think much of."

Says I in a tone of deep rebuke, "Instead of tendin' other folks'es motes, Thomas Jefferson, you had better take care of your own beams, you'll have plenty work, enough to last you one spell."

"And if you have got through with your breakfast," says his father, "you had better go and fodder the cows."

Thomas J. arose with alacraty and went to the barn, and his father soon drew on his boots and follered him, and with a pensive brow I turned out my dishwater.

I hadn't got my dishes more than half done, when with no warnin' of no kind, the door bust open, and in tottered Simon Slimpsey, pale as a piece of a white cotton shirt. I wildly wrung out my dishcloth, and offered him a chair, sayin' in a agitated tone, "What is the matter, Simon Slimpsey?"

"Am I pursued?" says he in a voice of low frenzy, as he sunk into a wooden bottomed chair. I cast one or two eagle glances out of the window, both ways, and replied in a voice of choked down emotion,

"There haint nobody in sight; has your life been attackted by burglers and incindiarys? speak, Simon Slimpsey, speak!"

He struggled nobly for calmness, but in vain, and then he put his hand wildly to his brow, and murmured in low and hollow accents—

"Betsey Bobbet."

I see he was overcome by as many as six or seven different emotions of various anguishes, and I give him pretty near a minute to recover himself, and then says I as I sadly resumed my dishcloth,

"What of her, Simon Slimpsey?"

"She'll be the death on me,," says he, "and that haint the worst on it, my sole is jeopardized on account of her. Oh," says he, groanin' in a anguish, "could you believe it, Miss Allen, that I—a member of a Authodox church and the father of 13 small children— could be tempted to swear? Behold that wretch. As

I come through your gate jest now, I said to myself 'By Jupiter, I can't stand it so, much longer.' And last night I wished I was a ghost, for I thought if I was a apperition I could have escaped from her view. Oh," says he, groanin' agin, " I have got so low as to wish I was a ghost."

He paused, and in a deep and almost broodin' silence, I finished my dishes, and hung up my dishpan.

"She come rushin' out of Deacon Gowdey's, as I come by jest now, to talk to me, she don't give me no peace, last night she would walk tight to my side all the way home, and she looked hungry at the gate, as I went through and fastened it on the inside."

Agin he paused overcome by his emotions, and I looked pityingly on him. He was a small boned man of about seventy summers and winters. He was always a weak, feeble, helpless critter, a kind of a underlin always. He never had any morals, he got out of morals when he was a young man, and haint been able to get any sense. He has always drinked a good deal of liquor, and has chawed so much tobacco that his mouth looks more like a old yellow spitoon than anything else. As I looked sadly on him I see that age, who had ploughed the wrinkles into his face, had turned the furrows deep. The cruel fingers of time, or some other female, had plucked nearly every hair from his head, and the ruthless hand of fate had also seen fit to deprive him of his eye winkers, not

8

one solitary winker bein' left for a shade tree (as it were) to protect the pale pupils below ; and they bein' a light watery blue, and the lids bein' inflamed, they

SIMON SLIMPSEY.

looked sad indeed. Owin' to afflictive providences he was dressed up more than men generally be, for his neck bein' badly swelled he wore a string of amber beads, and in behalf of his sore eyes he wore ear rings. But truly outside splendor and glitter wont satisfy the mind, and bring happiness. I looked upon his mournful face, and my heart melted inside of me, almost as soft as it could, almost as soft as butter in the month of August. And I said to him in a soothin' and encouragin' tone,

"Mebby she will marry the Editer of the Augur, she is payin' attention to him."

"No she wont," says he in a solemn and affectin' way, that brought tears to my eyes as I sot peelin' my onions for dinner. "No she wont, I shall be the one, I feel it. I was always the victim, I was always down trodden. When I was a baby my mother had two twins, both of 'em a little older than me, and they almost tore me to pieces before I got into trowses. Mebby it would have been better for me if they had," says he in a mewsin' and mournful tone—I knew he thought of Betsey then—and heavin' a deep sigh he resumed,

"When I went to school and we played leap frog, if there was a frog to be squshed down under all the rest, I was that frog. It has always been so—if there was ever a underlin' and a victim wanted, I was that underlin' and that victim. And Betsey Bobbet will get round me yet, you see if she dont, wimmen are awful perseverin' in such things."

"Cheer up Simon Slimpsey, you haint oblecged to marry her, it is a free country, folks haint oblecged to marry unless they are a mind to, it dont take a brass band to make that legal." I quoted these words in a light and joyous manner hopin' to rouse him from his dispondancy, but in vain, for he only repeated in a gloomy tone,

"She'll get round me yet, Miss Allen, I feel it." And as the dark shade deepened on his eye brow he said,

"Have you seen her verses in the last week's Augur?"

"No" says I "I haint."

In a silent and hopeless way, he took the paper out

of his pocket and handed it to me and I read as follers:—

### A SONG.

Composed not for the strong minded females, who madly and indecently insist on rights, but for the retiring and delicate minded of the sex, who modestly murmer, "we will not have any rights, we scorn them." Will some modest and bashful sisteh set it to music, that we may timidly, but loudly warble it; and oblige, hers 'till deth, in the glorious cause of wimmen's only true speah.   BETSEY BOBBET.

> Not for strong minded wimmen,
> Do I now tune up my liah;
> Oh, not for them would I kindle up the the sacred fiah.
> Oh, modest, bashful female,
> For you I tune up my lay;
> Although strong minded wimmen sneah,
> We'll conqueh in the fray.
>   CHORUS.—Press onward, do not feah, sistehs,
>       Press onward, do not feah;
>       Remembeh wimmen's speah, sistehs,
>       Remembeh wimmen's speah.
>
> It would cause some fun if poor Miss Wade
> Should say of her boy Harry,
> I shall not give him any trade,
> But bring him up to marry;
> And would cause some fun, of course deah maids,
> If Miss Wades'es Harry,
> Should lose his end and aim in life,
> And find no chance to marry.
>   CHORUS.—Press onward, do not feah, sistehs, &c.
>
> Yes, wedlock is our only hope,
> All o'er this mighty nation;
> Men are brought up to other trades,
> But this is our vocation.
> Oh, not for sense or love, ask we;
> We ask not to be courted,
> Our watch-word is to married be,
> That we may be supported.
>   CHORUS.—Press onward, do not feah, sistehs, &c.

Say not, you're strong and love to work;
Are healthier than your brothch,
Who for a blacksmith is designed;
Such feelins you must smothch;
Your restless hands fold up, or gripe
Your waist into a span,
And spend your strength in looking out
To hail the coming man.
    Chorus.—Press onward, do not feah, sistchs, &c.

Oh, do not be discouraged, when
You find your hopes brought down;
And when you meet unwilling men,
Heed not their gloomy frown;
Yield not to wild dispaih;
Press on and give no quartah,
In battle all is faih;
We'll win for we had ortch.
    Chorus.—Press onward, do not feah, sistchs,
        Press onward do not feah,
        Remembeh wimmen's speah, sisters,
        Remembeh wimmen's speah.

"Wall" says I in a encouragin' tone, "that haint much different from the piece she printid a week or two ago, that was about womans spear."

"It is that spear that is a goin' to destroy me," says he mournfully.

"Dont give up so, Simon Slimpsey, I hate to see you lookin' so gloomy and depressted."

"It is the awful detarmination these lines breathe forth that appauls me" says he. "I have seen it in another. Betsey Bobbet reminds me dreadfully of another. And I dont want to marry again Miss Allen, I dont want to," says he lookin' me pitifully in the face, "I didnt want to marry the first time. I wanted to be a bachelder, I think they have the easiest time of it, by half. Now there is a friend of mine, that never was married, he is jest my age, or that is, he is only half an hour younger, and that haint enough difference to make any account of, is it Miss Allen?" says he in a pensive, and enquirin' tone.

"No," says I in a reasonable accent. "No, Simon Slimpsey, it haint."

"Wall that man has always been a bachelder, and you ought to see what a head of hair he has got, sound at the roots now, not a lock missing. I wanted to be one, she, my late wife, came and kept house for me and married me. I lived with her for 18 years, and when she left me, he murmured with a contented look, "I was reconciled to it. I was reconciled for sometime before it took place. I dont want to say anything against nobody that haint here, but I lost some hair by my late wife," says he puttin' his hand to his bald head in a abstracted way, as gloomy reflections crowded onto him, "I lost a good deal of hair by her, and I haint much left as you can see," says he in a meloncholy way "I did want to save a lock or two for my children to keep, as a relict of me. I have 13 children as you know, countin' each pair of twins as two, and it would take a considerable number of hairs to go round." Agin he paused overcome by his feelin's, I knew not what to say to comfort him, and I poured onto him a few comfortin' adjectives.

"Mebby you are borrowin' trouble without a cause Simon Slimpsey! with life there is hope! it is always the darkest before daylight." But in vain. He only sighed mournfully.

"She'll get round me yet Miss Allen, mark my

SIMON OVERCOME.

words, and when the time comes you will think of what I told you." His face was most black with gloomy aprehension, as he reflected agin. "You see if she dont get round me!" and a tear began to flow.

I turned away with instinctive delicacy and sot my pan of onions in the sink, but when I glanced at him agin it was still flowin'. And I said to him in a tone of about two thirds pity and one comfort,

"Chirk up, Simon Slimpsey, be a man."

"That is the trouble," says he "if I wasn't a man, she would give me some peace." And he wept into his red silk handkerchief (with a yellow border) bitterly.

# FREE LOVE LECTURES.

It was a beautiful mornin' in October. The trees in the woods nigh by, had all got their new fall suits on, red and purple and orange, while further back, the old hills seemed to be a settin' up with a blue gauze vail on. There was a little mite of a breeze blowin' up through the orchard, where the apples lay in red and yellow heaps in the green grass. Everything looked so beautiful and fresh, that as I went out on the doorstep to shake the tablecloth, my heart fairly sung for joy. And I exclaimed to Josiah in clear, happy tones,

"What a day it is, Josiah, to gather the winter apples and pull the beets."

He says, "Yes, Samantha, and after you get your work done up, don't you s'pose you could come out and pick up apples a spell?"

I told him in the same cheerful tones I had formally used, "that I would, and that I would hurry up my dishes as fast as I could, and come out."

But alas! how little do we know what trial a hour may bring forth; this hour brought forth Betsey Bobbet. As I went to the door to throw out my dishwater, I see her comin' through the gate. I controlled myself pretty well, and met her with considerable calmness. She was in awful good spirits. There had been a lecture on Free Love to Jonesville; Prof. Theron Gasher had been a lecturin' there, and Betsey had attended to it, and was all full of the idee. She begun almost before she sot down, and says she,

Josiah Allens wife you cant imagine what new and glorious and soaring ideahs that man has got into his head."

"Let him soar," says I coldly, it dont hurt me."

Says she, "He is too soaring a soul to be into this cold unsympathizing earth, he ought by good right to be in a warmeh speah."

Says I coldly, and almost frigidly, "From what I have heard of his lecture I think so too, a good deal warmer."

Says she, "He was to our house yesterday, he said he felt dreadful drawed to me, a kind of a holy drawing you know, I neveh saw such a saintly, heavenly minded man in my life. Why he got into such a spirutal state—when motheh went out of the room a minute—he kissed me moah than a dozen times; that man is moah than half a angel, Josiah Allens wife."

8*

I gave her a look that pierced like sheet lightnin' through her tow frizzles and went as much as half through her brain.

"Haint Theron Gusher a married man?"

"Oh yes, some."

"Some!" I repeated in a cold accent. "He is either married or he haint married one or the other," and again I repeated coldly "is he a married man Betsey?"

"Oh yes, he has been married a few times, or what the cold world calls marrying—he has got a wife now, but I do not believe he has found his affinity yet, though he has got several bills of divorcement from various different wimmen trying to find her. That may be his business to Jonesville, but it does not become me to speak of it."

Says I "Betsey Bobbet!" and I spoke in a real solemn camp meetin' tone, for I was talkin' on deep principle," says I, "you say he is a married man—and now to say nothin' of your own modesty if you have got any and stand up onto clear principle, how would you like to have your husband if you had one, round kissin' other wimmen?"

"Oh," says she, "His wife will neveh know it, neveh!"

"If it is such a pious, heavenly, thing, why not tell her of it?"

"Oh Prof. Gusheh says that some natures are to

gross and earthly to comprehend how souls can meet, scorning and forgetting utterly those vile, low, clay bodies of ours. He does not think much of these clay bodies anyway."

"These clay bodies are the **best we** have got," says I, "And we have got to stay in 'em till we die, and the **Lord** tells us to keep 'em pure, so he can **come** and visit us in 'em. I don't believe the Lord thinks much of these holy drawin's. I know I don't."

Betsey sot silently twistin' her ottor colored **bonnet** strings, **and** I went **on, for** I felt it was my duty.

" Married men are jest as good as them that **haint** married for lots of purposes, such as talkin' with on **the** subject of religeon, **and** polytix and miscelanious subjects, **and helpin'** you out **of** a double wagon, and etcetery. But when it comes to kissin', marryin' spile men in my opinion for kissin' any other woman only **jest their** own wives."

"But suppose **a** man has **a** mere clay wife?" says Betsey.

**Says** I, "Betsey, Josiah Allen was goin' **to** buy a **horse** the other day that **the** man said was a 3 year **old;** he found by lookin' **at her teeth** that she was **pretty near 40**; Josiah didn't buy it. If a man don't **want to marry a clay** woman, let him try to find one **that** haint clay. I think myself that he will have a **hard time to** find one, but he has a perfect right to **hunt** as long as he is a mind to—let him," **says I in a**

liberal tone. "Let him hire a horse and sulkey, and search the country over and over. I don't care if he is 20 years a huntin' and comparin' wimmin a tryin' to find one to suit him. But when he once makes up his mind, I say let him stand by his bargain, and make the best of it, and not try afterwards to look at her teeth."

Betsey still sot silently twistin' her bunnet strings, but I see that she was a mewsin' on some thought of her own, and in a minute or so she broke out: "Oh, what a soaring sole Prof. Gusheh is; he soared in his lecture to that extent that it seemed as if he would lift me right up, and carry me off."

For a minute I thought of Theron Gusher with respect, and then agin my eye fell sadly upon Betsey, and she went on,

"I came right home and wrote a poem on the subject, and I will read it to you." And before I could say a word to help myself, she begun to read.

Him of the Free Love Republic.

BY BETSEY BOBBET.

If females had the spunk of a mice,
From man, their foeman they would arise,
Their darning needles to infamy send—
Their dish cloth fetters nobly rend,
From tyrant man would rise and flee;
Thus boldly whispered Betsey B.
   CHORUS.—Females, have you a mice's will,
      You will rise up and get a bill.

But sweeter, sweeter, 'tis to see,
When man hain't found affinitee,

## A SORT OF WAR CRY.

But wedded unto lumps of clay,
To boldly rise and soar away.
Ah! 'tis a glorious sight to see;
Thus boldly murmured Betsey B.
    Chorus.—Male men, have you a mice's will,
        You will rise up and get a bill

Haste golden year, when all are free
To hunt for their affinitee ;
When wedlock's gate opens to all,
The halt, the lame, the great, the small.
Ah! blissful houh may these eyes see—
These wishful eyes of Betsey B.
    Chorus.—Males! females! with a mice's will,
        Rise up! rise up! and get a bill.

For that will hasten on that day—
That blissful time when none can say,
Scornful, " I am moah married than thee!"
For *all* will be married, and all *won't be* ;
But promiscous like. Oh! shall I see
That *blessed* time, sighed Betsey B.—
    Chorus.—Yes, if folks will have a mice's will
        And will rise up and get a bill.

" You see it repeats some," says Betsey as she finished readin'. But Prof. Gusheh wanted me to write a him to sing at thier Free Love conventions, and he wanted a chorus to each verse, a sort of a war-cry, that all could join in and help sing, and he says these soul stirrin' lines

    Have you a mice's will,
      You will rise up and get a bill ;'

have got the true ring to them. I had to kind o' speak against men in it. I hated too, awfully, but Prof. Gusheh said it would be necessary, in ordeh to rouse the masses. He says the almost withering sarcasm of this noble song is just what they need. He says it will go down to posterity side by side with Yankee Doodle, if not ahead of it. I know by his countenance that he thought it was superior to Mr. Doodles him But what think you of it, Josiah Allen's wife?"

"I think" says I in a cautious tone, "that it is about off 'n' a piece with the subject."

"Don't you think Josiah Allen's wife that it would be real sweet to get bills from men. It is a glorious doctrine for wimmen, so freein' and liberatin' to them."

"Sweet!" says I hautily "it would be a pretty world wouldn't it Betsey Bobbet, if every time a woman forgot to put a button onto a shirt, her husband would start up and say she wasn't his affinitee, and go to huntin' of her up, or every time his collar choked him."

"Oh, but wimmen could hunt too!"

"Who would take care of the children, if they was both a huntin'?" says I sternly, "it would be a hard time for the poor little innocents, if there father and mother was both of 'em off a huntin'."

Before I could free my mind any further about Prof. Gusher and his doctrine, I had a whole houseful of company come, and Betsey departed. But before she went she told me that Prof. Gusher had heard that I was in favor of wimmen's rights and he was comin' to see me before he left Jonesville.

The next day he came. Josiah was to the barn a thrashin' beans, but I received him with a calm dignity.  He was a harmless lookin' little man, with his hair combed and oiled as smooth as a lookin' glass.

PROFESSOR GUSHER.

He had on a bell-crowned hat which he lifted from his head with a smile as I come to the door.  He wore a plad jacket, and round his neck and hangin' down his bosom was a bright satten scarf into which he had stuck 2 big headed pins with a chain hitched onto each of 'em, and he had a book under his arm.  He says to me most the first thing after he sot down,

"You believe in wimmin havin' a right dont you?"

"Yes Sir," says I keenly lookin' up from my knitin' work.  "Jest as many rights as she can get holt of, rights never hurt any body yet."

"Worthy statements," says he.  "And you believe in Free Love, do you not?"

"How free?" says I cooly.

"Free to marry any body you want to, and as long as you want to, from half a day, up to 5 years or so."

"No Sir!" says I sternly, "I believe in rights, but I dont believe in wrongs, of all the miserable doctrines that was ever let loose on the world, the doctrine of

Free Love is the miserable'st. Free Love!" I repeated in indignant tones," "it ought to be called free devlitry, that is the right name for it."

He sunk right back in his chair, put his hand wildly to his brow and exclaimed,

"My soul aches, I thought I had found a congenial spirit, but I am decieved, my breast aches, and siths, and pants." He looked so awful distressed, that I didn't know what did ail him, and I looked pityin' on him from over my spectacles and I says to him jest as I would to our Thomas Jefferson,

"Mebby your vest is too tight."

"Vest!" he repeated in wild tones, "would I had no worse trammels than store clothes, but it is the fate of reformers to be misunderstood. "Woman the pain is deeper and it is a gnawin' me."

His eyes was kinder rolled, and he looked so wilted and uncomfortable, that I says to him in still more pityin' accents,

"Haint you got wind on your stummuck," for if you have, peppermint essence is the best stuff you can take, and I will get you some."

"Wind!" he almost shouted, "wind! no, it is not wind," he spoke so deleriously that he almost skairt me, but I kep up my placid demeanor, and kep on knittin'.

"Wimmen," said he, "I would right the wrongs of your sect if I could. I bear in my heart the woes and pains of all the aching female hearts of the 19 centurys."

My knittin' dropped into my lap, and I looked up at him in surprise, and I says to him respectfully,

"No wonder you groan and sithe, it must hurt awfully."

"It does hurt," says he, "but it hurts a sensitive spirit worse to have it mistook for wind."

He see my softened face, and he took advantage of it, and went on.

"Woman, you have been married, you say, goin' on 15 years; hain't you never felt slavish in that time, and felt that you would gladly unbind yourself?"

"Never!" says I firmly, "never! I don't want to be unbound."

"Hain't you never had longings, and yearnings to be free?"

"Not a yearn," says I calmly, "not a yearn. "If I had wanted to remain free I shouldn't have give my heart and hand to Josiah Allen. I didn't do it deleriously, I had my senses." Says I, "you can't set down and stand up at the same time, each situation has its advantages, but you can't be in both places at once, and this tryin' to, is what makes so much trouble amongst men and wimmen. They want the rights and advantages of both stations to once—they want to set down and stand up at the same time, and it can't be did. Men and wimmen hain't married at the pint of the bayonet, they go into it with both their eyes open. If anybody thinks they are happier, and freer from care without bein' married, nobody compels 'em to be married, but if they are, they hadn't ought to want to be married and single at the same time, it is onreasonable."

He looked some convinced, and I went on in a softer tone,

"I hain't a goin' to say that Josiah hain't been tryin' a good many times. He has raved round some, when dinner wasn't ready, and gone in his stockin' feet considerable, and been slack about kindlin' wood. Likewise I have my failin's. I presume I hain't done always exactly as I should about shirt buttons, mebby I have scolded more'n I ort to about his keepin' geese. But if men and wimmen think they are marryin' angels, they'll find out they'll have to settle down and keep house with human critters. I never see a year yet, that didn't have more or less winter in it, but what does it say, 'for better, for worse,' and if it turns out more worse than better, why that don't part us, for what else does it say? 'Till death does us part,' and what is your little slip of paper that you call a bill to that? Is that death?" says I.

He quailed silently, and I proceeded on.

"I wouldn't give a cent for your bills, I had jest as lives walk up and marry any married man, as to marry a man with a bill. I had jest as lives," says I warmin' with my subject, "I had jest as lives join a Mormon at once. How should I feel, to know there was another woman loose in the world, liable to walk in here any minute and look at Josiah, and to know all that separated 'em was a little slip of paper about an inch wide?"

My voice was loud and excited, for I felt deeply what I said, and says he in soothin' tones,

"I presume that you and your husband are congenial spirits, but what do you think of soarin' soles, that find out when it is too late that they are wedded to mere lumps of clay."

I hadn't fully recovered from my excited frame of mind, and I replied warmly, "I never see a man yet that wasn't more or less clay, and to tell you the truth I think jest as much of these clay men as I do of these soarers, I never had any opinion of soarers at all."

He sank back in his chair and sithed, for I had touched him in a tender place, but still clinging to his free love doctrine, he murmered faintly,

"Some wimmen are knocked down by some men, and dragged out."

His meek tones touched my feelin's, and I continued in more reasonable accents.

"Mebby if I was married to a man that knocked me down and dragged me out frequently, I would leave him a spell, but not one cent would I invest in another man, not a cent. I would live alone till he came to his senses, if he ever did, and if he didn't, why when the great roll is called over above, I would answer to the name I took when I loved him and married him, hopin' his old love would come back again there, and we would have all eternity to keep house in."

He looked so depressted, as he sot leanin' back in his chair, that I thought I had convinced him, and he was sick of his business, and I asked him in a helpful way,

"Hain't there no other business you can get into, besides preachin' up Free Love? Hain't there no better business? Hain't there no cornfields where you could hire out for a scare-crow—can't you get to be United States Senator? Hain't there no other mean job not quite so mean as this, you could get into?

He didn't seem to take it friendly in me, you know friendly advice makes some folks mad. He spoke out kinder surly and says he, "I hain't done no hurt, I only want everybody to find their affinitee.

That riled up the blood in me, and says I with spirit,

"Say that word to me agin if you dare." Says I "of all the mean words a married woman ever listened to, that is the meanest," says I "if you say "affinitee" here in my house, agin, young man, I will holler to Josiah."

He see I was in earnest and deeply indignent, and he ketched up his hat and cane, and started off, and glad enough was I to see him go.

# ELDER WESLEY MINKLE'S DONATION PARTY.

About four weeks afterwards, I had got my kitchen mopped out, clean as a pin and everything in perfect order and the dinner started, (I was goin' to have beef steak and rice puddin',) and then I took a bowl of raisons and sot down to stun 'em, for I was goin' to bake a plum cake for supper. I will have good vittles as long as my name is Josiah Allen's wife. And it haint only on my own account that I do it, but I do it as I have observed before, from deep and almost cast iron principle. For as the greatest of philosiphers have discovered, if a woman would keep her table spread out from year to year, and from hour to hour, filled with good vittles, that woman would have a clever set of men folks round.

As I sot serenely stunnin' my raisons, not dreamin' of no trouble, I heard a rap at the door, and in walked Betsey Bobbet. I see she looked kinder curious, but I didn't say nothin', only I asked her to take off her things. She complied, and as she took out her tattin' and begun to tat, says she—

"I have come to crave your advise, Josiah Allen's wife. I am afraid I have been remissin' in my duty. Martin Farquar Tupper is one of the most sweetest poets of the ages. My sentiments have always blended in with his beautiful sentiments, I have always flew with his flights, and soahed with his soahs. And last night afteh I had retiahed to bed, one of his sublime ideahs come to me with a poweh I neveh befoah felt. It knocked the bolted doah of my heart open, and said in low and hollow tones as it entered in, 'Betsey Bobbet, you have not nevah done it.'"

Betsey stopped a minute here for me to look surprised and wonderin', but I didn't, I stunned my raisons with a calm countenance, and she resumed—

"Deah Tuppah remarks that if anybody is goin' to be married, thier future companion is upon the earth somewhere at the present time, though they may not have met him or her. And he says it is our duty to pray for that future consort. And Josiah Allen's wife, I have not neveh done it."

She looked agonized, as she repeated to me, "Josiah Allen's wife, I have neveh preyed for him a word. I feel condemned; would you begin now?"

Says I coolly, "Are you goin' to prey *for* a husband, or *about* one?"

Says she mournfully, "A little of both."

"Wall," says I in a cautious way, "I don't know as it would do any hurt, Betsey."

Says she, "I will begin to prey to-night. But that is not all I wished to crave your advise about. Folks must work as well as prey. Heaven helps them that help themselves. I am goin' to take a decided stand." Then she broke off kinder sudden, and says she, "Be you a goin' to the Faih and Donation to the Methodist church to-morrow night?"

"Yes," says I, "I am a layin' out to go."

"Well, Josiah Allen's wife, will you stand by me? There is not another female woman in Jonesville that I have the firm unwaverin' confidence in, that I have in you. You always bring about whateveh you set youh hands to do—and I want to know, will you stand by me to-morrow night?"

Says I in a still more cautious tone "what undertakin' have you got into your head now, Betsey Bobbet?"

"I am going to encourage the Editah of the Augah. That man needs a companion. Men are bashful and offish, and do not always know what is the best for them. I have seen horses hang back on the harness before now, I have seen geese that would not walk up to be picked. I have seen children hang back from pikery. The horses ought to be made to go! The geese ought to be held and picked! The children ought to take the pikery if you have to hold thieh noses to make them. The Editah of the Augah *needs* a companion, I am going to encourage that man to-morrer night and I want to know Josiah Allen's wife if you will stand by me."

I answered her in reasonable tones. "You know Betsey that I can't run, I am too fat, and then I am gettin' too old. Mebby I might walk up and help you corner him, but you know I can't run for anybody."

Jest then Josiah came in and the conversation dropped down viz: on the fare. Says Josiah, says he, "Brother Wesley Minkley is a honest, pure minded man and I shall go, and shall give accordin' to my ability, but I don't believe in 'em, I don't believe in doin' so much for ministers. The bible says let them live on the gospel; why don't they? The old 'postles wasn't always havin' donations and fares to get up money for 'em, and big sallerys. Why don't they live like the 'postles?"

LIVIN' ON GOSPEL.

Says I, "Josiah Allen you try to live on clear gospel

a spell, and see if your stommack wouldn't feel kinder empty." Says I, "The bible says the 'Laborer is worthy of his hire.'" Says I, "folks are willin' to pay their doctors and lawyers, and druggers, and their tin peddlers, and every body else only ministers, and if any body has a slave's life, it is a good conscientious minister." Says I, "Brother Wesley Minkley works like a dog."

"I don't deny it," says Josiah, "but why don't he live like the 'postle Paul?"

Says I, "the 'postle Paul didn't have to buy 40 or 50 yards of merymac callico and factory cloth every year. He didn't have to buy cradles and cribs, and soothin' syrup, for he didn't have any babys to be cribbed and soothed. He didn't have to buy bunnets, and gographys, and prunella gaters, and back combs, and hair pins, and etcetery, etcetery. He didn't have a wife and seven daughters and one son, as Brother Wesley Minkley has got." Says I, almost warmly, "Every other man, only jest ministers, has a hope of layin' up a little somethin' for their children, but they don't think of doin' that, all they expect is to keep 'em alive and covered up," and says I, "The congregation they almost slave themselves to death for, begrec'! that, and will jaw too if they hain't covered up, an' dressed up slick. Sister Minkley wants her girls to look as well as the rest of the girls in the Church. Says I, "The 'postle Paul wasn't a mother, Josiah,
9

not that I have anything against him," says I more mildly.

The conversation was interupted here by Shakespeare Bobbet comin' after Betsey, they had company. Betsey returned with him, but her last words to me was, in a low awful voice,

"Will you stand by me Josiah Allen's wife?" I sithed, and told her in a kind of a bland way, "I would see about it."

The donatin and fare occured Wednesday night, and Josiah and me went early, Thomas J. and Tirzah Ann bein' off to school. And I carried as much and as good as anybody there, though I say it that shouldn't. I carried as good vittles too as there was and I didn't scrimp in quantity neither.

We was a layin' out to carry 'em half a barrel of pork, and I made a big jar of butter and sold it, and got the money for it, five dollars, and I atted Josiah to sell the pork and get the money for that. Says I, "Brother Minkley and his wife have both come to years of understandin', and it stands to reason that they both know what they want better than we do, and money will buy anything."

Josiah kinder hung back, but I carried the day. And so we carried 15 dollars in a envelop, and told sister Minkley to open it after we got home. I didn't want 'em to thank us for it—it makes me feel just as mean as pusley. But some folks carried the litlest things. There was a family of 7 hearty men and women, and all they carried was a book mark out of perforated paper, and a plate of cookeys. There was 7 book marks, for I counted 'em, and 14 pair of slips for the minister's only boy, who is home from school. And this same young man, Whitfield Minkley, had 24 neck ties. Of course there was some other things, a few sassige or so, a little flour, and some dried blackberrys.

But it does beat all what simple things some folks will carry. Shakespeare Bobbet carried the minister a pair of spurs. Thinks' I to myself, "What is he goin' to use 'em on, the saw horse or the front gate?" For they have kep' him down so low, that he is too poor to own any other steeds.

And Betsey Bobbet brought him a poem of hers all flowered off round the edges, and trimmed with pink ribbon. I haint nothin' aginst poetry, but with a big family like Brother Minkley's, it did seem to me that there was other things that would be more nourishin' and go further.

After we had left our vittles in the procession room where we was goin' to eat, I marched into the meetin' house room which was full of folks, and Brother Minkley came up to talk with me. I felt low spirited, for Betsey's design wore on me. And when Brother Minkley took my hand in hisen, and shook it in the purest and most innocent manner, and said, "Sister Allen, what is the matter? are you havin' a xercise in your mind?"

Says I to him, "Yes, Brother Minkley, I be."

I turned the subject quickly then, for I abhor hippocrites, and I felt that I was a deceivin' him. For whereas he thought I was havin' a religous xcercise performin' in my mind, I was not; it was Betsey Bobbet's design that was a wearin' on me. So I waved off the subject quickly, though I knew that like as not he would think I was a backslidin' and was afraid he would ketch me at it. Thinks'es I, better let him think I am a slidin' back, I can endure false importations better than I can let myself out for a hyppocrite. I waved off the subject and says I,

"That was a beautiful sermon of yours last Sunday, Brother Minkley."

"You mean that from the text 'He overthrew the tables of the money changers,' and so forth; I am glad it pleased you, sister Allen. I meant to hit a blow at gamblin' that would stagger it, for gamblin' is a prevailin' to a alarmin' extent." And then says he, plantin' himself firmly before me, "Did you notice, sister Allen, the lucid and logical manner in which I carried up the argument from the firstly to the twenty-thirdly?"

I see then I was in for it. Brother Wesley Minkley haint got another fault on earth as I know on—only jest a catchin' his church members and preachin' his sermons over to 'em. But I have said 100 times that I am glad he has got that, for it sets me more at rest about him on windy days. Not that I really s'pose he will ascend, but if he hadn't got that fault I should be almost tempted to examine his shoulder blades occasionally, (on the outside of his coat,) to see if his wings was a spoutin', he is so fine and honest and unsuspicious.

When his sermons are so long that they get up into the twentiethlies, and thirtiethlies, as they jinerally do, I can't say but what it is a little wearin' on you, to stand stun still whenever he happens to catch you, in the store, or street, or doorstep, and have him preach 'em all over to you alone. You feel kinder curious, and then sometimes your feet will get to sleep. But on the present occasion I rejoiced, for it freed me for the time bein' from Betsey's design. He laid holt of that sermon, and carried it all up before me through the firstlys and the tenthlys, just as neat and regular as you could hist a barel up the chamber stairs, and had just landed it before the ninteenthly which was, "That all church members had ort to get together, and rastle with the awful vice of gamblin' and throw it, and tread onto it," when Betsey Bobbet appeared before us suddenly with a big bag before her and says she,

"Here is the grab bag, you must grab."

I never heard of the thing before, and it come so kind of sudden on me that I hung back at first. But there was a whole lot of folks lookin' on, and I didn't want to act odd, so I laid holt of it, and grabbed it with both hands as tight as I could towards the bottom. Betsey said that wasn't the way, and then her design so goaded her, that she bent forward and whispered in my ear,

"The Editah of the Augah got home to-nignt, he is expected here in half an hour, I expect you to stand by me Josiah Allen's wife."

I sithed heavy, and while I was a sithin' Betsey asked Elder Minkley to grab, and he, thinkin' no hurt, bein' so pure minded and unsuspicious, and of such a friendly turn, he threw both arms around the bag grabbed it, and held it tight. And then Betsey

THE ENEMY ATTACKTED.

explained it to us—you had to pay 25 cents and then you run your hand into the bag, and had jest what you happened to grab first.

Then at that minute I see the power of pure and cast iron principle as I never seen it before. Betsey

Bobbet and all other sorrows and sufferin' was for the minute forgot, and I was glad I had been born. With the look of a war horse when his mane tosses and he snorts, a smellin' of the battle field, Elder Wesley Minkley ketched the bag out of Betsey's tremblin' hand, threw it down onto the floor, and sot down on it. He looked peaceful then, he knew he had throwed the tempter, and got on to it, holdin' of it down. In the most tryin' and excitin' scenes of life, the good of the human race is my theme of mind, I am so wrapped up in it, and then, even in this glorious scene, I said to myself, "Ah would that Adam had served them apples in the same way."

Brother Minkley took out his red silk handkerchief and wiped his heroic, but sweaty face, for it was warm in the meetin' house, and he bein' a large portly man, principle had heat him up. And then such a sermon as he preached to Betsey Bobbet, it did my very soul good to hear, says he, "It is gamblin', and gamblin' of the very worst kind to, for it is gamblin' in the name of God."

"Oh" says Betsey, "deah and respected sir, the money is for you, and it is not gamblin', for there is not any wicked papeh cards connected with it at all, it is only a sort of pious raffling in harmless pincushions and innocent rag children."

Then did I see pure principle mountin' up higher and higher, his honest fat face grew fire red with it, and says he, "No raffled pincushions shall ever enrich me, I scorn lucre that is obtained in that way. Not one cent of money Betsey Bobbet will I ever take, that is realized from the sale of these ragged children. Not a ragged child shall be gambled for, for me, not a child."

We was right under the gallery, and at this minute a fish hook was let down not but a little ways from us, and Shakespeare Bobbet who stood by a basket full of things, hitched on a long huzzy all made of different kinds of calico, and it went up a danglin' over our heads. As he ketched sight of it, Brother Wesley Minkley started up and says he, to Betsey in tones that *would* be replied to,

"What does that mean?"

Says Betsey in almost tremblin' tones, "They pay ten cents for fishin' once."

Then says he in tones that sounded some like distant thunder,

"Do they know what they are goin' to get for thier money?"

"No sir," says she, and she quailed to that extent that I almost pitied her.

"More gamblin!" he cried in fearful tones. And then he sprung for the huzzy, and shouted up the gallery to Shakespeare Bobbet, "I forbid you to draw up this huzzy another step. I forbid this huzzy to be drawed up an inch further." He hung on to the

## THE GRAB-BAGS AND HUZZIES OVERCOME. 213

huzzy with both hands, and says he—with the fire of his old foregrandfather in his eye (who was an orderly

THE ELDER ON THE ALERT.

sargant in the Revolution) "I'll see if there is goin' to be huzzies gambled for in this way. I'll see if there is goin' to be such shameless doin's in my church!"

For the next half hour confusion rained. But pure principle conquered. In the language of scripture slightly altered to suit the occasion, "He overthrew the grab bags, and drove out the huzzies and fish hooks." When peace rained agin, I grasped holt of his hand, and says I almost warmly,

"You have done a good job brother, some folks may call it pious gamblin', but I never believed in it."

Whitfield Minkley come up at that very minute, and says he, "That is jest as I think," says he, in the language of Shakespeare, "'It is stealin' the livery horses of heaven, to carry the devil out a ridin'" or mebby I hain't got the very words, but it was somethin' to that effect.

Says I, "I never knew that Shakespeare Bobbet ever turned his mind that way," and then says I in a cordial way, "I am real glad you have got home Whitfield, I guess I am about as glad to see you as any body, unless it is your ma, and one or two others."

He thanked me and said it seemed good to get home agin, and then says he, "I suppose Tirzah Ann is well." His face as he said this was as red as his neck tie. But I didn't seem to notice it. I talked with him quite a spell about her, and told him both the children would be to home Saturday, and he must come up then, for Thomas Jefferson would be awful disappointed not to see him.

He looked awful tickled when I asked him to come, and he said he should certainly come, for he never wanted to see Thomas Jefferson so bad, in his life.

I don't make no matches, nor break none. But I hain't a goin' to deny, that sister Minkley and I have talked it over, and if things go on, as they seem to be a goin' between *her* Whitfield and *our* Tirzah Ann, there won't be no straws laid in their way, not a straw.

Whitfield was called off by one of his sisters, and

Brother Wesley Minkley standin' in front of me begun,

"Sister Allen, I am very much like you, I believe in actin' up to our professions, and as I was about to remark in my twentiethly," then that good, pure minded man begun agin jest where he left off. He had jest lifted up his left hand, and was pintin' it off with his right fore finger, and I was jest thinkin' that most likely I had got my night's job in front of me, when unxpected the Editer of the Augur come to speak to me, and Brother Wesley Minkley bein' a true gentleman, stopped preachin' to once, and went to talkin' to Josiah.

I looked sadly into the face of the Editer of the Augur, and sithed, for I knew that Betsey would soon begin to encourage him, and I pitied him.

He said "How de do?" to me, and I said in a absent minded way that "I was; and I hoped it was so with him." And then I sithed agin. And my two gray eyes looked sadly into his'en (which was butnut colored) for a spell, and then roamed off across the room onto Betsey. I seen her a fixin' on her waterfall more securely, and a shakin' out her greek bender, and tightnin' her horse hair bracelets, and her lips moved as if she was beginnin' to prey. And I knew he had got to be encouraged, and I felt for him.

The Editer of the Augur followed my mournful gaze, and I was surprised to see the change in his butnut eye as it met hers, from what it had been in more former times preceedin'. For whereas he had always looked at her with fear and almost agonizin' aprehension, as if he realized his danger, now he looked full in her face, as she smiled across the room at him, with a proud haughty and triumphant mene on him I could not understand. He gazed at her silently for I should think pretty near a half a minute and then he turned to me with a sweet, contented smile curvin' his moustache—which had been colored a new bright black,— and says he to me with a peaceful and serene look on to Betsey,

"How sweet it is Josiah Allen's wife for a noble but storm tosted bark to anchor in a beautiful calm. How sweet it is, when you see the ravenin' tempest a smilin' at you, I mean a lowerin' at you, in the distance, to feel that it can't harm you—that you are beyond its reach. To see it in its former dread power a drawin' near—" (Betsey had started to come towards us.) "and feel that you are safe from it. Josiah Allen's wife I feel safe and happy to night."

Betsey was stopped for the minute by Deacon Gowdey, but I knew it was only a momentary respite, and knowin' her design, how could I answer? I could only look gloomy into his face, and think sadly, Ah! how little we know when trials and dangers are ahead of us, how little we know when we are goin' to be encouraged.

But he continued on in the same sweet happy triumphin' tones,

"Josiah Allen's wife, I believe you are my friend."

"Yes! and your well wisher," and says I almost wildly, "whatever comes, whatever may happen to you, remember that I wished you well, and I pitied you."

"Instead of pityin' me, wish me joy," and he held out his right hand towards me.

I haint no hypocrite, and knowin' what I knew, how could I be so deceitful? I hung back and gripped holt of a breadth of my dress with my right hand.

Says he, "I am married, Josiah Allen's wife, I was married a week ago to-night."

I grasped holt of his right hand which he still held out, with my right hand, and says I, "you take a load offe'n my mind. Who too?"

Says he, "the prettiest girl in Log London where father lives."

My emotions paralyzed me for nearly a quarter of a minute, and then says I,

"Where is she?"

"To her folks'es," says he, "But she will be here next week."

Betsey drew near. He looked calmly and fearlessly at her, but he murmured gently, "The twins will be a wakin' up; I must be a goin'," and he gently retreated.

The first words Betsey said to me was, "Ketch hold of me Josiah Allen's wife, ketch hold of me, I am on the very point of swooning."

Then I knew what Deacon Gowdey had been a tellin' her. She looked like a blue ghost, trimmed off with otter color, for she had on a blue parmetta dress all trimmed with annato colored trimmin's. She murmured in almost incoherent words, somethin' about "her dearest gazelle bein' a dyin', and her wantin' to be took off to her buryin' ground." But I knew it was no time for me to show my pity; true friendship demanded firmness and even sternness, and when she asked me wildly agin to "ketch hold of her," I says to her coldly,

"Ketch holt of yourself, Betsey Bobbet."

"My lost, my dearest gazelle is a dyin'! my hopes are witherin'!" says she, shettin' up her eyes and kinder staggerin' up against the wall.

Says I in tones as cold as old Zero, or pretty nigh as cold as that old man,

"Let 'em wither."

But I see I must come out still more plainer, or she would make a public circus of herself, and says I pushin' her into a corner, and standin' up in front of her, so as to shet off the audience from her face, for she was a cryin', and she did indeed look ghostly,

"Betsey Bobbet the gazelle is married, and their hain't no use in your follerin' on that trail no longer. Now," says I, " take your bunnet and go home, and collect yourself together. And" says I, generously "I will go with you as far as the door."

## SHE SEEKS RELIEF IN POETRY. 219

So I got her started off, as quick, and as quiet as I could, and I guess there wasn't mor'n seven men and 14 wimmen that asked me as I came back in,

"If it was the Editer of the Augur, that Betsey was a cryin' about, and if I ever see such a idiot in my life?"

I answered 'em in a kind of blind way, and it broke up pretty soon.

When Josiah and me went home, as we passed Mr. Bobbet'ses, I looked up into Betsey's winder which fronted the road, and I see Betsey set by her table a

BETSEY SEEKS RELIEF.

writin'. Her lips were firmly closed and she was a cryin', her cheeks looked holler and I knew that her teeth was out, so I felt that she was writin' poetry. I was right, for in the next weeks *Gimlet* these verses came out. These lines was wrote on to the top of 'em:

"We do not wish to encourage the feeling of revenge in our fair contributor's fair breast, but this we will say, that on some occasions, revenge is a noble feeling and almost leans over against virtue's side. And though we do not wish to be personal—no one could scorn it more than we do—but we say, and we say it with the kindest feelings towards him, that the E—— of the A—— is a *villian*." Editor of the Gimlet.

A Desiah.

BY BETSEY BOBBET.

Methinks I soon shall pass away,
I have seen my last gazelle expiah;
Deah friends I do not wish to stay;
To be a ghost is my desiah.
Revenge is sweet as honey a most—
Methinks 'twere sweet to be a ghost.

I would not be a seraphim,
For far a sweeter sight would be
On bedpost sitting, twitting him,
Of his deceit and perfide;
I'd rathah be a dreadful ghost,
A sitting on a certain post.

I can give up my heavenly claim,
My seat upon the heavenly quiah;
I feel anotheh, wildeh aim—
To be a ghost is my desiah.
Ah, yes! I'd ratheh be a ghost,
And sit upon a certain post.

Methinks he'd coveh up his head
And groan and rithe, and maybe swear,
And sithe, "I wish she wasn't dead;"

But still I'll keep a sittin' theah.
As long as I remain a ghost,
I'll hang around a certain post.

Anotheh certain person may,
With terror wish she hadn't had
The wretch who made me pass away;
Maybe *she'll* wish I wasn't dead.
In vain! for still my dreadful ghost,
Shall glare on her from a certain post.

To think how I my brain have racked
On lays for him. My stomach cramp;
My bended form; my broken back;
My blasted hopes; my wasted lamp.
Oh, then I long to be a ghost,
To hang around a certain post.

My soul it pants, my crazed brain spins,
To think how gushed my fond heart's flow,
My sympathy for certain twins,
And then to think he used me so.
But soon! ah soon I'll be a ghost,
A haunting round a certain post.

## WIMMEN'S SPEAH.

One bright, beautiful day, I had got my mornin's work all done up, and had sot down to double some carpet yarn, and Josiah sot behind the stove, blackin' his boots, when Betsey come in for a mornin's call. She hadn't sot but a few minutes when says she,

"I saw you was not down to the lecture night before last, Josiah Allen's wife. I was sorry that I attended to it, but my uncle's people where I was visitin' went, and so I went with them. But I did not like it, I do not believe in wimmin's havin' any rights. I think it is real bold and unwomanly in her to want any rights. I think it is not her speah, as I remarked last night to our deah New Preacher. As we was a coming out, afteh the lecture, the fringe of my shawl ketched on to one of the buttons of his vest, and he could not get it off—and I did not try to, I thought it was not my place - so we was obleeged to walk close togatheh, cleah through the hall, and as I said to him, afteh I had enquired if he did not find it very lonesome here, says I, 'It is not wimmin's speah to vote,' and says I, 'do you not think it is woman's nature naturally to be clingin'?' 'I *do*,' says he, 'Heaven *knows* I *do*.' And he leaned back with such a expression of stern despair on to his classic features, that I knew he felt it strongly. And I said the truth. I do not believe wimmin ought to vote."

"Nor I nuther," says Josiah, "she haint got the rekrisite strength to vote, she is too fraguile."

Jest at this minute the boy that draws the milk came along, and Josiah, says he to me, "I am in my stockin' feet, Samantha, can't you jest step out and help Thomas Jefferson on with the can?"

Says I, "If I am too fraguile to handle a paper vote, Josiah Allen, I am too fraguile to lift 100 and 50 pounds of milk."

He didn't say nothin', but he slipped on his rubbers and started out, and Betsey resumed, "It is so revoltin' to female delicacy to go to the poles and vote: most all of the female ladies that revolve around in the high circles of Jonesville aristocracy agree with me in thinkin' it is real revoltin' to female delicacy to vote."

"Female delicacy!" says I, in a austeer tone. "Is female delicacy a plant that withers in the shadder of the pole, but flourishes in every other condition only in the shadder of the pole?" says I in a tone of witherin' scorn. " Female delicacy flourishes in a ball room, where these sensitive creeters with dresses on indecently low in the neck, will waltz all night with

FEMALE DELICACY.

strange men's arms round their waists," says I. " You have as good as throwed it in my face, Betsey Bobbet, that I haint a modest woman, or I would be afraid to go and vote; but you ketch me with a low neck dress on, Betsey Bobbet, and you will ketch me on my way to the Asylum, and there haint a old deacon, or minister, or presidin' Elder in the Methodist church, that could get me to waltz with 'em, let alone waltzin' with promiscuus sinners. And," says I in the deep, calm tone of settled principle, " if you don't believe it, bring on your old deacons and ministers, and presidin' Elders, and try me."

"You are gettin' excited, Samantha," says Josiah.

"You jest keep blackin' your boots, Josiah Allen, I haint a talkin' to you. Betsey, is it any worse for a female woman to dress herself in a modest and Christian manner, with a braige viel over her face, and a brass mounted parasol in her hand, and walk decently to the pole and lay her vote on it, than to be introduced to a man, who for all you know may be a retired pirate, and have him walk up and hug you by the hour, to the music of a fiddle and a base violin?"

"But if you vote you have got to go before a board of men, and how tryin' to delicacy that would be."

"I went before a board of men when I joined the meetin' house, and when I got the premium for my rag carpet, and I still live and call myself a respectable character, but," says I in a vain of unconcealed sarcasm " if these delicate ball characters are too modest to go in broad daylight armed with a umbrell before a venerable man settin' on a board, let 'em have a good old female board to take thier votes."

"Would it be lawful to have a female board?" says Betsey.

"Wimmen can be boards at charity schools—poor little paupers, pretty hard boards they find 'em sometimes—and they can be boards at fairs, and hospitals, and penitentarys, and picnics, and African missions, and would it be any worse to be a board before these delicate wimmen," says I, almost carried away with enthusiasm, "I would be a board myself."

"Yes you would make a pretty board," says Josiah, "you would make quite a pile of lumber." I paid no attention to his sarkastic remark, and Betsey went on.

"It would be such public business Josiah Allen's wife for a woman to recieve votes."

"I dont know as it would be any more public business, than to sell Episcopal pin cushiens, Methodist I scream, or Baptist water melons, by the hour to a permiscuus crowd."

But says Betsey, 'twould devouh too much of a female's time, she would not have time to vote, and perform the other duties that are incumbient upon her."

Says I, "Wimmen find time for thier everlastin' tattin' and croshain'. They find plenty of time for thier mats, and their tidys, their flirtations,

NO TIME TO VOTE.

thier feather flowers, and bead flowers, and hair flowers, and burr flowers, and oriental paintins, and Grecian paintins, and face paintins. They spend more time a frizzin' thier front hair than they would, to learn the whole constitution by heart; and if they get a new dress they find plenty of time to cut it all up into strips, jest to pucker it up and set it on agin. They can dress up in thier best and patrol the streets as regular as a watchman, and lean over the counter in dry good stores till they know every nail in 'em by heart. They find plenty of time for all this, and to go to all the parties they can hear of, and theatres and conserts, and shows of all kinds, and to flirt with ev-

DREADFUL SHORT OF TIME.

ory man they can lay holt of, and to cover their faces with their fans and giggle; but when it comes to an act as simple and short as puttin' a letter into the post office, they are dreadful short on it for time."

But says Betsey, "The study that would be inevitable on a female in ordeh to make her vote intelligably, would it not be too wearing on her?"

No! not a single bit; s'posin these soft, fashionable wimmen should read a little about the nation she lives in, and the laws that protects her if she keeps 'em, and hangs and imprisons her if she breaks 'em? I don't

NO TIME TO STUDY LAWS.

'know but it would be as good for her, as to pore over novels all day long," says I; "these very wimmen that think the President's bureau is a chest of draws where he keeps his fine shirts, and the tariff is a wild horse the senators keep to ride out on,—these very wimmen that can't find time to read the constitution, let 'em get on to the track of a love-sick hero and a swoonin' heroine, and they will wade through half a dozen volumes, but what they will foller 'em clear to Finis to see 'em married there," says I, warmin' with my subject, "Let there be a young woman hid in a certain hole, guarded by 100 and 10 pirates, and a young man tryin' to get to her, though at present layin' heavily chained in a underground dungeon with his rival settin' on his back, what does a woman care for time or treasure, till she sees the pirates all killed off with one double revolver, and the young woman lifted out swoonin' but happy, by the brave hero?" Says I, in a deep camp meetin' voice, "If there had been a woman hid on the Island of Patmos, and Paul's letters to the churches had been love letters to her, there wouldn't be such a thick coat of dust on bibles as there is now."

"But if wimmen *don't* read about the laws they'll know as much as some other folks do. I have seen men voters," says I, and I cast a stern glance onto Josiah as I spoke, "whose study into national affairs didn't wear on 'em enough to kill 'em at all. I have seen voters," says I with another cuttin' look at him, "that didn't know as much as their wives did." Josiah quailed a very little as I said this, and I continued on—" I have seen Irish voters, whose intellects wasn't tiresome to carry round, and whose knowledge concernin' public affairs wasn't so good as it was about rum, and who would sell their votes for a drink of whiskey, and keep it up all day, votin' and drinkin' and then drinkin' and votin', and I guess wimmen won't do any worse."

Betsey almost quailed before my lofty glance and voice, but continued on cleavin' to the subject—"How awful and revolting it would sound to hear the faih and softch sex talking about tariffs and caurkusses."

"I don't know," says I, "but I had as lives hear 'em talk about caurkusses, as to hear 'em backbitin' thier neighbors and tearin' the charicters of other wimmen into bits, or talkin' about such little things as wimmen will; why in a small place, a woman can't buy a calico apron without the neighborhood holdin' a inquest over it. Some think she ort to have it, some think it is extravagant in her, and some think the set flower on it is too young for her, and then they will all quarrel agin whether she ort to make it with a bib or not." Says I "the very reason why men's talk as a general thing is nobler than wimmen's, is because they have nobler things to think about." Says I "Betsey Bobbet, when did you ever know a passel of men to set down and spend a whole afternoon talkin' about each other's vest, and mistrustin' such a feller painted ; fill a woman's mind with big, noble sized thoughts, and she won't talk such little back bitin' gossip as she does now."

"Josiah Allen's wife," says Betsey, "I shall always say it is not woman's speah to vote."

"No," says Josiah, "it hain't ; wimmen would vote for the handsomest men, and the men that praised thier babys, they wouldn't stand up onto principal as men do, and then, how they would clog up the road 'lection day, tryin' to get all the news they could, wimmen have got such itchin' ears."

"Itchin' ears!" says I, "principle!" says I, in low but awful deep tones of voice," Josiah Allen, it seems to me, that I wouldn't try to stand up onto principle agin, till the pantaloons are wore out you hired a man with to vote your ticket." He begun to look sheepish at once, and I continued in still more awful accents, "talk about itchin' ears, Josiah Allen! here you have sot all the mornin' blackin' your boots, you have rubbed them boots till you have most rubbed holes through 'em, jest for an excuse to set here and hear me and Betsey Bobbet talk. And it hain't the first time nuther, for I have known you Josiah Allen, when I have had female visitors, to leave your work and come in and lay on that lounge behind the stove till you was most sweltered, pretendin' you was readin'."

"I *wuz* a readin'." says Josiah drawin' on his boots.

"I have ketched you laughin' over a funeral sermon, and a President's message, what is there highlarious in a funeral sermon Josiah Allen? What is there exhileratin' in a President's message?"

"Wall," says he, "I guess I'll water the steers."

"I should think you had better," says I coolly, and after he went out, Betsey resumed,

"Josiah Allen's wife, I still say it is not woman's speah to vote," and she continued, "I have got a few verses in my pocket, which I composed that night aftah I returned from the lecture, which embody into them the feelings of my soul concerning woman's speah. I went to my chamber, and let down my back haih, and took out my teeth, I always feel more free somehow, and poetic, with my hair down and my teeth out, and there I wrote these stanzeys, and seeing it is you, I will read them to you."

My firm and cast iron principles forbid my wishin' in a reckless way that I wasn't myself, and I was in my own house, and horspitality forbid my orderin' her in stern accents, not to read a word of 'em, so I submitted, and she read as follows:

WIMMEN'S SPEAH;<br>
Or whisperin's of nature to<br>
BETSEY BOBBET.

Last night as I meandered out<br>
To meditate apart,<br>
Secluded in my parasol,<br>
Deep subjects shook my heart.<br>
The earth, the skies, the prattling brooks,<br>
All thundered in my ear,<br>
"It is matrimony! it is matrimony<br>
That is a woman's speah."

Day with a red shirred bonnet on,
Had down for China started,
Its yellow ribbons fluttered o'er
Her head, as she departed;
She seemed to wink her eyes on me,
As she did dissapeah;
And say, "It is matrimony, Betsey,
That is a woman's speah."

A rustic had broke down his team;
I mused almost in teahs,
"How can a yoke be borne along
By half a pair of steers?"
Even thus in wrath did nature speak,
"Heah! Betsey Bobbet, heah!
It is matrimony! it is matrimony
That is a woman's speah."

I saw a paih of roses
Like wedded pardners grow;
Sharp thorns did pave thier mortal path,
Yet sweetly did they blow;
They seemed to blow these *glorious* words,
Into my *willing* eah;
"It is matrimony! it is matrimony
That is a woman's speah."

Two gentle sheep upon the hills;
How sweet the twain did run,
As I meandered gently on
And sot down on a stun;
They seemed to murmur sheepishly,
"Oh Betsey Bobbet deah,
It is matrimony! it is matrimony
That is a women's speah."

Sweet was the honeysuckles breath
Upon the ambient aih;
Sweet was the tendah coo of doves,
Yet sweeter husbands aih.
All nature's voices poured these words
Into my *willing* eah;
"B. Bobbet, it is matrimony
That is a woman's speah."

"The above are my sentiments," says she, as she folded up the paper.

"I am a married woman," says I, and I hain't got nothin' to say aginst marryin', especally when Josiah's back is turned, I don't believe in bein' underhanded. But there are a great many widows and unmarried wimmen in the world, what are they to do?"

"Let them take heed to these glorious and consoling words,

> "'It is matrimony, it is matrimony
> That is a woman's speah.'"

"Shet up about your speah's," says I, gettin wore out, "You may sing it Betsey Bobbet, and ministers may preach it, and writers may orate about it, that it is women's only speah to marry, but what are you goin' to do? Are you goin' to compel men to marry all the wimmen off?" says I, with a penetratin' look onto Betsey.

"I have seen wimmen that was willin' to marry, but the men wasn't forthcomin', what are they to do? What are the wimmen to do whose faces are as humbly as a plate of cold greens?" Says I, in stern tones, "Are men to be pursued like stricken dears by a mad mob of humbly wimmen? Is a woman to go out into the street and collar a man and order him to marry her? I am sick of this talk about its bein' a woman's only speah to marry. If it is a woman's only speah to marry, the Lord will provide her with a *man*, it

A WOMAN'S RIGHTS.

stands to reason he will. One that will suit her too, one that will come jest as nateral for her to leave all of the rest of the world and foller, as for a sunflower to foller on after the sun. One that she seems to belong to, jest like North and South America, joined by nature unbeknown to them ever sense creation. She'll know him if she ever sees him, for their two hearts will suit each other jest like the two halves of a pair of shears. These are the marriages that Heaven signs the certificates of, and this marryin' for a home, or for fear of bein' called a old maid, is no more marriage in the sight of God, no more true marriage, than the blush of a fashionable woman that is bought for ten cents an ounce and carried home in her pocket, is true modesty."

Here was a pause, durin' which Betsey quailed some, and I then resumed again, in the same lofty tones and I don't know but a little loftier, "There is but one thing that makes marriage pure and holy in the sight of God."

"And what is that?" says Betsey in an enquirin' tone.

"Love," says I, in a full clear tone, "Love, such as angels feel for one another, love, such as Samantha Smith felt for Josiah Allen, though *why* I loved him, Heaven knows, I don't. But I couldn't help it, and I would have lived single till them days we read of, if I hadn't. Though for what reason I loved him—" I continued mewsin'ly, and almost lost in deep retrospectin',—" I don't know. I don't believe in rehearsin' privacies and braggin' about such things, but in the name of principle I speak. A richer man wanted me at the same time, a man that knew half as much agin, at least, as Josiah. I no need to have wet the ends of my fingers in dishwater if I had married the other one, but I could'nt do it, I loved Josiah, *though why* "—and agin I plunged down into deep abstraction as I murmured to myself,—" though *why* I did, I don't know."

"In them days," says I, risin' up agin out of my revery, "In them days to come, when men and wimmen are independent of each other, marriage will be what it ought to be, for folks won't marry unless God unites their hearts so close they can't get 'em apart nohow. They won't be tackled together by any old rotten ropes of interest and accomidation, that are liable to break in to pieces any minute, and in them days, the hands of divorce writers won't be so lame as they be now."

"I cannot comprehend" says Betsey "how wimmen's votin', will change the reprehensible ideah of marryin' for a home, or for fear of being ridiculed about, if it will, I cannot see."

"Cant you see daylight Betsey Bobbet, when the sun is mountin' up into the clear horizeon?" Says I in a eloquent voice, " it stands to reason that a woman wont marry a man she dont love, for a home, if she is capable of makin' one for herself. Where's the disgrace of bein' a old maid, only wimmen are kinder dependent on men, kinder waitin' to have him ask her to marry him, so as to be supported by him? Give a woman as many fields to work in as men have, and as good wages, and let it be thought jest as respectable for 'em to earn *thier* livin' as for a man to, and that is enough. It riles me to hear 'em talk about wimmen's wantin' to wear the breeches; they don't want to; they like calico better than broadcloth for stiddy wear, they like muslin better than kersey mear for handsome, and they have a nateral hankerin' after the good opinon and admiration of the other sect, but they can do better without that admiration than they can without vittles."

"Yes" says Betsey "men do admire to have wimmen clingin' to 'em, like a vine to a stately tree, and it is indeed a sweet view."

"So 'tis, so 'tis," says I, I never was much of a clinger myself. Still if females want to cling, I haint no objection. But," says I, in reasonable tones, "as I have said more'n a hundred times, if men think that wimmen are obleeged to be vines, they ought to feel obleeged to make trees of themselves, for 'em to run up on. But they wont; some of 'em, they will not be trees, they seem to be sot against it. And as I have said what if a vine haint no tree convenient to cling to? or if she has, what if the tree she clings to happens to fall through inherient rotteness at the core, thunder and lightnin' or etcetery? If the string breaks what is to become of the creeper if it can't do nothin' but creep? Says I, "it is all well enough for a rich woman to set in a velvet gown with her feet on the warm hearth and wonder what makes the poor drunkard's wife down in the street, shiver. Let her be out once with her bare feet in the snow, and she'd find out. It haint the rich, happy, comfortable clingers I am talkin' in behalf of, but the poor shiverers outside who haint nothin' to cling to,"

"Women's speah"—began Betsey.

"Women's speah," says I interuptin' her in a magestic tone before which Betsey quailed imperceptably. "Women's speah is where she can do the most good; if God had meant that wimmen should be nothin' but men's shadders, He would have made gosts and fantoms of 'em at once. But havin' made 'em flesh and blood, with braens and souls, I believe He meant 'em to be used to the best advantage. And the talk about wimmen havin' to fight, and men wash dishes, if wimmen vote, is all shear nonsense. In the Baptist church where wimmen vote, I dont see as they act different from other wimmen, and I dont see as the Baptist men act any more sheepish than common men." Says I "it is jest as ridiculous to say it would make a woman act coarse and rampage round to vote, as to say that kissin' a pretty baby, or lovin' books and music and pictures, makes a man a hen huzzy."

Says I, carried away with powerful emotions, "you may shet a lion up for years, in a room full of cambric needles and tattin shettles, and you cant get him to do anything but roar at 'em, it haint a lion's nature to do fine sewin," says I. "And you may tie up a old hen as long as you please, and you cant break her of wantin' to make a nest, and scratch for her chickens." Says I—wavin' my right hand, slow and magestically— "you may want a green shade onto the front side of your house, and to that end and effect you may plant a acorn, and set out a rose bush, but all the legeslaters in creation cant make that acorn tree blow out with red posy's, no more can they make that rose bush stand up straight as a giant. And thier bein' planted by the side of each other—on the same ground and watered out of the same waterin' jug—dont olter thier natural turn. *They will both help shade the winder*, but do it in their own way which is different. And men and wimmen votin' side by side, would no more alter their natural dispositions than singin' one of Watts'es hymns together would. One will sing base, and the other air, so long as the world stands."

"Josiah Allen's wife," says Betsey, "I think your views are uronieus. We cannot think alike about clinging, we also diffeh in our views about caurkusses. When I considch that 'lections and caurkusses come once every yeah, then comes home the solemn feelin', how wearin' it would be for a female to drop all her domestic labohs and avocations, and be present at them. Josiah Allen's wife, let us sposen the case, sposen a women is a washin', or churnin' buttah, how could she leave this laboh to go and vote?" I was so wore out, that says I, "we *will* sposen the case, sposen a women is a fool, how can she talk common sense?" Says I, with so impatient a gesture that I broke off a thread, and had to tie it on agin "you are goin' over the same old ground agin of a woman's time," says I "wimmen can drop all thier domestic labors and go to fares—town fares, and county fares, and state fares if she can get to 'em. She will be on the ground in time to see the first punkin and bedquilt carried on to it, and she will stay to see the last horse, trot his last trot; she can find time for picnics and pleasure exertions, and celebrations, and 4th of July—that last, all day—and it would take about half a minute to vote." "But" says I, in the most grand and noble tone I had used yet. " Men haint took by the coat collar and dragged off to caurkusses and 'lections. they dont go unless they are a mind to, and I dont suppose wimmen would be drove there like a flock of sheep. They wouldn't want to go; only, when some great law was up concerning right and wrong, or her

THE WIFE AND MOTHER AT A PRIMARY.

own intrinsick interests, as givin a mother a equal right to her children, a right she earnt naturally, a deed God himself stamped with the great seals of fear and agony. Or bein' taxed without representation; which breaks the old constitution right into, in the middle, every time it is done. Or concernin' equal pay, for equal labor. I spose every female clerk and teacher and operator, who have half starved on about one third what men get for doin' the same work would be on hand. Like wise concerning Temperance, I spose every drunkards wife and mother and girl would go to the pole, that could get there. Poor things, under the Legislator they have enjoyed the right of sufferin'; sposen it lets 'em enjoy the right of suffragin' a spell, mebby they would find it as easy if not easier."

Jest at this minute we see the new Local Preacher, comin' down the road in a open buggy, and Betsey said to once she must be goin, for her folks would be a worryin' after her." Says I, as she hurried to the door,

"Mebby you will get a ride."

"Oh no," says she, "I had a great deal rather walk afoot, I think there is nothing like walking afoot for strengthenin' the mussles."

I am glad she felt so, for I see he didn't ask her to ride. But as she said, health is a blessing, and it is a treat indeed to have strong mussles.

# A TOWER TO NEW YORK DISCUSSED.

THE summer after the Donation and Fare dawned peacefully and fair on Jonesville and the earth. The weather was pleasant, and things seemed to go on as Sister Wesley Minkley and I could wish them to, between her Whitfield, and our Tirzah Ann. Thomas Jefferson every fortnight or so dressed up in his best and went in the direction of Lawyer Snow's. He *said* that "he went to a new protracted meetin' that they had jest started up that way." I don't say that he didn't, but I will say that they protracted 'em pretty late. I don't make no matches nor break none, but I must say that things look promisin' and agreable in the direction of the children. Whitfield Minkley, and Maggy Snow, is agreeable to me, *very*; so they be to Josiah.

Josiah thinks considerable of Maggy's bein' so forehanded. I say *myself* if she hadn't but one hand in the line of riches, or no hand at all, she would still be *my* choice. She is a straight-forward sensible girl—with no affectation, or sham about her. She reminds me of what Samantha Allen was, before she had changed her maiden name of Smith. Whether they are really engaged on not, I don't know, for Thomas J. is such a hand for fun that you can't find out anything from him no more than you could from the wind. But good land! there is time enough. The children shan't marry anybody in one good five years from now, if I have my say about it. But as I told Josiah, I remember we was a talkin' it over last fall, as we sot out a new orchard—I was a holdin' the trees for him and says I—"Josiah it is our duty to get apple trees and children started in the right direction, and then let them take their time to grow."

He said, "Yes, so it was."

He feels well about it, as I say, it is agreeable to us both, and then Josiah's crops looked well, the crows took a little of his corn, but it had come on, and bid fair to be a first rate crop. And as for his oats and barley and winter wheat, they couldn't be bettered.

The Editer of the Augur had brought home his bride, a good lookin' light complected woman, who seemed devoted to him and the two twins. They went to house keepin' in a bran new house, and it was observed that he bought a cottage bedstead that didn't have any posts, and life for him seemed blest and peaceful.

Betsey Bobbet did not pine away and expire as

might be expected by cursory readers of her last poem in the Jonesville Gimlet. But any deep philosipher who had made the Human Race, his (or her) study for any length of time, never worrys over such efushions, knowin' that affliction is like the measles, and if they break out freely in pimples and poetry, the patients are doin' well.

Betsey had been pretty quiet for her through the winter and spring, she hadn't made overtures only to two more—which was a little pill doctor, and a local preacher who had been sent round by the Conference. As she remarked to me, "It is so natural to get attached to your minister and your physician."

As I said the summer sun basked peacefully down and Jonesville almost asleep under her rays, seemed the abode of Repose. But where was there a Eden fenced in, but what Ambition let down the bars, or climbed over the fence. But this was a noble Ambition, a Ambition I was proud to see a gettin' over the fence. It was a Ambition that leaped over into my door yard the very day I heard the blessed tidings, that Horace Greeley was run up for President.

I had always respected Horace, he had always been dear to me. And when I say dear, I want it to be plainly understood—I insist upon it that it *shall* be understood—that I mean dear, in a scriptural, and political sense. Never sense I united myself to Josiah Allen, has my heart swerved from that man so much as the breadth of a horse hair. But Horace's honest pure views of life, has endeared him to every true lover of the Human Race, Josiah Allen's wife included. Of course we don't think alike on every subject. No 2 human bein's ever did. Horace and I differ on some things such as biled vittles, Wimmen's Rights, and cream biscuit. He don't believe in biled vittles, and it is my favorite beverage. He is a unbeliever in salaratus, I myself don't see how he makes cream biscuit fit to eat without it. And he—not havin' me to influence him—hadn't come out on to the side of wimmen's havin' a Right. But as a general thing, Horace Greeley was to be found onto the side of Right. He was onto the side of the weak, the down trodden. He was always a plottin' to do some good to somebody, and I felt that if the eyes of his spectacles could be once opened onto this subject of wimmen's havin' a Right, that he would be more help to us, than a army of banners. Months before he was run up for President I had felt this, and in the fall of 1871, as Josiah was a settin' by the fire alone, he a readin' the World and I a knittin' says I to him,

"Josiah are you willin' that I should go down to New York village on a tower, and have a talk with Horace about the Human race and wimmen's havin' a right?

Josiah didn't seem to be willin', he looked up from the World, and muttered somethin' about "Tammany's ring."

I dont know when the old Smith blood so riled up

in me as it did then. I remember I riz right up where I set in front of the stove, and waved my right hand, I was so excited, and says I,

"Josiah Allen if you have lived with me goin on 15 years, and if you haint no more confidence in me than to think I would accept a ring from old Tammany, then I will stay to home. Says I, Josiah Allen, I never mistrusted till this very minute that you had a jealous hair in your head; says I, you have fell 35 cents in my estimation to night, says I, you know Josiah Allen that I haint never wore no jewelrey sense I jined the Methodist meetin' house, and if I did, do you spose I would accept a ring from old Tammany, that sneakin' old Democrat? I hate old Tammany, I perfectly despise the old man."

I felt so imposed upon and worked up, that I started right off to bed and forgot to wind up the clock, or shet the buttery door, for I remember the clock run down and the cat eat the inside out of the custard pies. Wall from that time I never had opened my head to Josiah about goin' off on a tower. But I wrote Horace a letter on the subject of Wimmen's Rights, as good a letter as I knew how, beggin' him to follow the example of J. Allen's wife, and all other noble reformers and put his shoulder blades to the wheel."

His answer wasn't so satisfactory as I could have wished it was, and I knew I could do better to stand face to face with him. But as I say I dont know as I should ever have started up agin, if that great and good man hadn't been run up for President.

Now some thought it looked shiftless in the Democrats, and kinder poverty struck in 'em, to think they had got all out of President stuff, and had to borry some of the Republicans. But good land! where is there a housekeeper but what will once in a while get out of tea and have to borry a drawin' of her neighbors? If good honest, smart men was skurse amongst 'em, if they had got kinder run out of President timber, and wanted to borry a little, why it would have looked dreedful tight and unneighberly in the Republicans to have refused 'em, when they was well on it too for President stuff, they could have spared two or three jest as well as not, even if they never got 'em paid back. But the Democrats only wanted to borry one, and that was Horace. The Democrats thought everything of Horace because he put a bail onto Jeff Davis. Josiah said at the time that it raised him 25 cents or more in his estimation. At the same time it madded some of the Republicans. But it didn't me. You see I believe jest what I think is right, and pay no attention to what the other folks who are standin' on my doorstep may happen to believe.

Nobody that stands on my platform—let 'em stand as close to me as they are a mind to—not one of 'em is answerable to God for what thoughts and principles are performin' in my mind and soul. Josiah Allen's wife hangs on to nobody's apron strings only jest her own.

As far as the party on my doorstep believe what I think is right, I am with 'em heart and hand, but I am not one to shet up my eyes and walk up blindly and hang on to anybody's apron strings, not even Horace Greeley's, as anybody can see in the matter of biled vittles, Wimmen's Rights, and cream biscuit. To think you have got to believe every thing your party does, seems jest as unreasonable to me, as it would when you go out to pick greens, to pick skunk cabbage because cow cabbage is good and wholesome. Why skunk cabbage is pison, jest as pison as sikuta or ratsbane. Now the doctrine of free love as some folks preach it up, folks in both parties, why the smell of it is jest as obnoxious in my political and moral nostrals as the smell of sikuta is, and if anything smells worse than that, I don't want to go near it. Pick out the good and leave the bad, is my theme in greens and politix.

Now about puttin' that bail onto Jeff. Davis, though as I say it madded my party, I was glad he put it on. Jeff. was a mean critter no doubt, but I don't know as chokin' him to death with a rope would have made him any better. I say this idee of chokin' folks to death to reform 'em, is where we show the savage in us, which we have brought down from our barbarious ancestors. We have left off the war paint and war whoops, and we shall leave off the hangin' when we get civilized.

Says some to me, "Look at our poor Northern boys that suffered and died in Libby prison and Andersonville through Jefferson."

I says to 'em, "Would chokin' Jefferson bring 'em back? if so I would choke him myself.—not to kill him of course, but so he would feel it, I can tell you."

No! it was all over, and past. All the sin, and all the sorrow of the war. And God had out of it brought a great good to the black Africans, and the nation, in the way all good is generally brought, through sufferin' and tribulation. And if a nation is made perfect through sufferin' what should be the first lesson she should show to the world?

I say, it should be the lesson that Christ and his disciples taught, that of all Heavenly graces, charity is the greatest. The way I looked at it was this. The South that had been so braggin', and selfish, and overbearin', stood at the door of the proud and victorious North, like a beggar, harmless, destitute and ragged. Where is the rich happy woman that wouldn't give a nutcake to a sick beggar? I don't see myself how she could help givin' one, if she had any generosity and nobility and—nut-cakes.

Jeff Davis was all broke to pieces, and he wanted a

bail put onto him so life could grip holt of him agin, and carry him I hope towards that heaven he turned his back to, when he was a fightin' to uphold slavery. Horace helped put that bail on, and so did other noble men; and all the ministers in creation, of every persuasion, might all stand up in a row in our door yard, and preach to me 2 days, and then I wouldn't believe that H. G. would turn his hand to anything he thought was wrong.

If there was any fault in him about this, it was on the side of charity and mercy, and as a general thing that end of the board don't tip up any too far in this selfish world. As a general thing, folks don't teter on that end of the board so much as they do on the other.

So, as I said, when I heard that Horace was run up for President, I was so happy that my heart would have sung for joy if it had been anything of a singer, for now, thinks'es I, with that great and good and honest man for President, all he wants is the influence of Josiah Allen's wife to make him all the sufferin' nation needs. I felt that now the time had come for J. Allen's wife to come out boldly and put her shoulder blades to the wheel. I felt that if Horace could be perswaded to draw and Josiah Allen's wife to push, nothin' could hender that wheel from movin' right onward into Freedom. And so my principles, and the great doctrine so goared me, that I couldn't get no rest, I felt that I *must* see Horace before he got sot doun in the high chair, because you know when anybody gets sot doun they don't love to nestle round and make no changes. So I atted Josiah about it, but he didn't seem to be willin'. I didn't come right out and tell him how I was xcercised on Wimmin's Rights, knowin' he was a unbeliever, but I says to him,

"Josiah, Jonesville is a good village, but nobody wants to be tied doun even to a barell of sale molasses. Josiah, I do want to see some other village, I do want to go to New York on a tower."

Says he, "Samantha, what under the sun do you want to go for at your age, why do you want to start up and go a caperin' round the country?"

I thought a minute, and then says I, "I want to see Miss Woodhull, and give her a real talkin' to, about free love. I want to convince her she is in the wrong on it," and then says I in a kind of a blind way, "I have got other business that I feel that it is my duty to tend to."

But he didn't seem to be willin', and I wouldn't go without his consent. And so it went on, Josiah hangin' back, and my principles a goarin' me. It wore on me. My dresses begun to hook up looser on me, and finally one mornin', as I dallied over my second potatoe, and my third egg, not eatin' 'em with no appetite, Josiah says to me, "What does ail you, Samantha, you don't eat nothin', and you seem to be a runnin' doun."

Then I broached the subject to him agin. I expected

he would object. But he looked at me in a silent, melankolly way for about one minute, and half or three quarters of another, and then says he in a gentle but firm accent,

"Samantha if I can sell the old critter you can go."

So I was left in uncertainty (as it were) for I knew he wouldn't sell it for less than the price he had sot it, and no knowin' whether it would fetch it or not. But I felt in my heart a feelin' that I should go off on that tower. And so I gradually but silently began makin' preperations, I quietly and calmly took two breadths out of my brown alapaca dress and goared 'em and put a overskirt on to it, for I was determined not to go to New York village without a overskirt on to me. Not that I care about such triflin' things myself, but I felt that I was representin' a great cause, and I wasn't goin' to put our cause to open shame by not havin' on a overskirt. Men sometimes say that great and strong minded wimmen are slack in the matter of dressin' up, I was determined to show 'em that that weakness wasn't mine. I wasn't goin' to be all tattered out, with ends and tag locks of bows and pleatins, and tow curls and frizzles, but I felt there was a megium course to pursue, and I was determined to hit against it.

Then agin I felt that the color of my dress suited the great cause. I wasn't goin' rigged out in pink muslin, or sky-blue cambric, or anything of that sort. A good solid sensible brown seemed to be jest the thing. Black would have seemed too much in the mournin' line, as if we was despondent when we wasn't. White book muslin would have looked as if my principles was too thin, and I was too light and triflin', and didn't realize the great issues dependent on to me. No; brown alapaca with a overskirt I felt was jest what the anxious nation required of me, as I stood face to face with the future President of the United States—with my spectacles calmly gazin' into his'en, a influencin' him in the cause of Right.

Another reason, I wont deny, influenced me in tryin' to get a good pattern for my overskirt so as to have it set good. (I got it of Miss Gowdey and made it a little bigger round the waist,) I thought more'n likely as not Horace's and my picture would be took, and in the future would be hung up by the side of that good honest old Lincoln's Emancipation Proclamation.

"Josiah Allen's wife influencin' Horace in the Great Cause of Wimmen's Rights."

And though I haint vain, I thought how poor it would be, and what a eye sore to the nation if my dress didn't hang good. And how pleasin' it would be both to America and Josiah, to see me dressed in a noble and becomin' way. So I finished my overskirt, and silently done up my best petticoat, and in the same mysterious manner I put some tape trimmin' on to the bottom of it.

And so the long and tegus days passed away from me. I felt that suspense was a wearin' on me. Josiah see that it was. And on Saturday mornin' I see him pensively leanin' over the barn yard fence, mewsin' as it was, and pretty soon he hitched up the old mare, and went to Jonesville, and when he came back he says to me, in sorrowful tones but some composed.

"Samantha, you can start to-morrow if you want to, I have sold the old critter."

And then he added pensively. "I wish you would have a few griddle cakes for supper, with some maple molasses on to 'em."

# GOVERNED BY PRINCIPLES.

ON the next Monday mornin', I let loose to my feelins as it was, and begun to make open preparations. I baked up the best vittles the house afforded, for I determined Josiah should live like a king durin' his temporary widowerhood. Then after I got through bakin' and got the house clean as a pin, I commenced to fix a dress to wear on the journey, for of course I wasn't goin' to wear my best dress with a overskirt on the railway. I am a master hand for bein' careful of my clothes, and I knew it would almost spile one of my best dresses, but I had a calico dress as good as new. It was a dark blue ground work with a handsome sprig on it, and after I took up two tacks in it, I felt that it was jest the thing to wear on the tower.

I had jest put it on, and had got the lookin' glass onto the floor to see if it cleared the floor enough, when Thomas Jefferson come in, and says he,

"Your dress is too short, mother, I hate to see short dresses, they look so hihorsical."

I answered him with dignity as I looked over my shoulder into the glass,

"Samantha Allen, whose maiden name was Smith, haint a goin' to mop out the cars for the railroad company, free gratis for nothin'," and I added with still more impressive dignity, as I hung up the lookin' glass, "what you mean by hihorsical I don't know."

He said it was a compound word derived from the Greek, "high," to intoxicate, and "horsical," a race horse, which two words strained off from the dead language and biled down into English meant "hihorsical."

I told him "I didn't care for his Greek, I didn't care if it was dead, not a mite, I shouldn't cry over it," and I told him further, fixin' my gray eyes upon him serenely, "that there was two or three words that wasn't dead, that he would do well to strain off, and bile down, and take 'em for a stiddy drink."

He wanted to know what they was, and I told him plainly they was "Mind your own business."

He said he would bile 'em down, and take 'em stiddy as a clock, and pretty soon he started off for Jonesville—he had staid to home that day to help his father. And I went on with a serene face a makin' my preparations. Josiah didn't hardly take his eyes off of my face, as I made 'em. He sot in a dejected way, a claspin' the World in his two hands, with a sad look onto his face. He hated to think of my leavin' him, and goin' off on a tower. I see he did, and I says to him in a real affectionate tone,

"Josiah, haint there nothin' I can do for you in New York, haint you got any errands to the village?"

He rubbed his bald head in deep thought for a minute or two, and then says he, (he thinks everything of the World,) "The nigger barber's wife to Jonesville came pretty near runnin' away with another nigger last night; if you have time I should love to have you go to the Editer of the World and tell him of it. I am afraid," says he, and a gloomy, anxious look overspread his eye-brow, " I am afraid he haint heard of it."

I answered him in a soothin' tone, "That I guessed he had heard of it before now, I guessed it would be in the next week's World," and Josiah kinder chirked up and went out to work.

The next day I took ten pounds of butter, and 4 dozen of eggs and Josiah carried me to Jonesville to trade 'em out, to get necessarys for me to wear on my tower. I didn't begreech layin' out so much expense, neither did Josiah, for we both knew that as I was gettin' pretty well along in years; it wasn't likely I should ever go off on a tower agin. And then I had been prudent and equinomical all my days, and it wasn't no more than right that I should launch out now in a liberal way.

But all the time I was workin' over that butter, and all the time I was countin' out them eggs, Horace was in my mind. Hangin' such hopes on him as I hung, I felt that I must do somethin' openly, to give vent to my patriotic feelin's in regard to him.

I never had wore hats, for I felt that I was too old to wear 'em. But now as I was startin' off to Jonesville to get necessarys to wear on my mission to that great and good Horace, I felt that principle called on me to come out openly, and wear a white hat with a feather. And I felt that Josiah as the husband of Josiah Allen's wife, and the carrier of her to get them necessarys, must also wear one.

The father of Josiah, had left to him with other clothin', a large white fur hat. As the old gentleman hadn't wore it for some 40 or 50 years prior to and before his descase, ( he died when Thomas J. was a baby) it wasn't in the hight of fashion. But says I, "Josiah Allen in the name of Horace and principle will you wear that hat?"

Says he, "I hate to like a dog, for they will think I have stole the Baptist steeple, and am wearin' it for a hat." But seein' my sad dissapointed look, says he, "If you say so Samantha, I will wear it for once."

Says I with dignity, "It is not your wife, formally Samantha Smith, that says so, it is principle."

"Wall!" says he "fetch it on." Josiah was awful clever to me, I guess it is natural for all men to conduct themselves cleverer when they are about to lose their pardners for a spell.

The hat *was big*. I couldn't deny it. And Josiah

bein' small, with no hair to fill it up, as I lifted it up with both hands and set it onto him, his head went right up into it, the brim takin' him right across the bottom of his nose.

Says he, out from under the hat, "There hain't no use a talkin' Samantha, I can't never drive the old mare to Jonesville in this condition, blind as a bat."

But I explained it to him, that by windin' a piller-case, or somethin' round the top of his head, the hat would fit on, jest as you would fix a small cork into a big bottle.

So that bein' arrainged, my next thought was for my own hat, and I thought mournfully as I examined it, mine would be as much too small as his was too big; it was an old one of Tirzah Ann's, it was pure white, but it was small for *her*, and nobody could have got me even to have tried it onto my head, for love or money. But in such a nature as J. Allen's wife's, *principle* is all in all.

And as I looked in the glass and see how awfully I looked in it, a feelin' of grandeur—self sacrificin' nobility and patrotism swelled up in me, and made my face look redder than ever, I am naturally very fresh colored. And I felt that for the sake of Horace and principle, I could endure the burnin' sun, and mebby the scoffs and sneers of Jonesville, they bein' most all on the side of Grant. I took a old white silk bunnet linin' of mine, and put a new bindin' round the edge, it bein' formally bound with pink. And then after readin' a chapter in Foxes Book of Martyrs—a soul stirrin' chapter, concernin' them that was biled in oil and baked on gridirens for principle—I sallied out to get a feather to put onto it.

We hadn't no white feathers by us, and I shouldn't have felt like runnin' Josiah into any extra expense to buy one, if there had been a feather store in the door yard. But our old rooster "Hail the Day," as Thomas Jefferson calls him, had the most curlin'est, and foamin'est tail feathers you ever see, white as snow. And inspired by the most pure and noble and lofty sentiments that can animate the human breast, I chased up that old rooster for nigh onto half an hour. At last I cornered him behind the barn, and as I held him tight to my breast, and pulled out by main strength two long slim feathers, that quirled and waved in a invitin' manner, I says to him,

"This is hard for you, old Hail the Day. But you are not the rooster I take you to be, you are not like your mistress, if you are not willin' to suffer in the cause of Right."

He flopped his wings, when I let him go, and crowed nobly. I fixed the feathers in and we set out. But I was more scairt than hurt in the line of scoffs. As we went into Jonesville not a scoff did I see—not a single scoff. No! they all smiled as they looked at us, they see the power of principle, and they was proud of us. Some of 'em laughed, they admired us so.

VISIT TO JONESVILLE.

We drove up to the store and I went in with my butter and eggs, Josiah havin' business to the blacksmiths. The clerk looked at me, and he smiled, and says he,

"I see you are for Horace Greeley." He almost snickered but he checked himself, looked meachin, as he see my keen gray eye fixed onto his hat which he had on, it was a kind of a mice color, no principle shone on it of any kind.

"Yes," says I, "I am for Horace" and agin I looked keenly and searchin'ly at that hat, and says I "Be you on either side or be you on the fence?"

"Wall" says he "I am kinder on the fence at the present time. But I didn't get up there because I am a coward, I got up there through policy; when you are on the fence, you haint a steppin' on the feet of either party, it is a safe place, and it is a sightly place, you can see better than you can on the ground."

"When do you calculate to get off?" says I.

"Oh right after 'lection," says he. "I shall get off on the side that beats."

I see here was a chance for me to do good and says I,

"Young man, ridin' a fence never carried any man or woman into nobility or honor," says I, "you may saddle and bridle a fence with all the velvet cushioned caution, and silver mounted excuses, and shinin' policy you are a mind to, but you never could get Josiah Allen's wife on to it, she had ruther walk afoot," says I,

11*

"them brave warriors that go canterin' down life's battle field, leadin' on the forlorn hope in the cause of Right, don't go ridin' a fence."

He looked stricken, and I asked him in a milder tone to look at his green braige for viels. He took off that hat and threw it down behind the counter, and brought out the braige, and I bought right there on the spot a yard and a quarter of it. I then bought a pair of new cotton gloves, a good sized umbrella, a pair of morocco shoes, a pair of pink elastic garters, and two as good stockins as Jonesville afforded, and butter would pay for. I haint one to flounce the outside of the platter, and let the inside go bony and ragged. I haint no opinion of wolves on the outside, and sheep on the inside, I want to be sheep clear to the bone, in dress as well as principle. Wall, who should come into the store, jest as I was examinin' the green braige through my spectacles, but Betsey Bobbet. My purchases lay all round me on the counter, and says she,

"Josiah Allen's wife, what means this extravagant outlay of expendature?"

Says I, as coolly as if I went there every mornin' before breakfast,

"I am goin' to New York village on a tower."

She fairly screamed out, "What a coincidence!"

Says I calmly, "It haint no such thing, it is green braige for a viel. It is 75 cents a yard."

"You do not understand me, Josiah Allen's wife,"

says she. "I mean that it is so singulah and coinciding that I am goin' theah too. Cousin Melindy, she that married Ebenezah Williams, is just goin' with the consumption. And I felt that duty was a drawin' of me theah. As I told motheh, in case of anything's happenin', in case that Melindy should expiah, how sweet and soothin' it would be to Ebenezah to have somebody theah, that could feel for him. It would about kill Ebinezah to lose Melindy, and I feel that it would be so sweet and comfortin' for him to have somebody on hand to lean on;" she smiled sweetly as she continued, "there is almost a certainty that Melindy is about to be took from our aching hearts. But I fall back on the scripture, and on my duty, and try to feel as if I could give her up. When do you start?"

"Thursday mornin'," says I in a tone as cold as a grindstone in January, for I see what was before me.

She clasped her two hands and smiled on me two times, and cried out agin, "Oh, what anotheh coincidence! jest the day I was intending to embark. Oh," says she, "how sweet it will be for you to have a congenial companion on the way, as the poet Robinson Selkirk sweetly singeth,

'Oh solitude, where are the charms
Mr. Sage hath seen in thy face?'

Don't you say so, Josiah Allen's wife?"

"I respect Mr. Sage," says I, "he is a man I admire,

and Mr. Selkirk don't know beans," and I added in frigid tones, "when the bag is untied." I see that my emotions was a gettin' the better of me, I see my principals was a totterin'. I recollected that I was a member of the Methodist meetin' house, and the words of a him come back to me, with a slight change in 'em to suit the occasion.

> "Shall I be carried to New York,
> On floury bags of ease?"

I turned and shouldered my cross.

"Betsey we will set sail together Thursday mornin'." I then turned silently and left the store, for I felt than any further effort would have been too much for me.

Thursday mornin' found me to the depott in good season. Betsey also was on time. I didn't feel haughty nor at all proud, but still I felt that I was a independent householder startin' to New York village on a tower at my own expense. I see that all the car folks felt friendly towards me for thier was a pleasant smile on their faces every time they looked at me and Betsey.

I wasn't trimmed off so much as Betsey, but I looked well. I had on that good calico dress, a large black silk mantilly, a good shirred silk bunnet large enough to shade my face some, my bran new cotton gloves, my veil and my umbrell.

Betsey, I always thought put on too much to look well, howsomever everybody to their own mind.

She had on a pale blue parmetta dress, with flounces and puckers onto it, a overskirt and a greek bender of the same, trimmed with checkered delain, cut on a biasin,' a close fittin' bask of the delain, which was pink and yellow plaid and which was pinked out on the edge with a machine. She had on a white bobbinet lace hat, jest big enough to cover her bump of self-esteem, trimmed with red and yellow roses and long ends of otter colored ribbon and white lace, then she had long cornelian ear rings, a string of beads round her neck, and a locket and a big blue breast pin and a cornelian cross. A pair of new white cotton gloves, trimmed with two rows of broad white cotton edgin' five cents a yard—for I seen her buy it—and two horsehair bracelets. And with her new teeth and her long bran new tow curls, and waterfalls and frizzles all full of otter colored rosettes, I tell you she looked gay.

She says to me as she met my keen gaze.

"I don't know but what you think I am foolish Josiah Allen's wife, in enrobing myself in my best a coming on the road. But these are my sentiments. I knew we should get theah before night, and I should proceed at once to Ebinezah's, and if anything should be a happening, if it should be the house of mourning, I thought it would be so comforting to Ebinezah, to see me looking beautiful and cheerful. You know theah is everything in first impressions,

"I mean of course," she added hastily, that I am that sorry for poor lonely widdowers and especially Ebinezah, that if I could be a comfort to them, I would be willing to sacrifice a tablespoonful of my heart's best blood, much moah this blue parmetta dress. These are my sentiments Josiah Allen's wife."

Says I "coldly, I should know they was yours Betsey, I should know they was yours, if I should meet 'em in my porridge dish."

But the time drew near for the cars to bear me away from Josiah, and I began to feel bad.

I dont believe in husbands and wives partin' away from each other, one livin' in Europe, and one in New York village, one in Wall street, and the other on a Long Branch, one in Boston, and the other in North America. As the poet truly observes,

"When the cat is away the mice's will go to playin'."

As for me, I want my husband Josiah where I can lay my hand on him any time, day or night, I know then what he is about. Though so far as jealousy is concerned, Bunker Hill monument, and Plymouth Rock would be jest as likely to go to flirtin' and cuttin' up, as either of us. We have almost cast iron confidence in each other. But still it is a sweet and satisfyin' thought to know jest where your consort is, and what he is about, from hour to hour.

# THE FIRST PARTING IN 15 YEARS

Josiah and me didn't shed no tears as we each of us parted, though our hearts ached with anguish we both of us felt it our duty to be calm. I felt a tear risin' to my eye, but with a almost fearful effort I choked it back and said in low accents as we grasped holt of each others hands at partin',

"Good by, Josiah, remember to feed the hens, and keep the suller door shet up."

He too struggled nobly for composure and conquered, and in a voice of marble calm he said,

"Good by Samantha, dont spend no more money than is necessary."

The Ingin hitched to the front car give a wild yell, as if he felt our two woes—Josiah's and mine—and we parted for the first time in goin' on 15 years.

As I sunk back on the wooden bottomed car seat, perfectly onmanned by my efforts at commandin' myself, for the first time I felt regret at my wild and perilous undertakin'.

# MEETING GRANT AND COLFAX.

WE had to change cars about noon, as we went into the depot to get our tickets, the ticket man looked so kinder lonesome stuck in there alone, for all the world as if he had done somethin' and his mother had shet him up, that I thought I would make a little talk with him.

He favored Celestine Wilkins'es husband considerable, jest such a meachin' lookin' feller, and I knew Celestine's husband had a brother down this way somewhere, and so to kinder open a conversation with him, I asked him "If he ever had any relation that married a girl by the name of Gowdey?"

You ought to have heard how that feller snapped me up—he couldn't have answered me any shorter, if I had asked him to run away with me.

But thinks'es I to myself, he has got morbid through lonesomness. I pitied him shet up alone there, and so in a few minutes I begun agin.

"I didn't know but he was your brother, he has

a good deal such a meachin' look to him," and says I, "The country round here hain't so pleasant as Jonesville, do you think it is sir?"

"He didn't know or care nothin' about Jonesville."

His tone was sharper than that sword aged two, that the bible tells of.

Says I, "Young man you needn't take my head quite off, if you never did see Jonesville nor had any other advantages. I hain't to blame for it." And thinks'es I to myself, you may be lonesome for all of me, you may die of lonesomness for all I care, I shan't try to make any more talk with you to make your time pass off easier.

We got on to the cars agin and got a good seat. I wanted to set by an open winder, and Betsey didn't. I mistrust she thought the wind would take the kink out of her frizzles, and so she went on a seat or 2 ahead of me. There was a lot of fashionable lookin' folks came in too, and one of 'em came along and set right down in the seat with me, the cars bein' pretty full. She was dressed up like a doll, but she didn't act stuck up a mite, my opinion is, she knew what belonged to good manners, and I offered her some caraway, for I liked her looks. She took it and thanked me for it, and says I to make talk with her,

"Are you goin' far on the cars?"

She said, "She wasn't goin' far on this route, she was goin' to a waterin' place."

"How far?" says I.

"Oh 2 or 300 miles," says she.

"Good land!" says I, "Can't you find any water nearer hum? Why," says I, "I should think you would be choked before you got there." Says I, "Our cistern and well sometimes gives out in hot weather, but Josiah always draws water from the creek," why says I, full of pity for her, "If I hadn't any water to the house, and nobody to draw it for me I should rather drive myself to the creek and water myself 3 times a day, than to start off on the cars so far after it. Howsumever every body to their own mind."

She kinder laughed with her eyes, and, said somethin' about "seasides" and "sea bathin'" or somethin' and I felt it was my duty to say to her,

"You needn't go 300 miles for that, you can get good seasides to Jonesville for 75 cents. Tirzah Ann, Josiah's girl by his first wife, got one for that. I don't wear hats myself, except," says I with dignity, "in the cause of Right and for the good of the Human Race. And as for seein' bathin', I myself would go the other way, ruther than foller it up; howsumever everybody to thier own taste." But I kep' thinkin' of it, and I couldn't help breakin' out agin, and speakin' my mind; says I, in a good deal colder accents, "I would as soon go to a horse race—and sooner," for the more I thought of it the more I thought that no virtuous woman would start off 300 miles to see bathin' goin' on. I acted offish after that, and was sorry I had give her the caraway.

Her face looked red, and she started up and went back and sot down by some of her mates, and I was glad she did. She pretended to be a laughin', and she was talkin' to 'em awful busy; but I see one eye was on me the most of the time—she felt guilty.

At the very next station house two fellers come in that everybody seemed to be lookin' at, and payin' attention to. But they didn't seem to mind it. They come in and sot down right in the seat between me and Betsey.

After they had sot down, one of 'em took a cigar out of his pocket, and put it in his mouth. It wasn't lit, but he held it between his teeth as if it was a great comfort to him. Thinks-'es I, it is kinder queer works, but I can stand it if the R. R. Company can. But Betsey leaned her head back, and says to him,

"Was you aware, kind sir, that cigars was confiscated on the cars?"

He didn't say a word, but held on to it with his teeth as if it was dreadful comfortin' to him. And she asked him over again. But not a word did he say. I guess she asked him five times—but not a word did she get out of him. And then she turned to the feller with him, the smilin' chap, and says she,

"Is your companion a deaf male?"

He smiled. Agin she asked him,

"Is your pardner deprived of his eahs?"

"Oh no," says he, "he has got ears," and agin he smiled.

Thinks'es I, it is pretty queer works, but it is none of my business. I guess we had rode nigh on to an hour in jest that way, Betsey kinder oneasy and nestlin' round, I calm and placid in demeaniour and one of the men between us a holdin' that cigar in his mouth, as if it was indeed consolin', and the other one a smilin' blandly, at nothin' in particular. Everybody in the cars seemed to be a lookin' at 'em, and thinks'es I, it is no wonder, for of all the good natured lookin' men I ever see, he is the cap sheaf. Thinks'es I, I wish every ticket agent in the world could have his benine face to hang up before 'em, for a sampler, for if there was ever a race that had the appearance of bein' brought up on vinegar and ten-penny nails, it is them.

After a while, I got kinder hungry. My basket hung right up over them two men, and I rose up, and went to reach up for it, when the smilin' chap got up a smilin' and says he to me, "Can't I assist you, madam?" and he reached up smilin' as sweet as a rose, to take it down, when all of a sudden the handle slipped out at one end, and down come the contents right on to his face. One nut cake, a long, slim one, sot up straight on his nose, as handsome as you ever see a circus man ride a white horse. But most mournful of all, I had some biled eggs, and unbeknown to me, Tirzah Ann had took 'em out too quick, before they was

THE SMILIN' STRANGER.

much more than warmed through, and they broke onto his face and all run down into his whiskers. But if you will believe it, that blessed man smiled.

Thinks'is I to myself, "Good land! was there ever such a clever critter on earth?" I handed him a clean towel, and told him I was sorry. But he smiled, and said, "it wasn't any matter," and wiped his sweetly smilin' face, and handed the towel back smilin'."

The other feller never said a word, though one of the eggs broke onto the legs of his white pantaloons. Jest at this crisis, a tall man with whiskers came up, and said somethin, to 'em, and they got up and went to the other end of the car, where there was a lot of smart lookin' men. As they went by me the clever feller slipped on a piece of orange peel, and a most fell. But if you will believe it, the critter smiled.

I see that all of them smart lookin' men acted dreadful reverential towards the two, and I says to a bystander behind me,

"Can you tell me sir who that clever critter is, and the other one? Says he, "That is Skyler Colfax, and General Grant."

I rose right up in my seat, for at the mention of them two honored names, such emotions rushed onto me—that it drownded out fear, and all the shrinkin' bashfulness of my sect, and I forgot in that wrapped moment that I wasn't Josiah, and I advanced right onwards towards them two noble men. Every man round 'em see the lofty expression onto my face, and kinder fell back, and I walked right up and gripped Skylers'es hand with one of mine, while I held my umbrell in the other tremblin' with emotion.

"Skyler, I am glad Tirzah Ann took 'em out too quick."

He didn't know what I meant, but that blessed man smiled, and agin I spoke in the same tremblin' tones.

"I am glad they was rare done."

Agin he smiled, and agin I spoke, and I mastered my feelin's, with a effort, and spoke out loud and clear,

"The hen that laid them eggs, never shall do another day's work as long as my name is Josiah Allen's wife. I know jest which one laid 'em, for old speckle face's eggs are so big that we always keep 'em for our own use." Says I, "it makes me proud and happy to think I am the owner of that hen, for if it hadn't been for them eggs, I never should have felt so well acquainted with you. If it hadn't been for them eggs that broke onto your good and honored face, I never should have had the privilege of graspin' holt of your hand and sayin' to you what I now say, that though goodness and patience and faithfulness may be made light of by some, they are jest what is goin' to carry Uncle Sam triumphant onward, with a smilin' face, when the egg shells of uncivil war break on his honest face, and thier yelks run down into his whiskers."

Here my feelin's almost overcame me agin, and as

he smiled at me, and spoke kinder pleasant to me—and smiled agin, I turned silently away and grasped holt of General Grant'ses hand, and says I, in still more chokin' accents—

"Ulysses this is a proud day for Josiah Allen's wife," says I, "Ulysses how do you do?"

He didn't say nothin' but nodded kinder pleasant to me, and I says in the same almost tremblin tones for I knew he thought every thing of his relations. "How is Mr. Dents'es folks, are they all enjoying good health?" He nodded agin kinder pleasant but didn't say a word, and I proceeded on—

"Ulysses you have freed the land from war and bloodshed. Wherever the smoke of that peaceful cigar has smoked, it has drove before it the blood red cloud of war and treason." But says I, "that haint the main reason why I thought you ought to be President, and so I have told Josiah. I have said to Josiah more'n a hundred times that any man or woman ought to be President that knew enough not to talk when they hadn't nothin' to say. But—" says I, for even in that wrapped moment stern principle was the guide of J. Allen's wife—"That was when you was run up for President the first time; I go now for Horace Greeley, and so does Josiah."

There haint nothin' little and envious about Ulysses Grant, he didn't act mad a mite, he nodded to me agin as friendly as ever, and after invitin' them both in the name of Josiah, to make it thier home with us whenever they come to Jonesville, and sendin' my best respects to Julia and Mr. Dents'es folks, and Skylers'es wife Elliner, I retired to my seat and sot down.

When Betsey discovered who I had been talkin' with, she looked wild at the thought, but it didn't rouse in her, the spontanious emotions of patrotism it did in me. If a barell has been filled up with rain water, you can't expect to tap it and have it run strong beer. When any sudden circumstance taps folks'es minds, they will run out of 'em jest what they have been filled with, no more, no less. My mind was that filled with noble emotions of admiration and patrotism, that I entirely forgot for the minute that I was J. Allen's wife from Jonesville, But Betsey all the while remembered B. Bobbet, she also remembered her poetry. I don't believe a few earthquakes could make her forget that, her first words was after she recovered herself,

"I will make General Grant, that deah, sweet man, a present. Everybody does, that wants to get onto the right side of him. I will give him a piece of my poetry. If I remember rightly I have got one in my satchel bag, all printed out, with a running vine around the edges. There is 45 verses of it, and it is on the war. How fortunate that I brought it along." And as she dove her hands into her satchel bag, she continued dreamily,

"Mebby he is that liberal and generous turn with

"LET US HAVE PEACE."

his own folks, that after he has read it, he will give it to some of his wife's relations. Mebby there is a few widowehs among them," and then in a still more dreamy tone she murmured, " Betsey B. Dent, Washington, D. C." But anon or a little after, she roused out of this revery and takin' the poetry in her hand, she started down the car, and I bein' tired, leaned my head back against the side of the seat, and composed myself together.

I guess I had most got into a nap, when I heard a loud wrathful, eloquent voice, seemin'ly makin' a speech to some enimy. It started me up so that I rose right up onto my feet, and looked round, and there was that noble General, standin' up with his hands extended, layin' it down strong and decided. I knew what it was in $\frac{1}{2}$ a minute, Betsey Bobbet had done what a five years uncivel war couldn't do, nor a admirin' nation of 20 million souls. She had got him to makin' a speech, while Skyler who had smiled stidely for upwards of 40 years, stood lookin' on with a dark and awfully gloomy frown onto him.

I stood silent for some time lost in the sorrowful feelins the scene called forth, and then almost overcome with my pity for them, I wended my way towards them. As I drew nearer to them, I heard his words which he was pourin' out so eloquently and fluently, "Let us have peace, *Can't* we have peace ?" he was yellin' in such harrowin' tones, that there wasn't hardly a dry eye in my head as I listened.

12

"Have I escaped from the horrible danger of war, have I survived the open bullets of my enimies, and the well meanin' but almost fatal arrows of my friends, to expier in this way? To perish by poetry? Is there no sucker for me? *Cant* we have peace?" he screamed in a loud preachin' tone as he ketched sight of me, " Cant we have it, *say ?*"

He was almost delerious. But I laid my hand on his agitated elbow, and says I in soothin' tones.

" Yes Ulysses, you *shall* have a piece, you shall, Josiah Allen's wife will see to it, you *shall* have a piece."

And then I leaned down and whispered a few words into Betsey Bobbett's left ear, and she turned quicker'n a flash, and gathered up her poetry and rushed into the forward car.

As she disapeared, Skyler'ses face changed from that gloomy sinister frown, and agin he put on that smile that was upwards of 40 years old, but was still so sweet and fresh that I knew it was good for another 40 years—and the General grasped me by the hand sayin' in agitated tones,

"There was upwards of 50 of 'em, and she would read 'em." Says I soothingly, " I wouldn't think of it Ulysses, it is all over now. I was glad to show the gratitude the nation owes to you. I was glad of the chance to befriend you."

" Angel !" says he almost warmly. But I interupt-

## BETSEY OVERCOME BY STRATEGY. 287

ed him by sayin' in a tone of dignity. "I honor and respect you deeply Ulysses—but in the two names of Julia and Josiah, I must forbid your callin' me angel, or any other pet name."

I knew it was only his deep gratitude to me for rescuin' him from his peril that made him say it, for he and Julia think the world of each other. And the good solid principles, colored and morally struck in with tan bark in his early life, the muddy waters of political life haint been able to wash out, nor the gilt tinsel of fashionable life to cover up and destroy. I knew that even there in Washington Avenue, among all the big men there, he loved his wife, jest as much as if it was the fashion to love 'em. I knew all this, but still I felt that I must speak as I did, for principle with J. Allen's wife—as I have remarked more formally—is all in all.

I then turned and followed Betsey, not knowin' but what she would be a comin' back. What I whispered in her left ear was this, that her back hair was comin' down, and she bein' so bald, I knew it would fetch her down like a arrow in her breast.

They left at the next Station House, and Betsey and me proceeded onwards to New York village with no farther coincidences.

# AT NEW YORK, ASTERS'ES TAVERN.

THE cars didn't bust up nor break down, which surprised me some, but which I felt was indeed a blessin', and at ½ past six Betsey and me stood on the platform of the depott at New York village. As we stood there I would have swapped my last new cross barred muslin night cap in my satchel bag on my arm for a pair of iron ears. I should have been glad of the loan of a old pair for 16 seconds, if I couldn't got 'em no longer, the noise was so distractin' and awful.

Says I to myself, "Am I Josiah Allen's wife, or am I not?" some of the time I thought I was Josiah, I was so destracted. But though inwardly so tosted up and down, I kep a cool demeaniour outside of me. I stood stun still, firmly graspin' my satchel bag, my umberell and my green cap box—with my best head dress in it, till I had collected myself together, recolected what my name was, and where I was a goin'.

When my senses come back I thought to myself truly Josiah wasn't so far out of the way when he worried over old Tammany, for of all the shameless and brazen set, on the face of the earth, that set a howlin' round Betsey Bobbet and me was the shamelessest and brazenest.

Now I am naturaily pretty offish and retirin' in my ways, with strange men folks. I think it is becomin' in a woman to be so, instead of bold. Now when we sot sail from Jonesville, after we got well to ridin', a man came through the cars, a perfect stranger to me, but he reached out his hand to shake hands with me, jest as friendly and famelier as if I was his step mother. But I didn't ketch holt of his hand, as some wimmen would, I jest folded up my arms, and says I, coolly,

"You have got the advantage of me."

But he never took the hint, there he stood stun still in front of me holdin' out his hand. And seein' there was a lot of folks lookin' on, and not wantin' to act odd, I kinder took holt of his hand and shook it slightly, but at the same time says,

"Who under the sun you are I dont know—but you seem determined to get acquainted with me. Mebby you are some of his folks I haint never seen— are you related to Josiah on the Allen side or on the Daggett side?" Josiah's mother was a Daggett.

But before I could say any more he spoke up and

said all he wanted was my ticket. I was glad then I
had acted offish. For as I say, I dont believe in wimmen puttin' themselves forward and actin' bold. Not
that that stands in the way of their modistly claimin'
their honest rights. I have seen enough boldness
used by a passel of girls at one huskin' bee, or apple
cut, to supply 4 presedential elections, and the same
number of female caurkusses, and then have 5 or 6
baskets full left. Havein' these modest and reserved
feelins' in my soul—as firm as firm iron—what was
my feelins' as I stood there on that platform, when a
great tall villian walked up to me and yelled right up
close to my bunnet,

"Will you have a bus mom?"

If that man had the privilege of livin' several hundred years, he would say at the last 100, that he
never forgot the look I gave him as he uttered
these infamous words to me. It was a look calculated
to scorch a man to his very soul. It was a look calculated and designed to make a man sigh for some
small knot hole to creep through and hide him from
the gaze of wimmen. I'll bet 2 cents that he wont
insult another women in that way very soon. I give
him a piece of my mind that he wont forget in a
hurry. I told him plainly, "That if I wasn't a
married women and a Methodist, and, was free to kiss
who I was a mind to, I had jest as lives kiss a ana-
condy, or a boyconstructor, as him," and I says in

conclusion, "mebby you think because Josiah haint here to protect me, you can talk to me as you are a mind to. But, says I, "if I haint got Josiah with me I have got a good stout umberell." He quailed silently, and while he was a quailin' I turned to Betsey, and asked her if she was ready to start along, for as true as I live and breathe, I was afraid Betsey was so of that clingin turn, that she would be a kissen' some of them men in spite of my teeth, for thier was a lot of 'em besettin' her for a bus. A yellin' round her "have a bus?" Have a bus?" Jest as if that was jest what Betsey and me had come from Jonesville for. The miserable—lowlived creeters.

Betsey seemed to kinder hate to go, but I started her off. For no burdock bur ever stuck to a horse's mane, as Josiah Allen's wife sticks to a companion, a drawin' 'em along with her in the cause of Right. As we wended our way along, walkin' afoot, she wanted to know what tavern I was a goin' to put up to, and I told her "Mr. and Miss Asters'es tavern." Says she, "If it was not jest as it was, I would ask you to go to cousin Ebenezah's with me. But in the future it may be I shall be freer to act, than I be now. If I was a married female and had a home of my own heah, how happy I should be to welcome Jonesville to its blessed presincts. As deah Tuppah observes—"

But I interrupted her by sayin' coolly, "Betsey, I

have made up my mind to put up to Mr. Aster'ses, for Johnothan Beans'es ex-wife, Josiah's 2nd cousin, is Miss Aster'ses hired girl."

"Is she a widow?" says Betsey.

"She does a little in that line," says I in a cautious tone. "She is a vegetable widow." I wasn't goin' to say "grass widow" right out, though she *is* clear grass. For her husband, Johnothan Bean, run away with another woman 3 years ago this comin' fall, It was all printed out in the World at the time. At that very minute we turned on to Broadway, and Betsey was a sailin' on ahead of me in gay spirits, a laughin', and a talkin', and a quotin' Tupper, jest as happy as you please. But as we turned the corner, I stopped her by ketchin' holt of her Greek bender, and says I,

"I'd have a little respect into me, Betsey Bobbet," says I. "Less stand still here, till the funeral procession goes by."

So we put a funeral look onto our faces, and stood still a spell, and they streamed by. I thought my soul there was no end to the mourners. It seems as if we stood there decently and in order, with a solemn look onto our faces, becomin' the solemn occasion, for pretty nigh $\frac{1}{2}$ an hour. Finally I whispered to Betsey, and says I,

"Betsey, did you ever see such a gang of mourners in your life?"

I see her eyes looked kinder sot in her head, and she seemed to be not really sensin' what I said. She looked strange. Finally says she, "It is a sorrowful time, I am composin' a funeral owed, and I will repeat it to you soon."

I wanted to get her mind offen that idee, and I continued on a talkin',

"It must be some awful big man that is dead. Like as not it is the Governor of the United States or some deacon or other. Do see 'em stringin' along. But how some of the mourners are a behavin', and how gay some of the wimmen are dressed. If I had known there was goin' to be a funeral in the village, while I was here, some of the mourners might have had my black bombazeen dress, and my crape viel jest as well as not. I always make a practice of lendin' 'em on funeral occasions."

Jest then a little boy came sailin' by, with a segar in his mouth almost as big as *he* was. And I ketched holt of him, and whispered to him,

"Bub who is dead?" and says I, "be you one of the mourners?"

"Yes, old lady," says he, in a impudent tone, "I am out on a short mourn."

If it hadn't been for the mournful occasion, and for gettin' off'en my dignity, I would have spanked him, then and there; he laughed so impudent at me. But I let him go on, and then I took out my snowy 25 cent linen handkerchief and wiped off my heated face, and says I to Betsey,

"I am wore out; there hain't no end to this procession seemin'ly, we may as well go on, for I am beat out, we shall act as well as some of the mourners do any way, if we do walk on." So we wended on. Betsey's cousin lived not a great ways from Miss Asters'es, only it was down a little ways another street, up over a store. I told her "I guessed I wouldn't climb up them grocery stairs, I was so tuckered out, and then Miss Aster would most probable have supper about ready, and I didn't want to have her fuss to set the table over for me, or steep her tea over, and I felt that a cup of tea I must have."

I was kinder dreadin' goin' in alone, not bein' acquainted with Miss Aster, and I don't know when I have been tickleder, than I was to meet Jonothan Beans'es ex-wife, right on the sidewalk. She was real glad to see me too, for I befriended her when she first went to grass, (as it was) I took her right in for 3 weeks, and give her 2 pair of seamed stockins, and a lot of other things for her comfort.

She went right back with me. Of all the big houses I ever see, Mr. Asters'es house beat everything. I was determined not to act green and be a askin' questions, and so I didn't say a word. But I spose from the size of it, that Mr. Aster lets part of it for meetin' houses, and mebby they have a few select schools in it, and a few lunatick asylums, I should think they would need 'em, such a noise. But I didn't say a word.

Jonothan Beans'es ex-wife told me I must put my

name down on the Register before I went to my
room, I didn't object, nor I didn't ask no questions,
but I kep a pretty good look out. "Register!" I
knew I had heard somethin' that sounded like that,
connected with deeds, and I wasn't goin' to sign
away my property. I didn't know as it was so, but
I did have my thoughts, that mebby somebody had
told 'em I was comein' to the village, and they was
tryin' to get me to sign away my thirds, there is so much
iniquity in the world. But I kep my thoughts to
myself, and kep my eyes open. I jest looked over
the book pretty sharp, before I put my name down,
and I see it was all right. My room was on the
5th story, and I told J. Beans'es ex-wife that how
I was goin' to climb up them stairs I didn't know, I
was so tuckered out, I was sorry the minute I said
it, for I was afraid she would go and tell Miss Aster,
and Miss Aster would give up her bedroom to me, or
mebby she would make Mr. Aster sleep with one of
the boys, and have me sleep with her, and I wouldn't
have her put herself out for the world. And I spoke
up and says I,

"I guess I can weather it some way."

And she spoke up and says she, "Here is the
elevater, be carried up."

There was a big nigger comin' right towards us,
and I thought she meant him, for they have been called
such funny names ever since the war, that I thought

likely "Elevator" was one of 'em. But I jest put my foot right down to once, says I firmly,

"I haint a goin' to be lugged up stairs by that nigger." And then I was so afraid that he would hear it, and it would hurt his feelins, that I spoke right up pretty loud, and says I,

"It haint on account of the gentleman's dark complexion at all, that I object. But I don't think Josiah would like it, to have any other man carryin' me round in his arms."

But Johnothan Beans'es ex-wife explained it to me. There was a little room about as big as our smoke house, all fixed off neat as a pin, and all we had to do was to git in, and then we was histed right up in front of our room. I was awful glad to be carried up, but I have got some pity left into me, and I says to her, says I,

"Haint it awful hard for the man that is drawin' us up?" Says I, "Is it Mr. Aster, or is it his hired man?" and says I, "does he do it with a windlass, like a well bucket? or hand over hand, like drawin' up water out of a cistern with a pole?"

Johnathan Beans'es ex-wife said it was done by machinery, and she said, for I asked her the first thing, "that there wasn't no funeral, that there was jest such a crowd every day." I didn't believe her, but I was too beat out to contend. And glad enough was I, to stretch my weary limbs in a rockin' chair. J. Beans'es ex-wife said she would fetch me up a cup of tea, and my supper to me. She haint forgot the past.

She told me when she left me that night, to be dreadful careful about the gass, and not blow it out; she told me jest how it was done, and I'll bet Mrs. Aster herself couldn't do it any neater, for I thought of Josiah, and the thought of that man nerved me to do it right, so as not to die and leave him a gass widower, and a lonely man.

When I waked up in the mornin' such a noise as I heard. Why, I have thought sometimes when I was sleepy, that our old rooster "Hail the Day" makes an awful sight of noise. But good land! if all the roosters in the United States and Boston, had roosted right under my window, they couldn't have begun with it. My first thought as I leaped out of bed was, "Jonesville is afire." Then recollectin' myself, I grew calmer, and thought mebby Miss Aster had got breakfast ready, and was a hollerin to me. And growin' still more composed, I gin up that the tramplin' and hollerin' was down in the street. As I dressed me, I lay out my work for the day; thinks'es I, "Betsey Bobbet will be so took up with her mission to her cousin Ebenezer's, that I shall be rid of her." It was a sweet thought to me, and I smiled as I thought it. But alas! as the poet well observes, "How little we know what is ahead of us." Thinks'es I, as I turned the screw and let the water outen the side of the house to wash me, (Johnothan Beans'es ex-wife had showed me how the night before,) I must do all I can this day in the cause of Right. If I get that destracted here that I am threatened with luny, and have to leave before my time comes, I will go where duty calls me first and most. I should have been glad to have looked round the village, and got acquainted with some of Miss Aster'ses neighbors, but though I felt that the neighborin' wimmen might think I was real uppish and proud sperited, still I felt that I could better stand this importation than to desert the cause of Right for $\frac{1}{2}$ a minute. I felt that Horace, although nearly perfect in every other respect, needed Josiah Allen's wife's influence on a subject dear to that female's heart. And I felt that that deluded Miss Woodhull needed a true and pure principled female to show her plainly where she stood. Then I laid out to go to Isabella Beecher Hooker'ses. And the time was short, I knew with every fresh roar of destraction that come up from the street below, that the time of my stay in that village was short.

I was so almost lost in these thoughts, that I didn't see how late it was a gettin'. I had overslept myself in the first place, bein' so tuckered out the night before, and thinks'es I all of a sudden,

"What will Miss Aster think, my keepin' her from eatin' her breakfast so long?"

But inwardly, my mind was some composed by

thinkin' it was principle that had belated me. So I sailed down stairs. I had put on my best clothes, my headdress looked foamin', my overskirt stood out noble round my form. And it was with a peaceful mind though some destracted by the noise, that I wended my way to the breakfast table.

But instead of all of us a settin' to one table with Miss Aster to the head, a pourin' out tea, there was I'll bet, more'n a hundred little tables, with folks settin' round 'em, a eatin', and waiters a goin' all round amongst 'em, a waitin' on 'em. And every man waiter had got on one of his wives white bib aprons. Thinks'es I to myself, what a tussle I should have with Josiah, to get him to wear one of my aprons round the house when I had company; he is awful sot aginst wearin' aprons, it is all I can do to get one on to him when he is a churnin'.

Johnothan Beans'es ex-wife ketched my eye, as I went in, and she came and sot me down to a little table where there wasn't nobody. And then she was drawed off by somebody and left me alone. And I spoke out loud to myself,

"I'd like to know what I am goin' to eat, unless I lay to and eat stun china and glass ware." And ketchin' sight of the pepper box, I exclaimed almost convulsively,

"I never was much of a hand to eat clear pepper, and nothin' else."

A nigger come up to me at that minute, and said

somethin' in a frenchified accent about a cart bein' on my plate, or somethin' about a cart, and I see in a minute that he wanted to make out—because I come from the country—that I wanted a cart load of vittles. I don't know when I have been madder. Says I,

"You impudent creeter, you think because I am from the country, and Josiah haint with me, that you can impose upon me. Talk to me, will you, about my wantin' a cart load of vittles? I should be glad," says I in a sarcastic tone, "I should be glad to get somethin' a little more nourishin' than a three tined fork and a towel to eat, but I don't seem to run much chance of gettin' on it here."

Before he had time to say anything, J. Beans'es ex-wife came up, and said somethin' to me about lookin' at "Bill the Fair." I looked down on the table, and noticed then for the first time that there was a piece of poetry layin' there, seemin'ly cut out of some newspaper, I see that she wanted me to read it, but I told her, "That I wasn't much of a hand for poetry anyway, and Betsey Bobbet wrote so much that it made me fairly sick of it," and besides, says I, "I have left my specks up stairs, I forgot 'em till I got most down here."

But jest then I happened to think, mebby she had wrote it herself, I dont want to hurt nobody's feelins', and says I, in a pleasant tone,

"I presume "Bill the Fair," is a good piece of poetry, and if you haint no objection, I will take it home with me, and put it into Tirzah Ann's scrap book." She started off before I fairly got through speakin' and I folded up the poetry and put it into my pocket, and in a minute's time back she came with some first rate vittles. She knows what I like jest as well as I do, havin' lived with us a spell, as I said, when she first went to grass. She knows jest what a case I am for store tea; but she asked me what kind of tea I wanted, and I spoke right out before I thought,

"Anything but sage tea, I cant bear that."

But then I happened to think I see they was all a drinkin' coffee round me, I knew they was by the smell. And I thought mebby from her speakin' to me in that way that she meant to give me a little hint that Miss Aster was out of store tea, and says I, kinder loud for she had started off. "If Miss Aster is short on it for store sea, she needn't fuss for me, she need'nt borry any on my account, I can drink sage tea if I set out to."

But I thought to myself, that I had rather have brought a drawin' of tea in my pocket clear from Jonesville, than to have gone without it; while I was jest thinkin' this, Jonothan Beans'es ex-wife came back with a first rate cup of tea, strong enough to bear up a egg.

The more I looked round and see the droves of hungry folks, the sorrier I felt for Miss Aster. And I spoke to J. Beans'es ex-wife as she brought me my last vittles, says I, "If there is a woman on the face of the hull earth I am sorry for, it is Miss Aster, how on earth can she ever cook enough to fill this drove of folks?" says I, "How can she ever stand up under it?" And carried almost away with my sympathy, I says to Jonathan Beans'es ex-wife,

"You tell Miss Aster from me that she needn't make no fuss about the dinner at all, I will eat a picked up dinner, I had jest as lives as not, I didn't come down here to put her out and make her any trouble."

I heard a little noise to one side of me, and I looked round and there was a feller and two girls a snickerin' and laughin', right at me. They was rigged out awful fashionable, but I guess their brains had run to their hair mostly, the girls on their heads, and hisen on his face, such sights of it. But I don't believe they was very well off, for every one of 'em had broke one eye off'en their spectacles, and they lifted up that one eye, and looked at me through it, a laughin' at the same time as if they would split. But it didn't put me out a bit, I glared back at 'em, as sharp as they did at me, and says I,

"Laugh away if you want to, I know what it is to cook over a hot cook stove in the summer time, it tuckers anybody out, even if they have got good help, and I am sorry for Miss Aster."

They snickered worse than ever, and I got mad, and says I,

"I don't wonder you laugh! there haint no more pity and humanity in the whole lot on you, than there is in a three tined pitchfork, and no wonder when you see somebody that has got a little pity and generosity into 'em, it is more of a amusement and novelty to you than a circus would be."

As I said this, I rose up in almost fearful dignity, and sailed away from the table up to my room.

As I opened the door I heard a dreadful curious noise, a kind of a gurglin' gushin' sound, and when I opened the door, of all the freshets I ever see, I had forgot to turn back the little screw, and the water was a gushin' out all over. Jonothen Beans'es ex wife, happened to come along jest then, and she sent up a nigger with a mop, and a lot of cloths, and I turned to, and helped him, she told me not to, but says I,

"Josiah Allen's wife haint one to shirk when there is work to do," and says I, "you tell Miss Aster, after I get through here, I had jest as lives come down and help her wash up the breakfast dishes as not," says I, lookin' thoughtfully at my overskirt, I don't really want to put my hands into the dish water on account of my dress, but I had jest as lives wipe 'em as not."

But J. Beans'es ex wife said there wasn't no need of my helpin', and so after I got my room all slicked up and my bed made (she told me to leave my bed, but I wusn't goin' to act so slack) I sot down a minute to rest, before I set sail in the cause of Right.

I was jest a thinkin' that Betsey Bobbet was safe in

the house of mournin', and there was a sweet and satisfied smile on my face, as I thought it, when all of a sudden the door opened, and in she walked. My heart sunk pretty near ½ an inch. But I ketched holt of my principles, and says I,

"What is the matter Betsey?" For she looked as if she had been cryin' her eyes out. "Is your cousin no more? has Ebineezah suicided himself?"

"No moah!" says she in a indignant tone. "She is gettin, well, and Ebineezah is as happy as a king about it, she has been takin' cod liveh oil, and "Cherry Pectorial," and they have cured her, I hate Cherry Pectorial, and cod liveh oil, they are nasty stuffs."

Says I, in a insinuatin' tone, "you are goin' back there haint you?"

"No!" says she indignantly, "I wont stir a step back, they are so tickled about her gettin' bettah, that they don't use me with no respect at all." And there was a tear in her eye as she added in sorrowful tones, "Ebineezah told me that if it hadn't been for that cod liveh oil, he should have been a widowah, and a lonely man to day. No!" says she takin' off her hat and throwin' it in a angry fierce way onto the bed, "I wont stir a step back, I wont stay anotheh minute in the same house with cod liver oil, I perfectly despise it."

I see there was no use a arguin' with her, the arrow had struck too deep, I see my fate, Betsey had got to accompany me on my high and lofty mission. For a minute I thought wildly of escape, of gettin' her out of the room on some errent for a minute, and then tyin' the sheets together and lowerin' myself down from the winder. But better feelin's rose inside of me, Betsey was a human bein', I, belonged to the meetin' house. All these nobler emotions tied up my tongue, I said nothin' but I turned and concluded the wild tumult of my feelin's, by takin' the gingham case off'en my umberell I was goin' to carry with me, and put-

ON THE STREET.

tin' on my bunnet we started out for our promenade.

# MEET DR. MARY WALKER.

NO cambric needle ever had its eye sot any keener and firmer onto the North pole, than Josiah Allen's wife had her keen gray eye aimed at the good of the Human Race, so I thought I would go and see Horace first. But Jonothan Beans'es ex-wife told me he had gone away for the day, to some great rally in a neighborin' village. I didn't have the least idee what she meant by "rally," but I answered her in a bland way that "I hoped he would have good luck and get quite a mess of it," and then says I, "It won't make a mite of difference with me, I can go to Miss Woodhulls'es first."

Betsey was rampent to go to the Theater, "Barnums Amusement," and the "Centre of the Park," and some of the meetin' houses with big steeples, and other places of amusement. But I says to her as we wended our way on, "Betsey, these old bones of mine will repose in Jonesville to-morrer night as, the poet saith, 'In my own delightful feather bed.'

And Betsey, they couldn't rest there, if they looked back and see that they didn't do all they could while here, for the advancement of the Race, and for improvin' of my own mind. Says I, "I didn't come to this village for vain pleasure, I have got a high mission to perform about, and a mind to improve upon.

I thought we would jest run in a few minutes to Miss Hookers'es, but her hired girl says to me at the door says she,

"Miss Hooker is engaged."

I looked the hired girl full in the face, and says I,

"What of it, what if she is?"

Then says the hired girl, "She hain't to home."

Says I, "Why didn't you say so, in the first out, and not go to beatin' round the bush." Says I, for I was determined to do all the good I could to the Human Race, "Miss Hooker is a first rate woman, and it haint a hired girl's place to talk about her mistress'es family matters and love affairs."

When we got to Miss Woodhulls'es we went up the front doorsteps, and I knocked to the door, Betsey says, "Ring the bell."

Well says I, "I hain't particuler, hand it along." I thought mebby she had got one in her pocket, and wanted me to ring it to pass away the time, while we was standin' on the doorstep a waitin' for Miss Woodhull to come and open the door.

But Betsey reached by me, and took holt of a little

silver nub, by the side of the door, put there for a orniment, and pulled it.

Says I, "Don't be so impatient Betsey. She'll be here in a minute, don't go to foolin' and tearin' the house down to pass away time."

Jest at that minute a little Black African came to the door, he looked impudent at us, and says he,

"Miss Woodhull hain't to home," and he shet the door right in our faces. We was jest goin' down the doorsteps, when the door opened agin, and a little ligger came out, that at the first view baffled me. Says I to myself, "Is it a man, or is it a woman?" It had a woman's face but a man's pantaloons. I was baffled. But Josiah Allen's wife hain't one to give up the ship while there is $\frac{1}{2}$ a plank left. I was determined to get all the knowledge I could while on my tower. I was determined to get information on every deep and mysterious subject I could. And so I walked up to it, and says I in a low voice and polite as I could, for fear of hurtin' its feelins'.

"Be you a man sir?" or a women mom?"

It wasn't mad a bit, (I say *it*, for I didn't know then in what gender to put it.) It looked me so pleasant in the face, and yet so searchin'ly, that I was kinder flustrated, and says *I*, in a kind of awe struck tone,

I hope you wont be offended, I only ask for information. Be you a masculine, femenine or neutral gender?"

It smiled agin, jest as pleasant as one of my glass jars of maple sugar, and then it opened its mouth and said,

"I am Dr. Mary Walker."

I dont know when I have been so tickled; nothin' is sweeter than knowledge to the inquirin' mind, when it has been baffled. Says I,

"Mary I am glad to see you." and I give her hand such a shakin' that it looked red as a beet when I leggo. Says I,

"I am gladder to see you than I would be to see any nephew or neice I have got in the world. I am as glad to see you as I would be to see any brother or sister of mine."

Says she, "I cant recall your countenance."

Says I, Mary, I am Josiah Allen's wife."

"Oh!" says she, "I have read your eloquent orations on wimmin' havin' a right. I am happy to make your acquaintance." Then and there I introduced Betsey.

Says she, "Did you call to see Miss Woodhull?"

"Yes," says I, "I wanted to talk to her, for she is in the wrong, but she haint to home."

Says she, "she is to home, and you shall see her, a few friends of the cause, have met here to-day, but they are about all gone." She went right up the doorsteps agin, and instead of knockin', she ketched holt of that silver nob, that Betsey had been a foolin' with. Mary was so excited that she didn't really

13

know what she was about, or else she would have made some move towards gettin' in to the house. But it was jest as well, for that impudent faced little Black African happened to come to the door agin jest at the right time. And she spoke up kinder sharp like,

"Show these ladies into the parlor, they are friends of mine, and Miss Woodhull will be glad to see 'em."

He looked as if he would sink, and I didn't care if he did, clear through to the suller. I should have been glad to have seen him sunk.

I looked severe at him after I had gripped Mary's hand, and parted with her. He held the door open awful polite, and in a kind of a apoligy way he murtered somethin' about,

"Sposin' Miss Woodhull was engaged."

Says I pretty sharp, "Sposin she is engaged, is that any reason you should turn Betsey and me out doors?" Says I, I didn't keep our folks'es doors locked up when I got engaged to Josiah." Says I, "sposen Miss Woodhull is engaged, she ought to have been engaged, and married, years ago."

I was in the wrong, and I see it, and ketched holt of my principles convulsively, for I see that my indignant emotions towards that little lyin' imp was a shakin' 'em. I hadn't no right to be a speakin' aginst the woman of the house to their hired help. I felt as mean as pusley to think I had done it, and says I, mildly,

"I am glad Miss Woodhull is engaged to be married, it takes a load offen my mind," says I, "I presume she will settle down and make a real likely woman."

At that minute, a door opened right across the hall, and a man come out and shet it agin, and he ketched right holt of my arm, the first thing, and says he,

"Come, Marier Jane, or Marier Ann," says he, "I can't really call to mind your precise name this minute, but I think it is Marier any way, or mebby it is Mary Ann. Come, Mary Ann, it is time to be a goin' home."

I looked at him with almost fearful dignity, and I says to him with a air so cold that he must have thought it blowed off of Greenland's icy mountain,

"Leggo of my arm!"

But he never budged a inch, and I jest raised my umberell, and says I, "If you don't leggo of my arm, I'll make you leggo."

Then he leggo. And he stood back a little, but he looked piercin'ly and searchin'ly into my face, and says he,

"You are my wife, haint you?"

Then again I spoke with that fearful dignity, and that cold and icy air, 50 degrees under Mr. Zero it was, if it was a degree.

"No Sir! I am proud and happy to say I am not your wife, I am Josiah Allen's wife."

He looked real meachin, and says he, "I beg your pardon mom, but I've only been married to my last wife a few hours, havin' got a divorce from a former companion after dinner yesterday, and I have been so busy since, that I haven't really got the run of her face yet, though I thought" he added dreamily, "that I should know that nose agin any where."

I see that he was imposin' on me. But I wasn't goin' to have my nose throwed in my face by him, and says I, "I am aware that my nose is a pretty sizeable one. But," says I, in about as sarcastic a voice as I ever used in my life "it is a nose that haint never been wore off, and made smaller a pokin' into other folks'es affairs. Pokin' round a tryin' to find wives where there haint none."

"But mom, I was married between daylight and dark, and–"

But I wouldn't stay to hear another word of his apoligys, I jest turned my back onto him, when the door opened agin, and a woman came out, and I'll be hanged if her nose didn't look like mine—a honorable Roman. The man looked at her in a kind of a undecided way, but she walked right up and took holt of his arm, and he brightened up, and says he. "Are you goin' home now Mary Ann?"

"Yes," says she, "but my name haint Mary Ann, it is Mehitable."

"Wall," said he, "I knew there was a M in it." And he walked off with her, with a proud and triumphant mene.

## INTERVIEW WITH THEODORE AND VICTORY.

THE young black African opened the door and says he, "Josiah Allen's wife, and Betsey Bobbet, mom." He had asked us our names jest before he opened it.

Miss Woodhull was a standin' pretty near the door, a talkin' with 3 wimmin as we went in. But she come forward immediatly and put out her hand. I took it in mine, and shook it a very little, mebby 3 or 4 times back and forth. But she must have felt by that cool, cautious shake, that I differed from her in her views, and had come to give her a real talkin' to.

One of the wimmen she was a talkin' to, had jest about as noble a lookin' face as I ever see, with short white curls a fallin' all round it. The beholder could see by the first glance onto that face, that she hadn't spent all the immortal energies of her soul in makin' clover leaf tattin', or in cuttin' calico up into little pieces, jest to sew 'em togather agin into blazin' stars and sunflower bedquilts. It was the face of an earnest noble woman, who had asked God what He wanted her to do, and then hadn't shirked out of doin' it. Who had gripped holt of life's plough, and hadn't looked back because the furrows turned over pretty hard, and the stumps was thick.

She knew by experience that there was never any greensward so hard to break up, as old prejudices and customs; and no stumps so hard to get round as the ridicule and misconceptions of the world. What made her face look so calm then, when she was doin' all this hard work? Because she knew she was makin' a clearin' right through the wilderness that in the future was goin' to blossom like a rosa. She was givin' her life for others, and nobody ever did this since the days of Jesus, but what somethin' of his peace is wrote down on thier forwards. That is the way Elizabeth Cady Stanton looked to me, as Miss Woodhull introduced me and Betsey to her, and to the two other ladies with her.

One of the other wimmen I fell in love with at first sight, and I suppose I should have been jest so partial to her if she had been as humbly as one of the Hotentots in my old Olney's Geography, and I'll tell you why, because she was the sister of H. W. Beecher. As a general thing I don't believe in settin' folks up, because they happen to have smart relations. In the words of one of our sweetest and noblest writers, "Because a man is born in a stable it don't make him a horse." Not as a general thing, it don't.

But not once in 100 years does Nature turn out such a man as H. W. B. It takes her longer than that to get her ingregiences and materials togather to make such a pure sweet nature, such a broad charity, and such a intellect as hisen. Why, if the question had been put to me before I was born, whether I would be born his sister, or the twin sister of the queen of England, I'd never give a second thought to Miss Victoria Albert, not but what I respect the Widder Albert deeply, I think she is a real nice woman. But I had ruther be his sister than to be the sister of 21 or 22 other kings. For he is a king not make by the layin' on of earthly hands, he is God's own annointed, and that is a royalty that can't be upsot. So as I remarked I s'pose Isabella Beecher Hooker would have looked pretty good to me any way.

The other lady was smart and sensible lookin', but she was some like me, she wont never be hung for her beauty. This was Susan B. Anthony. Betsey Bobbet sot down on a chair pretty nigh the door, but I had considerable talk with Susan. The other two was awful long discussin' some question with Miss Woodhull.

Susan said in the course of her remarks that "she had made the 'Cause of Wimmen's Rights,' her husband, and was going to cleave to it till she died."

I told her I was deeply interested in it, but I couldn't marry myself to it, because before gettin' acquainted with it, I had united myself to Josiah."

We had considerable reasonable and agreeable talk, such as would be expected from two such minds as mine and hern, and then the three ladies departed. And Miss Woodhull came up to me agin kinder friendly, and says she,

"I am glad to meet you Josiah Allen's wife," and then she invited me to set down. As I turned round to get a chair I see through a door into another room where sot several other wimmen—some up to a table, and all dreadful busy readin' papers and writin' letters. They looked so business-like and earnest at thier work, that I knew they could not have time to back-bite thier neighbors, and I was glad to see it. As I took my seat I see a awful handsome gentleman settin' on a sofa—with long hair put back behind his ears,— that I hadn't ketched sight of before. It was Theodore Tilton, and Miss Woodhull introduced him to Betsey and me. He bowed to Betsey, but he came forward and took my hand in his'en. I couldn't refuse to take it, but I looked up in his handsome face with a look about two thirds admiration, and one of sorrow. If the handsomest and best feathered out angel, had fell right over the walls of heaven into our dooryard at Jonesville, I couldn't have give it a more piercin', and sort of pitiful look than I did him. I then turned and silently put my umberell in the corner and sot down. As I did so, Miss Woodhull remarked to Mr. Tilton,

HARD AT WORK.

"She is a Strong Wimen's Righter, she is one of us."

"No, Victory; I haint one of you, I am Josiah Allen's wife." Then I sithed. And says I, "Victory you are in the right on it, and you are in the wrong on it," and says I, "I come clear from Jonesville to try to set you right where you are wrong." Says I, almost overcome with emotion. "You are younger than I Victory, and I want to talk with you jest as friendly as if I was your mother in law."

Says she, "Where do you think I am in the right, and where do you think I am in the wrong?"

Says I, "You are right in thinkin' what a solemn thing it is to bring up children as they ought to be. What an awful thing it is to bring the little creeters into the world without their votin' on the subject at all, and then neglect 'em, and abuse 'em, and make their poor little days awful long in the world, and then expect them to honor you for it. You are right in your views of health, and wimmin's votin' and etcetery—but you are wrong Victory, and I don't want you to get mad at me, for I say it with as friendly feelins' as if I was your mother in law,—you are wrong in this free love business, you are wrong in keepin' house with two husbands at the same time."

"Two husbands! it is false; I was divorced from him, and my husband and I found him perishing in the streets, and we took him home and took care of

13*

him 'till he died. Which would the Lord have done Josiah Allen's wife, passed by on the other side, or took pity on him?

"I don't know what the Lord would have done Vicory, but I believe I should have sent him to a good horsepittle or tarven, and hired him took care of. I never could stand it to have another husband in the same house with me and Josiah. It would seem so kind o' curious, somethin' in the circus way. I never could stand it never."

"There have been a good many things Josiah Allen's wife that you have not been required to stand, God and man united you to a good husband whom you love. But in your happiness you should'nt forget that some other woman has been less fortunate. In your perfect happiness, and harmony—"

"Oh!" says I candidly, "I don't say but what Josiah and me have had our little spats Victory. Josiah will go in his stockin' feet considerable and—"

But she interrupted of me with her eyes a flashin',

"What would you say to livin' with a man that forgot every day of his life that he was a man, and sunk himself into a brute. Leaving his young wife of a week for the society of the abandoned? What would you say to abuse, that resulted in the birth of a idiot child? Would you endure such a life? Would you live with the animal that he had made himself? I married a man, I never promised God nor man that I would love, honor and obey the wild beast he changed into. I was free from him in the sight of a pure God, long enough before the law freed me."

I let her have her say out, for Josiah Allen's wife is one to let every man or mouse tell thier principles if they have got any. And if I was conversin' with the overseer of the bottomless pit, (I don't want to speak his name right out, bein' a Methodist), I would give him a chance to get up and relate his experience. But as she stopped with her voice kinder choked up, I laid my brown cotton glove gently onto her shoulder, and says I,

"Hush up Victory," says I "wimmen must submit to some things, they can pray, and they can try to let thier sorrows lift 'em nearer to heaven, makin' angels of 'em."

Here Mr. Tilton spoke up and says he, I don't believe in the angels exclusively, I don't see why there shouldn't be he angels, as well as she ones."

I was tickled, and I looked at him approvin'ly, and says I,

"Theodore you are the first man with one exception that I ever see that felt that way, and I respect you for it." Says I, "men as a general thing think that wimmen have got to do up all the angel business there is done. Men seem to get the idee that they can do as they are a mind to and the Lord will wink at 'em. And there are lots of things that the world thinks would be awful coarse in a woman, but is all right in a man. But I don't believe a man's cigar smoke smells any sweeter to the Lord than a woman's would. And I don't believe a coarse low song, sounds any sweeter and purer in the ears of angels, because it is sung in a base voice instead of a sulfereno. I never could see why men couldn't do somethin' in the angel line themselves, as well as to put it all on to the wimmen, when they have got everything else under the sun to do. Not but what " says I, " I am willen' to do my part. I never was a shirk, and Josiah Allen will tell you so, I am willin' to do my share of the angel business." And says I, in a generous way, " I would do it all, if I only had time. But I love to see justice and reason. Nature feathers out geese and gander's equally, or if there is any difference the gander's wings are the most foamin' lookin'. Men's shoulders are made jest the same way that wimmen's are; feathers would look jest as well on 'em as on a woman, they can cultivate wings with jest as little trouble. What is the purest and whitest unseen feathers on a livin' angel's hidden wing, Theodore and Victory? They are purity, goodness, and patience, and men can grow these unbeknown feathers jest as easy as a woman can if they only set out."

I had spoke real eloquent, and I knew it, but I felt that I had been carried away slightly by my emotions, from the mission I had come on—to try to convince Miss Woodhull where she was wrong.  And so after a minutes silence, I broke out agin mildly, for I felt that if I give way to anger or impatience my mission was lost.

"Another thing you are wrong in Victory, is to think you can be lawfully married without any minister or justice of the peace.  I knew that all you needed was to have it set before you plain by some female that wished you well; you are wrong in it Victory, and I tell you so plain, and to show you that I am your well wisher, I thought after I had convinced you that you was in the wrong, I would make you this offer.  That if you and Col. Blood will go home with Betsey and me, Elder Wesley Minkley shall marry you right in my parlor, and it shan't cost you a cent, for I will pay him myself in dried apples."

Says she, "I don't want any ceremony, I want the only tie to hold me to my husband to be love, the one sacred tie."

"Love is a first rate tie," says I, mildly, holdin' on to my temper first rate, "upwards of 15 years ago, I give one of the most remarkable proofs of it, that has ever been seen in this country;" (and for a minute my mind wandered off onto that old revery, *why* did I love Josiah Allen?) But collectin' my mind together I spoke onwards, with firm and cast iron principle.  "Still, although I felt that sacred tie unitin' Josiah and me in a double beau knot that couldn't be untwisted, the first time we met, still, if Elder Wesley Minkley hadn't united us at the alter—or mother's parlor, I should have felt dreadful floatin' round in my mind. It would have seemed too curious and onstiddy kinder, as if Josiah and me was liable to fall all to pieces at any time, and waver off in the air like two kites that had broke loose from thier strings." Says I, firmly, "Thier would be a looseness to it, I couldn't stand."

She said I would get accustomed to it, and that custom made many things seem holy that were unholy, and many things sinful that were pure in the sight of God.

But still I murmured with a sad look, but firm as old Bunker Hill, "I couldn't stand it, Victory, it would seem too much like a circus."

"And then agin, Victory, you are in the wrong of it about divorces. 'What God has joined togather let no man put asunder.'"

Says she, "Josiah Allen's wife, if divorces were free to-morrow, would you get one from Josiah?"

"Never!" says I, and my best dress most bust open at the breast, (them biases always was took up a little too snug) at the idee of partin' from Josiah.

"Well, what is it that would hold you so fast to each other that nothin' but death could separate you? was it the few words you said before the minister?"

"It was love, Victory! love, that wouldn't let me

eat a mite, nor sleep a wink, if I couldn't put my hand onto Josiah Allen any time day or night."

"Then," says she, "why not give other good men and women credit for bein' actuated by the same sentiments? Those that God has joined togather, no man can put asunder. Those who are really married heart and sole, would never separate, it would only correct abuses, and separate those that man, and not God, had joined togather."

Says I, "Victory, is there any particular need of folks lettin' man join 'em togather, when God hasn't?" says I; "if folks was obleeged to marry, there would be some sense in such talk," says I, "they haint no business to marry if they don't love each other. All sin brings its punishment, and them that commit the crime aginst thier own sole, of marryin' without love, ought to be punished by unhappiness in thier domestic relations, what else can they expect?" says I. "Marriage is like baptism, now some folks say it is a savin' audnence, I say nobody haint any right to be baptised unless they are saved already. Nobody haint any business to put on the outward form of marriage, if they haint got the inward marriage of the spirit."

"Some folks marry for a home," says she.

"Wall, they haint no business to," says I warmly. "I had ruther live out doors under a umberell, all my days."

"Those are my sentiments exactly, Josiah Allen's

wife. But you can't deny that people are liable to be decieved."

"If they are such poor judges the first time, what would hender 'em from bein' decieved the next time, and so on, ad infinitum, to the twentieth and thirtieth time?" says I firmly. "Instead of folks bein' tied together looser, they ought to be tied as tight agin. If folks knew they couldn't marry agin, how many divorces do you suppose there would be? No doubt there are individual cases, where there is great wrong, and great sufferin'. But we ought to look out for the greatest good to the greatest number. And do you realize, Victory, what a condition society would be in, if divorces was absolutely free? The recklessness with which new ties would be formed, the lovin' wimmen's hearts that would be broken by desertion, the children that would be homeless and uncared for. When a fickle man or woman gets thier eyes onto somebody they like better than they do thier own lawful pardners, it is awful easy to think that man, and not God, has jined 'em. But let folks once get the idee into thier heads, that marriage is a solemn thing, and lasts as long as thier lives do, and they can't get away from each other, they will be ten times as careful to live peacible and happy with thier companions." Says I, "When a man realizes that he can if he wants to, start up and marry a woman before breakfast, and get divorced before dinner, and have a new one before supper time, it has a tendency to make him onstiddy and worrysome."

Says I, " Victory, men are dreadful tryin' by spells, do you suppose I have lived with one for upwards of 15 years, and hain't found it out? But suppose a mother deserts a child because he is wormy, and tears his breeches. She brought him into the world, and it is her duty to take care of him. Do you suppose a store keeper ought to take back a pink calico dress, after you have made it up, and washed it because the color washes out of it, you ought to have tried it before it was cut off. I married Josiah Allen with both eyes open, I didn't wear spectacles then, I wasn't starved to it nor thumbscrewed into it, and it is my duty to make the best of him."

Says she, " When a woman finds that her soul is clogged and hampered, it is a duty she owes to her higher nature to find relief."

Says I, " When a woman has such feelin's, instead of leavin' her lawful husband and goin' round huntin' up a affintee, let her take a good thoroughwert puke. Says I, in 9 and ½ cases out of 10, it is folkes'es stomachs that are clogged up insted of their souls. Says I, there is nothin' like keepin' the stomach in good order to make the moral sentiments run good. Now our Tirzah Ann, Josiah's girl by his first wife, I kinder mistrusted that she was fallin' in love with—" I almost said it right out Shakespeare Bobbet, but

I thought of Betsey, and turned it "with a little feller that hadn't hardly got out of his roundabouts, she bein' at the same time in pantalettes. Well I give her a good thoroughwert puke, and it cured her, and if his mother," says I with a keen look onto Betsey, as I thought of my night of troubles, "If his mother had served him in the same way, it would have saved some folks a good deal of sufferin'."

I see that agin I was wanderin' off'en the subject, and I says in a deep solemn tone,

" I don't believe in this divorcin'."

Mr. Tilton spoke up for most the first time, and says he, "I think you are wrong in your views of divorce, Josiah Allen's wife."

I looked into his handsome face and my feelin's rose up strong I couldn't throw 'em, they broke loose and says I, in almost tremblin' tones,

"It is you that are in the wrong on it, Theodore," says I, "Theodore, I have read your poetry when it seemed as if I could ride right up to heaven on it, though I weigh 200 and 10 pounds by the steelyards. There is one piece by the name of "Life's Victory." I haint much of a hand for poetry, but I read it for the first time when I was sick, and it seemed as if it carried me so near to heaven, that I almost begun to feather out. And when I found out who the author was, he seemed as near to me as Thomas Jefferson, Josiah's boy by his first wife. Theodore, I have kept

## I ALMOST WEPT.      329

sight of you ever sense, jest as proud of you, as if you was my own son-in-law, and when you went off into this free love belief I felt bad." I took out my white 25 cent handkerchif, for a tear came within I should say half or three quarters of a inch from my eye-winkers. I held my handkerchif in my hand, the tear come nearer and nearer—he looked agitated—when up spoke Miss Woodhull.

"It is perfectly right; I believe in free divorce, free love, freedom in everything."

I jest jammed my handkerchif back into my pocket, for that tear jest turned round and traveled back to where it come from. I thought I had used mildness long enough, and I says to her in stern tones,

"Victory, can you look me straight in the spectacles, and say that you think this abominable doctrine of free love is right?"

"Yes mom, I can, I believe in perfect freedom."

Says I. "That is what burglers and incendiarys say," says I, "that is the word murderers and Mormans utter," says I "that is the language of pirates. Victory Woodhull."

She pretty near quailed, and I proceeded on, "Victory, there haint but one true liberty, and that is the liberty of the Gospel, and it haint Gospel liberty to be surrounded by a dozen husbands'es and ex-husbands'es," says I, this marryin' and partin' every day or to, haint accordin' to Skripter."

Says she in a scornful tone, "What is skripter?" If I had been her mother I would have spanked her then and there. But I wasn't, and I jest turned my back to her, and says I, "Mr. Tilton you believe the bible don't you?"

"Yes mom, I do, but the bible justifies divorce."

"Yes," says I, "for one cause, and no other, and the Saviour says that whosoever marries a woman put away for any but the bible cause, commits adultery, and I don't believe in adulteration, nor Josiah don't either. But says I, convulsivly, "You know a man will part with a woman nowadays if the butter don't come quick, and she will part with him if he don't hang up the bootjack. Is that bible Theodore?" Says I, "don't the bible say that except for that one reason, man and wife are married till death parts 'em. Says I, "is a lawyer in a frock coat, with a lot of papers stickin' out of his breast pocket, death?" Says I, "tell me Theodore is he death?"

He looked convinced, and says he, "No mom, he haint."

"Well then, what business has that little snip of a livin' lawyer to go round tryin' to make out he is death? tell me?" says I almost wildly.

I see my emotions was almost carryin' me off, and I ketched holt of my dignity, and continued in deep solemn tones,

"True marriage is a sacred thing, and it is a solemn

thing, it is as solemn as bein' baptized. And if you are baptized once in the way you ought to be, it is enough. But the best way you can fix it, it is a solemn thing Victory. To give your whole life and soul into the keepin' of somebody else. To place all your hopes, and all your happiness in another human bein' as a woman will. A true woman if she loves truly, never gives half of her heart or three quarters, she gives it all. She never asks how much shall I get back in money and housen and finery? or whether she could do better in another direction. No; True Love is a river that runs onward askin' no questions of anybody, sweepin' right on with a full heart. And where does that river empty Theodore and Victory?"

They both looked as solemn as a protracted meetin', almost, as I looked at 'em, first one, then the other, through my specs; but they didn't reply. Says I, in a deep solemn tone, the name of the place where that river emptys is Eternity." Says I, That river of True Love as it flows through the world gets riley sometimes, by the earthly mud on its banks. Sometimes it gets mad and precipitates itself over precipices, and sometimes it seemin'ly turns backward a spell. But in its heart it knows where it is bound for, it keeps on growin' broader, and deeper, and quieter like, and as it jines the ocian it leaves all its mud on the banks, for God cleanses it, and makes it pure as the pure waters it flows into."

I felt real eloquent as I said this, and it seemed to impress 'em as I wanted it to. They both of 'em have got good faces. Though I didn't like their belief, I liked their looks. They looked sincere and honest.

Agin I repeated, "Marriage is a solemn thing."

I heard a deep sithe behind me, and a sorrowful voice exclaimed,

"It is solemn then both ways, you say it is solemn to marry, and I know"—here was another deep sithe "I *know* it is solemn not to." It was Betsey, she was a thinkin' of the Editer of the Augur, and of Ebineezer, and of all the other dear gazelles, that lay cold and lifeless in her buryin' ground. I felt that I could not comfort her, and I was silent. Miss Woodhull is a well bread woman, and so to kinder notice Betsey, and make talk with her, says she,

"I believe you are the author of these lines
'If wimmen had a mice's will,
They would arise and get a *bill?*'"

"Yes" says Betsey, tryin' to put on the true modesty of jenious look.

Miss Woodhull said "she had heard it sung to several free love conventions."

"How true it is" says Betsey glancin' towards Mr. Tilton, "that deathless fame sometimes comes by reason of what you feel in your heart haint the best part of you. Now in this poem I speak hard of man, but I didn't feel it Miss Woodhull, I didn't feel it at the time, I wrote it jest for fame and to please Prof. Gusheh. I love men" says she, glancin' at Mr. Tilton's handsome face, and hitchin' her chair up closer to his'en.

"I almost worship 'em."

Theodore began to look uneasy, for Betsey had sot down close by the side of him and says she,

"Did you ever read the soul stirrin' lines that Miss Woodhull refers to, I will rehearse them to you, and also three others of 25 verses apeice which I have wrote since on the same subject."

I see a cold sweat begin to break on his white and almost marble forward, and with a agitated move he ketched out his watch and says he,

"I have a engagement."

Says Betsey, beseechin'ly layin' her hand on his coat sleeve, "I can rehearse them in 26 or 27 minutes, and oh how sweet your sympathy would be to me, let me repeat them to you deah man."

A haggard look crept into his handsome eyes, and says he, wildly turnin' 'em away, "It is a case of life and death," and he hurried to the door.

But Betsey started up and got ahead of him, she got between him and the door, and says she, "I will let you off about hearin' the poetry—but oh! listen to my otheh prayer."

"I *wont* listen to your prayer," says he, firmly.

"In the name of the female wimmen of America

who worship you so, pause, and heah my prayer."

He paused deeply agitated, and says he. "In their name I will hear you, what is your request Betsey Bobbet?"

She clasped her hands in a devotional way, and with as beseechin' and almost heart meltin' a look as a dog will give to a bone held above its head, she murmured,

"A lock of youh haih deah man, that I may look at it when the world looks hollow to me, a lock of youh haih to make my life path easier to me."

I turned my spectacles on which principle sot enthroned, towards 'em, and listened in awful deep interest to see how it would end. Would he yield or not? He almost trembled. But finally he spoke.

"Never! Betsey Bobbet! never!" and he continued in low, agitated tones, "I have got jest enough to look well now."

My heart throbbed proudly, to see him comin' so nobly through the hot furnace of temptation, without bein' scorched. To see him bein' lifted up in the moral steelyards, and found full weight to a notch. But alas! Jest as small foxes will gnaw into a grape vine, jest so will dangerous and almost loose principles gnaw into a noble and upright nature unbeknown to them.

Agin Betsey says in harrowin' tones, at the same time ketchin' holt of his coat skirts wildly,

"If you can't part with any more, give me one haih, to make my life path smootheh."

Alas! that my spectacles was ever bought to witness

BETSEY'S PRAYER.

the sad sight. For with a despairin', agonized countenance such as Lucifer, son of Mr. Mornin' might have wore as he fell down, Theodore plucked a hair out of his foretop, threw it at Betsey's feet, and rushed out doors. Betsey with a proud, haughty look, picked it up, kissed it a few times, and put it into her portmoney.

But I sithed.

I hadn't no heart to say anything more to Victory. I bid her farewell. But after we got out in the street, I kept a sithin'.

14

# A WIMMEN'S RIGHTS' LECTURER.

AS we wended our way back to Miss Asters'es to dinner, Betsey said she guessed after all she would go and take dinner to her cousin Ebeneezer's, for her Pa hadn't give her much money. Says she,

"I hate to awfully. It is revoltin' to all the fineh feelings of my nature to take dinneh theah, afteh I have been so—" she stopped suddenly, and then went on agin. "But Pa didn't make much this yeah, and he didn't give me much money, he nor Ma wouldn't have thought they could have paid my faih heah on the cars, if they hadn't thought certain, that Ebeneezah's wife would be took from us, and I—should do my duty by coming. So I guess I will go theah and get dinneh."

Thinks'es I to myself, "If your folks had brought you up to emanual labor, if they had brought you up to any other trade only to get married, you might have money enough of your own to buy one dinner

## I RECEIVE A VISIT. 837

independent, without dependin' on some man to earn it for you." But I didn't say nothin', but proceeded onwards to the tavern where I put up. When I got there I met Johnothan Beane'es ex wife, and says she,

"Oh, I forgot, there is a lady here that wanted to see you when you got back."

"Who is it," says I.

"It is a female lecturer on wimmen's rights," says she.

Well, says I, "Principle before vittles, is my theme, fetch her on."

Says she, "Go into your room and I'll tell her you have come, and bring her there. She is awful anxious to see you."

Well, says I, "I'm visible to the naked eye, she won't have to take a telescope," and in this calm state of mind I went into my room and waited for her.

Pretty soon she came in.

Jonothan Beans'es ex wife introduced us, and then went out. I rose up and took holt of her hand, but I give it a sort of a cautious shake, for I didn't like her looks. Of all the painted, and frizzled, and ruffled, and humped up, and laced down critters I ever see, she was the cap sheaf. She had a hump on her back bigger than any camel's I ever see to a managery, and no three wimmen ever grew the hair that critter had piled on to her head.

I see she was dissapointed in my looks. She looked

dreadful kinder scornful down onto my plain alpaca, which was made of a sensible length. Her's hung down on the carpet. I'll bet there was more'n a bushel basket of puckers and ruffles that trailed down on to the floor behind her, besides all there was on the skirt and waist.

She never said a word about my dress, but I see she looked awful scornful on to it. But she went on to talk about Wimmen's Rights, and I see she was one of the wild eyed ones, that don't use no reason. I see here was another chance for me to do good—to act up to principle. And as she give another humiliatin' look onto my dress, I become fully determined in my own mind, that I wouldn't shirk out from doin' my duty by her, and tell her jest what I thought of her looks. She said she had just returned from a lecturin' tower out in the Western States, and that she had addressed a great many audiences, and had come pretty near gettin' a Wimmen's Right's Governor chosen in one of the States. She got to kinder preachin' after a while, and stood lookin' up towards the cealin', and her hands stretched out as if she was a lecturin'. Says she,

"Tyrant man shan't never rule us." Says I, "I haint no objection to your makin' tyrant man better, if you can—there is a chance for improvement in 'em—but while we are handlin' 'motes,' sister, let us remember that we have got considerable to do in the line of 'beams.'" Says I, "To see a lot of immortal

ON A LECTURIN' TOWER.

wimmen together, sometimes, you would think the Lord had forgot to put any brains into their heads, but had filled it all up with dress patterns, and gossip, and beaux, and tattan."

"Tyrant man has encouraged this weakness of intellect. He has for ages made woman a plaything; a doll; a menial slave. He has encouraged her weakness of comprehension, because it flattered his self love and vanity, to be looked up to as a superior bein'. He has enjoyed her foolishness."

"No doubt there is some truth in what you say, sister, but them days are past. A modest, intelligent woman is respected and admired now, more than a fool. It is so in London and New York village, and" says I with some modesty, "it is so in Jonesville."

"Tyrant man," began the woman agin. "Tyrant man thinks that wimmen are weak, slavish idiots, that don't know enough to vote. But them tyrants will find themselves mistaken."

The thought that Josiah was a man, came to me then as it never had before. And as she looked down from the cealin' a minute on to my dress with that scornful mene, principle nerved me up to give her a piece of my mind.

Says I, "No wonder men don't think that we know enough to vote when they see the way some wimmen rig themselves out. Why says I, a bachelder that had always kept house in a cave, that had read about both and hadn't never seen neither, would as soon take you for a dromedary as a woman."

She turned round quicker'n lightnin', and as she did so, I see her hump plainer'n ever.

Says she, "Do you want to insult me?"

"No," says I, "my intentions are honorable, mom."

"But," says I, puttin' the question plain to her, "would you vote for a man, that had his pantaloons made with trails to 'em danglin' on the ground, and his vest drawed in to the bottom tight enough to cut him into, and his coat tails humped out with a bustle, and somebody else's hair pinned on the back of his head? Would you?" says I solemnly fixin' my spectacles keenly onto her face. "Much as I respect and honor Horace Greeley, if that pure-minded and noble man should rig himself out with a bustle and trailin' pantaloons, I wouldn't vote for him, and Josiah shouldn't neither."

HOW WOULD YOU LIKE IT?

But she went right on without mindin' me—"Man has always tried to dwarf our intellects; cramp our souls. The sore female heart pants for freedom. It is sore! and it pants."

Her eyes was rolled up in her head, and she had lifted both hands in a eloquent way, as she said this, and I had a fair view of her waist, it wasn't much bigger than a pipe's tail. And I says to her in a low, friendly tone. "Seein' we are only females present, let me ask you in a almost motherly way, when your heart felt sore and pantin' did you ever loosen your cosset strings? Why," says I, "no wonder your heart feels sore, no wonder it pants, the only wonder is, that it don't get discouraged and stop beatin' at all."

She wanted to waive off the subject, I knew, for she rolled up her eyes higher than ever, and agin she began "Tyrant man"—

Agin I thought of Josiah, and agin I interrupted her by sayin' "Men haint the worst critters in the world, they are as generous and charitable agin, as wimmen are, as a general thing."

"Then what do you want wimmen to vote for, if you think so?"

"Because I want justice done to every human bein'. Justice never hurt nobody yet, and rights given through courtesy and kindness, haint so good in the long run, as rights given by law. And besides, there are exceptions to every rule. There are mean men in the world as well as good ones. Justice to wimmen won't prevent charitable men from bein' charitable, generous men from bein' generous, and good men from bein' good, while it will restrain selfishness and tyrany. One class was never at the mercy of another, in any respect, without that power bein' abused in some instances. Wimmen havin' the right to vote haint a goin' to turn the world over to once, and make black, white, in a minute, not by no means. But I sincerely believe it will bring a greater good to the female race and to the world."

Says I, in my most eloquent way, "There is a star of hope a risin' in the East for wimmen. Let us foller on after it through the desert of the present time, not with our dresses trailin' down onto the mudy ground, and our waists lookin' like pismires, and our hair frizzled out like maniacs. Let us go with our own hair on our heads, soberly, decently, and in order; let us behave ourselves in such a sober, christian way, that we can respect ourselves, and then men will respect us."

"I thought" says she, that you was a pure Wimmen's Righter! I thought you took part with us in our warfare with our foeman man! I thought you was a firm friend to wimmen, but I find I am mistaken."

"I *am* a friend to wimmen," says I, "and because I am, I don't want her to make a natural born fool of herself. And I say agin, I don't wonder some-

## DRESS AND STATESMANSHIP. 345

times, that men don't think that wimmen know enough to vote, when they see 'em go on. If a woman don't know enough to make a dress so she can draw a long breath in it, how is she goin' to take deep and broad views of public affairs? If she puts 30 yards of calico into a dress, besides the trimmin's, how is she goin' to preach acceptably on political economy? If her face is covered with

FEMALE STATESMANSHIP.

paint, and her curls and frizzles all danglin' down onto her eyes, how can she look straight and keenly into foreign nations and see our relations there? If a woman don't know enough to keep her dress out of the mud, how is she goin' to steer the nation through the mud puddle of politics? If a woman humps herself out, and makes a camel of herself, how is she goin' through the eye of a needle?"

I said these last words in a real solemn camp meetin' tone, but they seemed to mad her, for she started right up and went out, and I didn't care a cent if she did, I had seen enough of her. She ketched her trail in the door and tore off pretty nigh a yard of it, and I didn't cry about that, not a mite. I don't like these bold brazen faced wimmen that go a rantin' round the country, rigged out in that way, jest to make themselves notorious. Thier names hadn't ought to be mentioned in the same day, with true earnest wimmen who take thier reputations in thier hands, and give thier lives to the cause of Right, goin' ahead walkin' afoot through the wilderness, cuttin' down trees, and diggin' out stumps, makin' a path for the car of Freedom, that shall yet roll onward into Liberty.

As soon as she was gone, I went down and eat my dinner, for I was hungry as a bear. At the dinner table Jonothan Beans'es ex wife asked me "what I would like for desert."

I told her "I hadn't turned my mind much that way, for I hadn't no idee of goin' into the desert business, I wouldn't buy one any way, and I wouldn't take one as a gift if I had got to settle down, and live on it. But from what I had heard Thomas Jefferson read about it, I thought the desert of Sarah was about as roomy and raised as much sand to the acre as any of 'em."

Says she, turnin' the subject, " will you have pie or puddin'."

I couldn't see then, and I have thought about it lots sense, I don't see what started her off onto Gography all of a sudden.

After dinner I thought I would rest a spell. My talk with that female lecturer had tired me out. Principle is dreadful tuckerin' to any body, when you make it a stiddy business. I had rather wash, any time, than to go off on a tower of it as I was. So I went to my room and sot down real comfortable. But I hadn't sot more'n a minute and a half, when Betsey Bobbet came, and nothin' to do, but I must go to Stewarts'es store with her. I hung back at first, but then I happened to think, if Alexander should hear—as of course he would—that I had been to the village and hadn't been to his shop, he would have reason to feel hurt. Alexander is a real likely man, and I didn't want to hurt his feelin's, and it haint my way to want to slight anybody. And then I had a little tradin' I wanted to do. So take it all together, I finally told Betsey I would go with her.

## ALEXANDER'S STORE.

I HAD heard it was considerable of a store, but good land! it was bigger than all the shops of Jonesville put together, and 2 or 3 10 acre lots, and a few meetin' houses. But I wouldn't have acted skairt, if it had been as big as all Africa. I walked in as cool as a cowcumber. We sot down pretty nigh to the door and looked round a spell. Of all the sights of folks there was a comin' in all the time, and shinin' counters all down as fur as we could see, and slick lookin' fellers behind every one, and lots of boys runnin' round, that they called " Cash." I says to Betsey,

"What a large family of boys Mr. Cash'es folks have got, and they must some of 'em be twins, they seem to be about of a size."

I was jest thinkin' in a pityin way of their mother: poor Mrs. Cash, and how many pantaloons she would have to put new seats into, in slidin' down hill time, when Betsey says to me,

"Josiah Allen's wife, hadn't you better be purchasing your merchandise?" Says she, "I will set here and rest 'till you get through, and as deah Tuppah remarked, 'study human nature.'" She didn't have no book as I could see to study out of, but I didn't make no remarks, Betsey is a curious critter, anyway. I went up to the first counter—there was a real slick lookin' feller there, and I asked him in a cool tone, "If Mr. Stewart took eggs, and what they was a fetchin' now?"

He said "Mr. Stewart don't take eggs."

"Well," says I, "what does he give now for butter in the pail?"

He said "Mr. Stewart don't take butter."

"Well," says I, in a dignified way, "It haint no matter, I only asked to see what they was a fetchin' here. I haint got any with me, for I come on a tower." I then took a little roll out of my pocket, and undone 'em. It was a pair of socks and a pair of striped mittens. And I says to him in a cool, calm way,

"How much is Mr. Stewart a payin' for socks and mittens now. I know they are kinder out of season now, but there haint no danger but what Winter will come, if you only wait long enough."

He said "we don't take em."

I felt dissapointed, for I did want Alexander to have 'em, they was knit so good. I was jest thinkin' this over, when he spoke up agin, and says he, "we don't take barter of no kind." I didn't know really what he meant, but I answered him in a blind way, that it was jest as well as if they did, as fur as I was concerned, for we hadn't raised any barter that year, it didn't seem to be a good year for it," and then I continued on—"Mebby Mr. Stewart would take these socks and mittens for his own use." Says I, "do you

DON'T TAKE BARTER.

know whether Alexander is well off for socks and mittens or not?"

The clerk said "he guessed Mr. Stewart wasn't sufferin' for 'em."

"Well," says I in a dignified way, "you can do as you are a mind to about takin' 'em, but they are colored in a good indigo blue dye, they haint pusley color, and they are knit on honor, jest as I knit Josiah's."

"Who is Josiah?" says the clerk.

Says I, a sort of blindly, "He is the husband of Josiah Allen's wife."

I would't say right out, that I was Josiah Allen's wife, because I wanted them socks and mittens to stand on their own merits, or not at all. I wasn't goin' to have 'em go, jest because one of the first wimmen of the day knit 'em. Neither was I goin' to hang on, and tease him to take 'em. I never said another word about his buyin' 'em, only mentioned in a careless way, that "the heels was run." But he didn't seem to want 'em, and I jest folded 'em up, and in a cool way put 'em into my pocket. I then asked to look at his calicos, for I was pretty near decided in my own mind to get a apron, for I wasn't goin' to have him think that all my property lay in that pair of socks and mittens.

He told me where to go to see the calicos, and there was another clerk behind that counter. I didn't like his looks a bit, he was real uppish lookin'. But I wasn't goin' to let him mistrust that I was put to my stumps a bit. I walked up as collected lookin' as if I owned the whole caboodle of 'em, and New York village, and Jonesville, and says I,

"I want to look at your calicos."

"What prints will you look at?" says he, meanin' to put on me.

Says I, "I don't want to look at no Prince," says I,

"I had ruther see a free born American citizen, than all the foreign Princes you can bring out." Says I, "Americans make perfect fools of themselves in my mind, a runnin' after a parcel of boys, whose only merit is, they happened to be born before thier brothers and sisters was." Says I, "If a baby is born in a meetin' house, it don't make out that he is born a preacher. A good smart American boy like Thomas Jefferson, looks as good to me as any of your Princes." I said this in a noble, lofty tone, but after a minute's thought I went on,

"Though, if you have got a quantity of Princes here, I had as lives see one of Victory's boys, as any of 'em. The widder Albert is a good housekeeper, and a first-rate calculator, and a woman that has got a Right. I set a good deal of store by the widder Albert, I always thought I should like to get acquainted with her, and visit back and forth, and neighbor with her."

I waited a minute, but he didn't make no move towards showin' me any Prince. But, says he,

"What kind of calico do you want to look at?"

I thought he come off awful sudden from Princes to calico, but I didn't say nothin'. But I told him "I would like to look at a chocklate colored ground work, with a set flower on it."

"Shan't I show you a Dolly Varden," says he.

I see plainly that he was a tryin' to impose on me,

talkin' about Princes and Dolly Varden, and says I with dignity,

"If I want to make Miss Varden's acquaintance, I can, without askin' you to introduce me. But," I continued coldly, "I don't care about gettin' acquainted with Miss Varden, I have heard her name talked over too much in the street. I am afraid she haint a likely girl. I am afraid she haint such a girl as I should want my Tirzah Ann to associate with. Ever sense I started from Jonesville I have heard that girl talked about." 'There is Dolly Varden!' and 'Oh look at Dolly Varden!' I have heard it I bet more' a hundred times sense I sot out. And it seems to me that no modest girl would be traipsin' all over the country alone, for I never have heard a word about old Mr. and Miss Varden, or any of the Varden boys. Not that it is anything out of charicter to go off on a tower. I am off on a tower myself," says I, with quite a good deal of dignity, "but it don't look well for a young girl like her, to be streamin' round alone. I wish I could see old Mr. and Miss Varden, I would advise the old man and woman to keep Dolly at home, if they have any regard for her good name. Though I'm afraid," I repeated, lookin' at him keenly over my specs, "I'm afraid it is too late for me to interfere, I am afraid she haint a likely girl."

His face was jest as red as blood. But he tried to

turn it off with a laugh. And he said somethin' about her "bein' the style," and "bein' gay," or somethin'. But I jest stopped him pretty quick. Says I, givin' him a awful searchin' look,

"I think jest as much of Dolly as I do of her most intimate friends, male or female."

He pretended to turn it off with a laugh. But I know a guilty conscience when I see it as quick as anybody. I haint one to break a bruised reed more than once into. And my spectacles beamed more mildly onto him,

DOLLY VARDEN.

and I says to him in a kind but firm manner.

"Young man, if I was in your place, I would drop Dolly Varden's acquaintance." Says I, "I advise you for your own good, jest as I would Thomas Jefferson."

"Who is Thomas Jefferson?" says he.

Says I, in a cautious tone, "He is Josiah Allen's child, by his first wife, and the own brother of Tirzah Ann."

## A DREADFUL DISCOVERY.

I then laid my hand on a piece of choklate ground calico, and says I, "This suits me pretty well, but I have my. doubts," says I, examinin' it closer through my specs, I "mistrust it will fade some. What is *your* opinion?" says I, speakin' to a elegantly dressed woman by my side, who stood there with her rich silk dress a trailin down on the floor.

"Do you suppose this calico will wash mom?"

I was so busy a rubbin' the calico to see if it was firm cloth, that I never looked up in her face at all. But when I asked her for the third time, and she did'nt speak, I looked up in her face, and I haint come so near faintin' sence I was united to Josiah Allen. *That woman's head was off!*

The clerk see that I was overcome by somethin', and says he, "what is the matter?"

I could'nt speak, but I pinted with my forefinger stiddy at that murdered woman. I guess I had pinted at her pretty nigh half a minute, when I found breath and says I, slowly turnin' that extended finger at him, in so burnin' indignant a way, that if it had been a spear, he would have hung dead on it.

"That is pretty doin's in a Christian country!"

His face turned red as blood agin—and looked all swelled up, he was so mortified. And he murmured somethin' about her "bein' dumb," or a "dummy" or somethin'—but I interrupted him—and says I,

"I guess you would be dumb yourself if your head was cut off." Says I, in awful sarcastic tones,

"It would be pretty apt to make any body dumb."

Then he explaned it to me. That it was a wooden figger, to hang thier dresses and mantillys on. And I cooled down and told him I would take a yard and 3 quarters of the calico, enough for a honorable apron.

Says he, "We don't sell by retail in this room."

I give that clerk then a piece of my mind. I asked him how many aprons he supposed Tirzah Ann and I stood in need of? I asked him if he supposed we was entirely destitute of aprons? And I asked him in a awful sarcastic tone if he had a idee that Josiah and Thomas Jefferson wore aprons? Says I, "any body would think you did." Says I, turnin' away awful dignified, "when I come agin I will come when Alexander is in the store himself."

I joined Betsey by the door, and says I, "Less go on to once."

"But" says she, to me in a low mysterious voice; "Josiah Allen's wife, do you suppose they would want to let me have a straw colored silk dress, and take thier pay in poetry?"

Says I, for the land's sake Betsey, don't try to sell any poetry here. I am wore out. If they wont take any sacks and mittens, or good butter and eggs, I know they wont take poetry."

She argued a spell with me, but I stood firm, for I wouldn't let her demean herself for nothin'. And finally I got her to go on.

# A HARROWIN' OPERATION.

ALL I could do and say, Betsey would keep a goin' into one store after another, and I jest trailed round with her 'till it was pitch dark. Finally after arguin' I got her headed towards her cousin's.

It was as late as half past eight when I got back to Miss Asters'es. As I went by the parlor door, I heard a screechin' melankoly hollerin'. Thinks'es I to myself, " somebody's hurt in there, some female I should think, by the voice." I thought at first I wouldn't interfere, as there was enough to take her part, for the room seemed to be chuck full. So I was goin' on up to my room, when it come to my ears agin, louder and more agonizin' than ever. I couldn't stand it. As a female who was devoted to the cause of Right, I felt that in the behalf of my sect I would see what could be done. I kinder squeezed my way in, up towards the sound, and pretty soon I got where I could see her. Then I knew she was crazy.

She looked bad. Her dress seemed to be nice silk,

## 358  A POOR MANIAC.

but it jest hung on to her shoulders, and she had strung a lot of beads and things round her neck—you know how such poor critters will rig themselves out—and she had tore at her hair so she had got it all streamin, down her neck. Her face was deathly white, only in the middle of her cheeks there was a

A HARROWIN' SCENE.

feverish spot of fire red. Her eyes was rolled up in her head. She looked real bad.

She had got to the piano in some way, and there she set a poundin' it, and yellin'. Oh how harrowin' it was to the nerves, it made my heart almost ache to

see her.  There was a good many nicely dressed
wimmen and men in the room and some of 'em
was leanin' over the poor girl's shoulders, a lookin' at
her hands go, and some of them wimmen's dresses
was hangin' down off their shoulders, so that I
thought they must have been kinder strugglin' with
the maniac and got 'em all pulled down and torn open,
and they looked most as crazy as she did.

The poor girl didn't know a word she was sayin' but
she kep a mutterin' over somethin' to herself in a
unknown tongue.  There wasn't no words to it.  But
poor thing, she didn't sense it.  Some of the time she
would be a smilin' to herself, and go on a mutterin'
kinder low, and then her worse fits seemed to come
on in spasms, and she would go to poundin' the piano
and yellin'.  And I see by the way her hands went
that she had got another infirmity too.  I see she had
got Mr. Vitus'es dance.  It was a sad sight indeed.

As I see the poor thing set there with her dress
most off of her, jest a hangin' on her shoulders, right
there before so many men, I though to myself, what
if was my Tirzah Ann there in that condition.  But
one thing I know as long as Josiah Allen's wife lived,
she wouldn't go a wanderin' round half naked, to be
a laughin' stock to the community.  I took it so right
to myself, I kep a thinkin' so, what if it was our Tirzah
Ann, that there wasn't hardly a dry eye in my head.
And I turned to a bystanter, standin' by my side, and

says I to him in a voice almost choked down with emotion,

"Has the poor thing been so long? Can't she get any help?"

Jest that minute she begun to screech and pound louder and more harrowin' than ever, and I says in still more sorrowful accents, with my spectacles bent pityin'ly on her,

"It seems to come on by spasms, don't it?"

She kinder held up in her screechin' then, and went at her mutterin' agin in that unknown tongue, and he heard me, and says he,

"Beautiful! hain't it?"

That madded me. I give that man a piece of my mind. I told him plainly that it "was bad enough to have such infirmities without bein' made a public circus of. And I didn't have no opinion of anybody that enjoyed such a scene and made fun of such poor critters."

He looked real pert, and said somethin' about my "not havin' a ear for music."

That madded me agin. And says I, "Young man, tell me that I hain't got any ears agin if you dare!" and I ontied my bonnet strings, and lifted up the corner of my head dress. Says I, "What do you call that? If that hain't a ear, what is it? And as for music, I guess I know what music is, as well as anybody in this village." Says I, "you ought to hear

## TIRZAH ANN AS A MUSICIAN. 361

Tirzah Ann sing jest between daylight and dark, if you want to hear music." Says I, "her organ is a good soundin' one everybody says. It ought to be, for we turned off a good two year old colt, and one of our best cows for it. And when she pulls out the tremblin' stopple in front of it, and plays psalm tunes Sunday nights jest before sundown, with the shadders of the mornin' glory vines a tremblin' all over her, as she sings old Corinth, and Hebron, I have seen Josiah look at her and listen to her till he had to pull out his red bandanna handkerchief and wipe his eyes."

"Who is Josiah?" says he.

Says I, "It is Tirzah Ann's father." And I continued goin' on with my subject. "No medder lark ever had a sweeter voice than our Tirzah Ann. And when she sings about the 'Sweet fields that stand dressed in livin' green,' she sings it in such a way, that you almost feel as if you had waded through the 'swellin flood,' and was standin' in them heavenly medders. Tell me I never heard music! Ask Whitfield Minkley whether Tirzah Ann can sing Anna Lowery or not, on week day evenin's, and old Mr. Robin Grey. Ask Whitfield Minkley, if you don't believe me. He is a minister's only son, and he hadn't ought to lie."

The little conceited feller's face looked as red as a beet. He was a poor lookin' excuse any way, a uppish, dandyfied lookin' chap, with his moustache turned up

15

at the corners, and twisted out like a waxed end. He pretended to laugh, but he showed signs of mortification, as plain as I ever see it. And he put up his specs, and I'll be hanged if he hadn't broke one eye offen 'em, and looked at me through it. But I wasn't dawnted by him, not a bit. I didn't care how close he looked at me. Josiah Allen's wife hain't afraid to be examined through a double barreled telescope.

Just then a good lookin' man with long sensible whiskers and moustache, hangin' the way the Lord meant 'em to, and who had come up while I was a speakin' this last—spoke to me and says he,

"I am like you madam, I like ballads better than I do opera music for the parlor."

I didn't really know what he meant, but he looked good and sensible lookin' and so says I in a blind way,

"Yes like as not."

Says he, "I am very partial to those old songs you have mentioned."

Says I "They can't be bettered."

Before I could say another word, that poor crazy thing begun agin, to yell, and pound and screech, and I says to him,

"Poor thing! couldn't there be somethin' done for her? If her mind can't be restored, can't she get help for Mr. Vitus'es dance?"

And then he explained it to me, he said she wasn't crazy, and didn't have Mr. Vitus'es dance. He said she was a very fashionable young lady and it was a opera she was singin'."

"A operation," says I sithin' "I should think as much! I should think it was a operation! It is a operation I don't want to see or hear agin." And says I anxiously, "Is it as hard on everybody as it is on her? Does everybody have the operation as hard as she has got it?"

He kinder smiled, and turned it off by sayin' "It is the opera of *Fra Diovole*."

"Brother Devel" says the conceited little chap with the waxed end moustache.

"'The Operation of the ——'" on account of my connection with the M. E. church, says I, "I will call it David." But they both knew what I meant. "The operation of the— the David. I should think as much."

And I don't know as I was ever more thankful than I was when I reflected how my pious M. E. parents had taught me how to shun that place of awful torment where the —— David makes it his home. For a minute these feelin's of thankfulness swallered these other emotions almost down. But then as I took another thought, it madded me to think that likely folks should be tormented by it on earth. And I says to the little feller with the waxed end moustache,

"If that operation is one of the torments that the —— the David keeps to torment the wicked with, it is a burnin' shame that it should be used beforehand, here on earth, to torment other Christian folks with.

I didn't wait for him to answer, but I turned round with a real lot of dignity, and sailed out of the room. It was with a contented and happy feelin' the next mornin' that I collected together my cap box, and spectacle case, packed my satchel bag with my barred muslin night cap and night gown, and put my umberella into its gingham sheath (for it was a pleasant mornin') and set, as you may say, my face homewards. I thought I would proceed right from Horace's to the depott, and not come back agin to Miss Aster'ses. I paid my bill with a calm demeaner, though it galled me to see 'em ask such a price.

Jonothan Beans'es ex wife seemed to hate to have me go, she is one that don't forget the days when she first went to grass. I told her to tell Miss Aster just how it was, that I felt as if I must go, for Josiah would be expectin' me. But I would love to stay and get acquainted with her. But she had so much on her hands, such a gang to cook for, that I knew she didn't have no time to visit with nobody. And I told her to be sure and tell Miss Aster, that she mustn't feel particuler at all because we hadn't visited together—but she must pay me a visit jest the same. Then I sent my best respects to Mr. Aster and the boys, and then I set out. Jest by the front door I met Betsey, and we both set sail for Horace's.

## A VISIT TO HORACE.

IT was with a beatin' heart that I stood at the door of the shop where Horace'es papers are made. And though he haint printed 'em alone since he was run up, as he did more formally, they told me I would be apt to find him at his old office.

I was jest a goin' to knock when a boy came out, and says I,

"Bub, I want to see Horace."

"Horace who?" says he.

"Horace Greeley," says I.

"Wall" says he, "I will take up your card."

I see then that he was a tryin' to empose upon me. I haint naturally warlike, but I can stand up on my dignity, straight as a cob when I set out. Says I,

"I'll have you know that I am a member of the Methodist meetin' house." Says I, warmly, "I dont know one card from another, and I'm glad I dont. Says I, "I presume there are wimmin here in the village, as old as I be, that set up to play cards till 9 or 10 o'clock at night. But thank fortin' I haint one of 'em." Says I, "Young man, I detest card playin', it ends in gamblin'. Now" says I firmly, "you jest tell me where Horace is, or I'll know the reason why!"

He see I was'nt to be trifled with, any more, He muttered somethin' about *his* not bearin' the blame. But he went up stairs, and we followed tight to his heels, and the minute he opened the door we went in. Horace had'nt dressed up much, for I spose he did'nt expect us. But if he had been dressed up in pink silk throughout, it wouldn't have made no difference to my feelin's as I ketched sight of that noble and benign face, that peaceful innocent mouth, that high forward, with the hair a curlin' round the sides of it, like thin white clouds curlin' round the side of a mountain in Ingun summer.

I use that figger of speech, because his face looked on the mountain plan, firm, and grand and decided. And I put in the Ingun summer, because you know jest how a mountain will look standin' a considerable ways above you on the first of October—kind o' mellow and peaceful and benign. But you realize all the time, that under all the green and shady growth of its mosses and evergreens, it has been growin' gradual but stiddy through the centuries. Under all that viel of shinin' blue gawze, wove out of mist one way, with a warp of sunshine, under all the mellow colerin' the time of the year has give it, there is a good strong back bone of solid rock in the old mountain, that couldn't be broke by all the hammers in creation.

That was jest my idee of his face, a mountain in Indgun summer, facin' the sunrise. Standin' up so high that it ketches a light on its forward before the world below gets lit up. Firm, solid principles with the edge took off of 'em, and kinder topped off with the experiences, and gradual convictions and discoveries of a noble life. And all softened down by the calmness and quiet of the time of day, and the fall of the year. That was the way Horace Greeley's face looked to me as I got a full view of it as he set to his desk a writin'.

In the dead of night on my own peaceful goose feather bed at home, I had made a speech all up in my mind for that glorious occasion, when 2 firm and true principled minds should meet—which was Horace's mind and mine. For though we conflict in some things, the good of the Human Race is as dear as our apples is, in our eyes. But at the first sight of that noble face, my emotions got up and overpowered me so, that I forgot every word of my speech, and all I could say was, in thick tones of feelin' and principle,

"Horace, I have come."

His face grew almost black with fear and anger.

He sprang up, and waved me back with his right hand and shouted to me,

"It is in vain madam! you are the 94th woman who has been here to-day after office. Female lobsteress depart! Get thee behind me Sa— female!"

Says I with deep emotion, "Horace you dont know me! I am not a female lobsteress! I am Josiah Allen's wife."

He came forward and shook hands with me, and says he, "I know you will excuse my vehemence, when I tell you, I am almost devoured by office seekers!" He cleared a path through the papers on the floor to some chairs, but as we set down, he continued in tremblin' tones, for it seemed as if he couldn't forget his troubles,

"Foxes and woodchucks have holes, but a candidate for the Presidency can't find none small enough to hide in, I *did*, says he sithin deeply," I *did* have a few peaceful, happy hours in the suller of my dwellin' house ;" he paused, overcome by sad recollections, and says I, deeply sympathizin' and interested,

"What broke it up Horace?"

"They found the out door suller way; so, says he sithin agin, I lost that peaceful haven."

"Wall" says I, tryin' to soothe his agitation,

"You're one in a high, noble place, Horace."

"Yes!" says he, "but it places anybody under a very strong light—a very strong light. I have never

INTERVIEW WITH HORACE.

done anything out of the way sense I was first born, but what I have seen it in the papers. I tore my pantaloons once," says he, gloomily, " in gettin' over the fence at the early age of 2 and a half, and I bit my mother once at the age of 7 months a nursin', I could wish these two errors of my past to be forgotten by the world and overlooked, but in vain. I am taunted with 'em on every side. I never threw a boot jack at a tom cat in the dead of the night, but what my picture has been took in the act, I never swore a oath to myself in the depths of my own stomach, but what I have seen that unspoken oath in the papers. I never jawed Mrs. Greeley about my shirt buttons," he continued, sadly, " in the depths of our secluded chamber, but what it has been illustrated with notes."

As he spoke of jawin' about shirt buttons, I says to myself, " How much! how much human nature is alike in all men," and I says aloud,

" How much you remind me of Josiah."

" Of Josiah!" says he, and that name seemed to make him remember himself, and to come nobly out of his gloomy reflections. " Josiah, he is your husband! Oh yes, Josiah Allen's wife! I am glad to meet you, for although I couldn't comply with the request your letter contained, yet it convinced me that you are a sincere friend to the human race."

" Yes," says I, " Horace, I am, and I want you to consider my request over agin."

15*

But he interrupted me hurriedly, seemin, to want to turn my mind from that subject.

"What do you think of Fourier's system, Josiah Allen's wife?" says he, lookin' at me languidly over his specks.

Says I, "I never see Mr. Fourier. How can I tell you any thing about the old man's health, whether his system is all right, or whether he is enjoyin' poor health. Horace, I come to talk with you on more important things."

But he continued placidly, hopin' to draw my mind off,

"What do you think of Darwin's idees?"

"Darwin who?" says I. "Darwin Gowdey? I don't know any other Darwin, and I never mistrusted that he had any idees, he is most a natural fool."

Says he, "about our descendin' from a monkey?"

Says I, with dignity, "I don't know how it is with you, but I know that I couldn't descend from a monkey, never bein' on one's back in my whole life." Says I, "I never looked well in the saddle any way bein' so hefty. But," says I, in a liberal way, "if you, or anybody else wants to ride monkeys, you have the privilege, but I never had no leanin' that way." And agin, says I, in agitated tones, "you needn't try to take my mind off'en the deep and momentous subject on which it is sot, by talkin' about ridin' monkeys. Horace I have come clear down here to the village on purpose to ask you to examine your platform, and see if there hain't no loose boards in it where some of the citizens of the United States, such as wimmen can fall through. Platforms, that are built over the deep waters, ought to be sound, and every board ought to be nailed down tight, so that nobody— not even the smallest and weakest—can fall through and get drownded." Says I, " Your door step is most all good solid timber, but I feel there is one old, mouldy, worm eaten board that is loose in it." And with emotion renderin' my voice weak as a cat, says I, " Horace, I want you to examine your door step and lay down a new board, and I will help you do it. I come a purpose to."

He see it was vain to turn the current of my thoughts round, and says he in a decided way,

" You must have become aware of my views from the contents of my letter. You got my letter?" says he in a enquirin' tone.

" Yes," says I, " we have framed it and got a glass over it, jest because it was your writin', but there seemed to be a mistake in it; it seemed to be wrote to Josiah."

" Says he, " What did you make it out to be?"

Says I, " it seemed to run as follers—' I don't want to purchase any more shoats.' "

" Josiah did have a uncommon kind of pigs, and we thought mebby you had heard that Josiah wanted to sell you one, though it was a mistake, for he swapped a couple with Deacon Gowdey for a yearlin' heifer, and he didn't have no more left than he wanted to keep over."

He said we didn't read it right. It read, 'I don't approve of any wimmen's votes.' And says he, leanin' back in his chair, "That is the ground I take, I don't believe in Wimmen's Rights. I don't see what rights they want—more'n they have now."

Then I dove right into the subject that was the nearest to my heart (with the exception of Josiah) and says I, "Horace, we want the right of equal pay for equal labor. The right of not bein' taxed without representation. The right of not bein' compelled, if she is a rich woman, of lettin' her property go to support public men, who are makin' laws that are ruinin' them she loves best, such as givin' licences to ruin body and souls. The right to stand by the side of all good and true soles in the nation, and tryin' to stop this evil spirit of intemperance and licentiousness that is runnin' rampant through the land. The right to—"

I don't know how much longer I should have gone on, but in the noble forgetfulness of yourself that always accompanies genius, I had riz up, and by an unguarded wave of my right hand a wavin' in eloquence I tipped over my umberell. Horace picked it up (he is a perfect gentleman at heart) and says he,

"Set down Josiah Allen's wife, don't fatigue yourself too much."

Rememberin' myself, I sot down, and Horace, pensively wipin' his brow with his lead pencil, went on to say,

"I admit there is some truth in what you say, Josiah Allen's wife. I admit, as a truthful man should, that whatever wimmen has laid thier hands to, such as churches, hospital work, foreign missionary work, ragged schools, Sunday schools, charity balls and fairs, and Good Templars, they have done more than men in thier efforts and good influence. They are more patient than men; they are not so strong, but they are more persistent. When they once get a plan in thier heads, they are awful to hold on—if they can't accomplish it in one way, they will take another."

"Says I," that is jest what Josiah says. He says, 'I always have my own way.'"

"I admit, that whenever wimmen have been admitted in any public affairs, they have had a puryfyin', and softnin' and enoblin' influence. But I deny that votin' and havin' a voice in public affairs is goin' to better the condition of either wimmen or the nation."

Says I, "Horace, the old White House needs puryfyin' more than any horsepittle or meetin' house in creation." And says I, "Let wimmen lay to, and help clean house." Says I, "let her try her hand for one year, and see what she can do."

Says Horace, goin' on placidly with his own thoughts, "It is not the change that would be wrought in public affairs I dread, so much as the change in the wimmen themselves, if they should mingle in the wild vortex of political life. I have two daughters, and rather than have them lose all thier delicacy, and enter political life and mount the rostrum, I would lay them in thier grave. I don't believe," says he, with great decision, "I don't believe in wimmen leadin' off into politics, and mountin' the rostrum."

I interupted him with a earnest tone; "you needn't twit me of that, no more Horace. I don't want to mount no rostrum. I had ruther give Josiah 20 curtain lectures than to give half of one to the public, there would be more solid satisfaction in it. But as far as indelicacy is concerned, it is no more immodest for a woman to lead off in politics than to lead off one of your indecent German waltzes with a man." Says I, "you men think it hain't indelicate for wimmen to go with you to balls, and to theatres, and into the wild vortex of the ocean a bathin' with you—and to post offices, and to fires, and fairs, and horse races, and to church, and to heaven with you. But it is awful to go and drop a little slip of white paper into a box, once a year with you."

Says Horace wavin' off that idee, "Woman holds in her arms a more powerful ballot than she can in her hands. Let her mould her baby boy, so that in the future his mother will vote through him."

Horace looked noble as he said this. His silver mounted spectacles shone with pure feelin' and principle. "But" says I, in a reasonable tone,

"How can wimmen mould children, if she haint got any to mould? I haint got any of my own, and lots of wimmen haint." Says I, "such talk is unreasonable, how can she go to mouldin', when she haint got the materials?"

"Let them influence thier husbands then," says he, "the influence of wimmen over men, is wonderful, and they can in this way wield a almost sovereign power. And they do in many instances exert this indirect power in an eminent degree."

Says I, finally, "I don't believe in no underhand proceedin,' I never did. The idee of wimmen bein' underhand, and go to mouldin' men on the sly, I don't believe in it." Says I, "accordin' to your own story Horace, wimmen have a influence in politics now."

"Wall—yes—a sort of a indirect influence in thier families, as it were."

Says I, "Horace can you look me straight in the spectacles and deny that there is wimmen's influence in politics at Washington to day?" Says I, "look at them female lobsteresses there." Says I, "one handsome, brilliant, unprincipled bad woman will influence 14 common men where a modest humbly well wisher of her sect will one." And says I, warmly, for the thought of these female lobsteresses always madded me—" I should be ashamed if I was in some of them Senator's places, makin' laws about the Mormans."

I see my deep principle was a floatin' me off into a subject where as a female I didn't want to go, and so I choked back the words I was about to utter which was, " I had jest as lives jine a Morman, as to jine one of them." I choked it back, and struggled for calmness, for I was excited. But I did say this,

"I think good wimmen ought to have a chance with bad ones in political affairs. For there is more good wimmen in the land than there is bad ones, but now the bad ones have it all thier own way."

Horace wiped his brow gently with his lead pencil, and said in a thoughtful accent,

"There may be some truth in what you say Josiah Allen's wife. I confess I never looked at it in exactly this light before."

Says I, in a triumphant glad tone, "That is jest what I told Josiah. Says I, "Josiah, Horace is all right, there never was a better meanin' man on the face of the earth than Horace is. All he wants is to have some noble principled woman to set him right in this one thing."

I see in a minute that I had made a mistake. Men hate to be dictated to by a woman, they hate to, like a dog. I see by his lowery brow that I had put the wrong foot forrerd. For the time bein' the sage and the philosifer sunk down in his nature, and the *man* spoke in the usual manlike way.

"I say wimmen's brains are too weak to grasp public matters. They have remarkable intuitions I grant. A woman's insight or instinct or whatever you may term it, will, I grant, fly over a mountain and discover what is on the other side of it, while a man is gettin' his gunpowder ready to make a tunnel through it. But they are not logical, they have not the firm grasp of mind, the clear comprehension requisite to a voter?

Says I, "Horace, which has the firmest grasp—the clearest comprehension, a earnest intelligent christian woman, or a drunken Irishman?" Says I, "Understand me Horace, I don't ask which would sell thier votes at the best lay, or vote the most times in one day—I dare say the man would get ahead of the woman in these respects, bein' naturally more of a speculator—and also bein' in practice. You know practice makes perfect. I don't ask you this. But I ask you and I want you to answer me Horace, which would be in the best condition for votin', Elizabeth Cady Stanton gettin' up off of her religious knees in the mornin' after family prayers, and walkin'—with the Constitution in one hand and the Bible in the other—coolly and sensibly to the pole, or Patrick oh Flanegan comin' out of a drunken wake, and staggerin' up against the pole with a whisky bottle in one hand and a club in the other, when he didn't know nothin' in the first place, and then had lost half or 3 quarters of that, in the liquer some clear minded, logical man give him, for votin' a few dozen times for him?"

At this question Horace quailed a very little. But it was not the quail of a weak man, there was principle in that quail, and a determination to argue to the end, which is one of the characterestics of that great and good man. She that was Samantha Smith also possesses some of this spirit.

"Set down, Josiah Allen's wife and don't fatigue yourself too much," says Horace, for almost carried away by my emotions, I had riz' up and stood on my feet agin.

And he went on, "You put the case in a very strong light Josiah Allen's wife. That is one of the peculiar weaknesses of your sect. You dont possess sufficient moderation. You exaggerate too much."

Says I, "publishin' a daily paper for 20 years, has a tendency to make any man a good judge of exaggeration, and if you see by my symptoms that I have got it, I haint a goin' to deny it. But you haint answered my question yet Horace."

Says he "Josiah Allen's wife, my mind is firmly made up on this subject. And nothin' upon earth will ever change it. I am fully convinced that woman's enterin' into public duties would result in makin' her coarse and unfeminine, and make her lose her love for home and husband. And then, suppose she were eligible for public offices: imagine a lady blacksmith! a lady constable! a lady president! it is absurd, Josiah Allen's wife."

Says I, "Horace, you are too smart a man to bring

up such poor arguments. You dont see a little sickly, literary, consumptive, broken backed blacksmith or constable. Men choose the occupations most congenial, and suitable for them, and wimmen would do the same, anyway. Rosa Bonheur chooses to live out doors half the time among cattle and horses, and I presume she haint half so afraid of 'em as Mr. A. Tennyson would be. I have heerd Thomas Jefferson read about 'em both. I dont suppose any woman would be compelled to be made a constable of, though if they was, I presume men would submit to be incarcerated by 'em as quick as they would by a male man."

"As for the idee of a lady president, I dont know as it would be any more absurd than a lady queen. Victory sets up pretty easy in her high chair, there dont seem to be anything very absurd about the Widder Albert. You say public duties makes a woman coarse, and forgetful of home and husband. Horace, look for one minute at the Widder Albert. Where will you find among your weak fashionable wimmen, so lovin' a wife, so devoted a mother? Where will you find a bigger housefull of children, brought up better than hern? She has had more public duties to perform than goin' once a year by the side of her husband, and votin' for Justice and Temperance. But did these public duties, that she performed so well, wean her from her husband?" Says I, "did they take up her mind so that she didn't almost break her heart when he died?" says I, "Do you think a honest desire to live a full life—to use every power that God has given you—to do your very best for God and humanity, do you think that this desire modestly and consistently carried into action, will make a woman coarse and unwomanly, any more than this present fashionable education, to flirt and simper and catch a rich husband?"

Says I, "You seem to think that votin' is goin' to be such a weight onto a woman that it will drag her right down from her home into public and political affairs and leave her there. Such talk is simple, for love and domestic happiness will be the other weight to the steelyards, as long as the world stands, and keep a woman's heart and mind jest as straight as a string. Votin' haint a goin' to spile any woman at all, be she married, or be she single, and there is a class at the mercy of the world, fightin' its hard battle alone—it will *help* them. The idee of its hurtin' a woman to know a little somethin', is in my mind awful simple. That was what the slaveholders said about the black Africans—it would hurt 'em to know too much. That is what Mr. Pope says to day about his church members. But I say that any belief, or custom that relies on oppression and ignorance and weakness to help it on in any degree, ought to be exploded up. Beautiful weakness and simplicity, haint my style at all in the line of wimmen. I have seen

## BEAUTIFUL SIMPLICITIES. 383

beautiful simplicities before now, and they are always affected, selfish critters, sly, underhanded, their minds all took up with little petty gossip and plottin's. Why they can't set a teacup on the table in a openhearted noble way. They have to plot on some byway to get it there, unbeknown to somebody. Their mouths have been drawed so into simpers, that they couldn't laugh a open generous laugh to save their lives. Always havin' some spear ready under their soft mantilly, to sweetly spear some other woman in the back. Horace, they haint my style. Beautiful weakness and simplicity may do for one evenin' in a ball room. But it dont wear well for all the cares and emergencies that come in a life of from 40 to 50 years. Was George Washington's mother any the less a industrious equinomical and affectionate wife and mother, because she took a interest in public affairs?" And says I, with a lower and more modest tone, " Is Josiah Allen's wife on that account any the less devoted to Josiah?"

He knew I was perfectly devoted to that man. He set mewsin' silently for a time seemin'ly on somethin' I had said heretofore, and finally he spoke up. " The case of Victory is very different. A crown that descends on a hereditary head is a different thing."

" So 'tis," says I, " But the difference is on the wrong side, for sposin' it descends onto the head of a hereditary fool—or a hereditary mean woman. If a woman was voted for it would be for goodness, or some other good quality."

Says Horace, wavin' off that idee and pursuin' after his own thoughts. "Man is sometimes mistaken in his honest beliefs, but Nature makes her laws unerringly. Nature intended the male of every species to take the preeminence. Nature designed man to be at the head of all public affairs. Nature never makes any mistakes."

"Nature made queen bees Horace. Old Nature herself clapped the crown on to 'em. You never heard of king bees, did you? Industrious equinomical critters the bees are too. The public duties of that female dont spile her, for where will you find housework done up slicker than hern? Where will you find more stiddy, industrious, equinomical orderly doin's through a whole nation than she has in hern? All her constituents up to work early in the mornin', home at night too, jest as stiddy as the night comes. No foreign spy's can come prowlin' 'round her premises—speculators on other folks'es honey haint encouraged,—tobacco is obnoxious to 'em. Only one thing I dont approve of, if food is skurce, if the females don't get honey enough to last the whole hive, all winter, they slaughter the male bees in the fall to save honey. I dont approve of it; but where will you find a great nater that haint got its peculiar excentricities? This is hern. She wants to dispose of the drones as they call

the lazy husbands of the workin' wimmen, and she
thinks killin' is the easiest way to dispose of 'em. I
say plainly I dont approve of it, it dont seem exactly
right to kill a husband to save winterin' him, it would
seem better to me to get divorces from 'em and set
'em up in business in a small way. But as I said,
where is there a nater that haint got a weakness?
*this* is hern. But aside from this where will you find
a better calculator than she is? No dashin' female
lobsteresses pullin' the wool over the eyes of *her*
Senators. No old men bees gaddin' 'round evenin's
when their confidin' wives think they are abed
dreamin' about their lawful pardners—no wildcatish-
ness, and smokin' and drunkenness, and quarellin' in
*her* Congress. You can't impeach *her* administration
no how, for no clock work ever run smoother and
honester. In my opinion there has a great many
men set up in their high chairs that would have done
well to pattern after this Executive female."

As I finished, flushed with several different emotions, Horace rose up and grasped me by the hand,
and says almost warmly,

"I am glad to have met you, Josiah Allen's wife,
you have presented the subject in a new, and eloquent
light. I admire eloquence wherever I meet it."

The praise of this great, and good man was like
manny to an Isrealitess. My breast almost swelled
with proud and triumphant emotions. But even then,

in that blissful moment, I thought of Josiah, no rock was ever firmer than my allegience to that man, I withdrawed my hand gently from his'en, and I said to him, with a beamin' face,

"You grasped holt of my hand, Horace, with the noblest and purest of feelin's, but I don't think Josiah would like to have me shake hands so often with any man."

Says he, "I honor your sentiments, Josiah Allen's wife, I think you are a firm principled woman, and a earnest, well wisher of your sect. But I do think you are in a error, I honestly think so. The Creator designed woman for a quiet, home life, it is there she finds her greatest happiness and content. God gave her jest those faculties that fit her for that life. God never designed her to go rantin' round in public, preachin' and lecturin'."

"Says I, "Horace, I agree with you in thinkin' that home is the best place for most wimmen. But you say that wimmen have great influence, and great powers of perswasion, and why not use them powers to win men's soles, and to influence men in the cause of Temperance and Justice, as well as to use 'em all up in teasin' thier husbands to buy 'em a summer bunnet and a pair of earrings? And take such wimmen as Anna Dickinson—what under the sun did the Lord give her such powers of eloquence and perswasion for, if He didn't calculate to have her use 'em?

Why you would say a human bein' was a fool, that would go to work and make a melodious piano, a calculatin' to have it stand dumb forever, holdin' back all the music in it not lettin' any of it come out to chirk folks up, and make 'em better. When a man makes a cheese press, he don't expect to get music out of it, it hain't reasonable to expect a cheese press to play Yankee Doodle, and old Hundred. I, myself, wasn't calculated for a preacher.

I believe the Lord knows jest what He wants of his creeters here below from the biggest to the littlest. When He makes a grasshopper, He makes it loose jinted, on purpose to jump. Would that grasshopper be a fullfillin' his mission and doin' God's will, if he should draw his long legs up under him, and crawl into a snail's house and make a lame hermit of himself?"

Says Horace, in reasonable accents, "No, Josiah Allen's wife, no, he wouldn't."

"Wall," says I, "likewise with birds, if the Lord hadn't wanted the sing to come out of thier throats, He wouldn't have put it into 'em. And when the Lord has put eloquence, and inspiration, and enthusiasm into a human sole, you can't help it from breakin' out. I say it is right for a woman to talk, if she has got anything to say for God and humanity. I have heard men and wimmen both, talk when they hadn't nothin' to say, and it is jest as tiresome in a man, as it is in a woman in my opinion.  Now I never had a call to preach, or if I had, I didn't hear it, only to Josiah, I preach to him considerable, I have to. I should feel dreadful curious a standin' up in the desk, and takin' my text, I don't deny it, but," says I, in deep tones, "if the Lord calls a woman to preach—let her preach, Horace."

"Paul says it is a shame for a woman to speak in public," says Horace.

Oh what a rush of idees flowed under my foretop as Horace said this, but I spoke pretty calm, and says I,

"I hain't nothin' aginst Mr. Paul, I think he is a real likely old bachelder.  But I put the words, and example of Jesus before them of any man, be he married, or be he single."

"Men will quote Mr Paul's remarks concernin' wimmen not preachin', and say he was inspired when he said that, and I say to 'em, "how is it about folks not marryin', he speaks full as pinted about that?" "Oh!" they say, "he wazzn't inspired when he said that," and I say to 'em, "how can you tell—when a man is 18 or 19 hundred years older than you be—how can you tell when he was inspired and when he wazzn't, not bein' a neighbor of his'en."  And after all, Mr. Paul didn't seem to be so awful set on this subject, for he went right on to tell how a woman's head ought to be fixed when she was a prayin' and a prophecyin'.  But

## CHRIST'S EXAMPLE. 389

in my opinion, all that talk about wimmen was meant for that church he was a writin' to, for some reason confined to that time, and don't apply to this day, or this village—and so with marryin'. When a man was liable to have his head cut off any minute, or to be eat up by lions, it wazzn't convenient to marry and leave a widder and a few orphan's. That is my opinion, other folks have thiern. But let folks quarell all they have a mind to, as to whether Mr. Paul was inspired when he wrote these things, or whether he wazzn't, this *we know*, that Jesus is a divine pattern for us to follow, and He chose a woman to carry the glad tidin's of His resurrection to the bretheren. There was one woman who received her commission to preach right from the Almighty.

How dare any man to try to tie up a woman's tongue, and keep her from speakin' of Him, when she was His most tender and faithful friend when He was on earth. It was wimmen who brought little children that He might bless 'em. Did He rebuke 'em for thus darin' to speak to Him publicly? No; but He rebuked the men who tried to stop 'em.

It was a women who annointed His feet, wet 'em with her tears, and wiped 'em with the hairs of her head. It was very precious ointment—but none too precious for Him she loved so. Some logical clear minded men present, thought it was too costly to waste on Him. And again Jesus rebuked 'em for troublin' the woman. It was in comfortin' a woman's lovin' achin' heart that Jesus wept. It was wimmen that stood by the cross to the very last and who stood by his grave weepin', when even Joseph had rolled a great stun aginst it and departed. And it was wimmen who came to the grave agin in the mornin' while it was yet dark. And it was a woman that He first revealed Himself to after He rose. What if Mary had hung back, and refused to tell of Him, and the glory she had seen. Would He have been pleased? No; when God calls a woman to tell of the wonders of His love and glory that He has revealed to her out of the darkness of this life, in the Lord's name let her answer. But let her be certain that it is the Lord that is callin' her, there is lots of preachers of both sects in my opinion that pretend the Lord is a callin' 'em, when it is nothin' but their own vanity and selfishness that is hollerin' to 'em."

For pretty near ½ or ¾ of a minute, Horace set almost lost in deep thought, and when he broke out agin it was on the old theme. He said "wedlock was woman's true spear. In the noble position of wife and mother, there lay her greatest happiness, and her only true spear." He talked pretty near nine minutes, I should think on this theme. And he talked eloquent and grand, I will admit, and never did I see spectacles shine with such pure fervor and sincerity as hisen. It impressed me deeply. Says he in conclusion, " Marriage is God's own Institution. To be the wife of a good man, and the mother of his children, ought to be a woman's highest aim, and purest happiness. Jest as it is man's highest happiness to have a woman entirely dependant on him. It rouses his noblest and most generous impulses, it moves his heart to do and dare and his arm to labor—to have a gentle bein' clingin' to his manly strength."

His eloquence so impressed me, that I had no words to reply to him. And for the first time sense I had begun to foller up the subject, my mind wavered back and forth, as Bunker Hill monument might, in a eloquent earthquake. I says to myself, "mebbe I am mistaken, mebbe marriage is woman's only true spear." I didn't know what to say to him, my spectacles wandered about the room, and happened to light onto Betsey—(I had been so took up with my mission to Horace that I had forgot to introduce her) and as they lit, Horace, who saw I was deeply impressed, repeated something about "clingin'" and I says to him in a foolish and almost mechanical tone,

"Yes Horace, I have seen clingers, here is one."

Betsey riz right up, and come forrerd, and made a low curchy to him, and set down tight to him, and says she,

"Beloved and admired Mr. Horace Greeley, I am Betsey Bobbet the poetess of Jonesville, and you speak my sentiments exactly. I think, and I know that wedlock is woman's only true speah. I do not think wimmen ought to have any rights at all. I do not think she ought to want any. I think it is real sweet and genteel in her not to have any rights. I think that to be the clinging, devoted wife of a noble husband would be almost a heaven below. I do not think she ought to have any other trade at all only wedlock. I think she ought to be perfectly dependent on men, and jest cling to them, and oh how sweet it would be to be in that state. How happyfying to males and to females that would be. I do not believe in wimmen having their way in anything, or to set up any beliefs of their own. For oh! how beautiful and perfectly sweet a noble manly mind is. How I do love your intellect, dearest Mr. Horace Greeley. How is your wife's health dear man? Haint I read in the papers that her health was a failing? And if she should drop off, should you think of entering again into wedlock? and if you did, should you not prefer a woman of genius, a poetess, to a woman of clay?"

Her breath give out here, and she paused. But oh what a change had come over Horace's noble and benign face, as Betsey spoke. As she begun, his head was thrown back, and a eloquent philosofical expression set onto it. But gradually it had changed to a expression of dread and almost anger, and as she finished, his head sunk down onto his breast, and he sithed. I pitied him, and I spoke up to Betsey, says I, "I haint no more nor less than a clay woman, but

I know enough to know that no man can answer 25 or 26 questions to once. Give Horace time to find and recover himself."

Betsey took a bottle of hartshorn and a pair of scissors, outen her pocket, and advanced onto him, and says she in tender cooin' tones. "Does your intellectual head ache? Let me bathe that lofty forwerd. And oh! dearest man, will you hear my one request that I have dreampt of day and night, will you—will you give me a lock of your noble hair?"

Horace rose up from his chair precipitately and come close to me and sot down, bringin' me between him and Betsey, and then he says to her in a fearless tone, "You can't have a hair of my head, I haint got much as you can see, but what little I have got belongs to my wife, and to America. My wife's health is better, and in case of her droppin' off, I should't never marry agin, and it wouldn't be a poetess! though" says he wipin' his heated forwerd,

"I respect 'em as a Race."

Betsey was mad. Says she to me, "I am a goin. I will wait for you to the depott." And before I could say a word, she started off. As the door closed I says in clear tones, "Horace, I have watched you for years—a laborin' for truth and justice and liftin' up the oppressed, I have realized what you have done for the Black African. You have done more for that Race than any other man in America. and I have re-

FILLIN' WOMAN'S SPEAH UNDER DIFFICULTIES.

light of new discoveries. As you rise higher above the earth you see stars you couldn't ketch sight of in a suller way. And the worlds cry of fickle mindedness, may be the angels war whoop, settin' us on to heavenly warfare'."

Horace seemed agin to be almost lost in thought, and I waited respectfully, for him to find and recover himself. Finally he spake,

"I have been sincere Josiah Allen's wife, in thinkin' that matrimony was woman's only spear, but the occurances of the past 25 or 30 minutes has convinced me that wimmen may be too zealous a carryin' out that spear. I admit Josiah Allen's wife, that any new state of public affairs that would make woman more independent of matrimony, less zealous, less reckless in handlein' that spear, might be more or less beneficial both to herself, and to man."

Here he paused and sithed. He thought of Betsey. But I spoke right up in glad and triumphant tones,

"Horace, I am ready to depart this minute for Jonesville. Now I can lay my head in peace upon my goose feather pillow."

I riz up in deep emotion, and Horace he riz up too. It was a thrillin' moment. At last he spoke in agitated tones, for he thought still of what he had jest passed through.

"My benefactor, I tremble to think what might have happened had you not been present." And he **ran his forefinger** through his almost snowy **hair.**

"My kind preserver, I want to give you some little token of my friendship at parting. Will you accept as a slight token of my dethless gratitude, 'What I know about Farming,' and two papers of lettice seed?"

I hung back, I thought of Josiah. But Horace argued with me, says he, " I respect your constancy to Josiah, but intellect—spoken or written—scorns all the barriers of sex and circumstance, and is as free to all, as the sunshine that beats down on the just and the unjust, the Liberal Republicans and the Grant party, or the married and the single." Says he, " take the book without any scruples, and as for the lettice seed, I can recommend it, I think Josiah would relish it."

Says I, " On them grounds I will accept of it, and thank you."

As we parted at the door, in the innocence of conscious rectitude, we shook hands, and says I, "Henceforth, Horace you will set up in a high chair in my mind, higher than ever before. Of course, Josiah sets first in my heart, and then his children, and then a few relations on my side, and on hisen. But next to them you will always set, for you have been weighed in the steelyards, and have been found not wantin'."

He was to agitated to speak, I was awful agitated too. Our silver mounted spectacles met each other in a last glance of noble, firm principled sadness, and so Horace and I parted away from each other.

# A SEA VOYAGE.

AFTER I left Horace, I hastened on, for I was afraid I was behind time. Bein' a large hefty woman, (my weight is 200 and 10 pounds by the steelyards now) I could not hasten as in former days when I weighed 100 pounds less. I was also encumbered with my umberell, my satchel bag, my cap box and "What I know about Farming." But I hastened on with what speed I might. But alas! my apprehensions was too true, the cars had gone. What was to be done? Betsey sat on her portmanty at the depott, lookin' so gloomy and depressted, that I knew that I could not depend on her for sukker, I must rely onto myself. There are minutes that try the sole, and show what timber it is built of. Not one trace of the wild storm of emotions that was ragin' inside of me, could be traced on my firm brow, as Betsey looked up in a gloomy way and says,

"What are we going to do now?"

No, I rose nobly to meet the occasion, and said in a voice of marbel calm, "I dont know Betsey." Then I sot down, for I was beat out. Betsey looked wild, says she, "Josiah Allen's wife I am sick of earth, the cold heartless ground looks hollow to me. I feel jest reckless enough to dare the briny deep." Says she, in a bold darin' way,

"Less go home on the canal."

The canal boat run right by our house, and though at first I hung back in my mind, thinkin' that Josiah would never consent to have me face the danger of the deep in the dead of the night, still the thought of stayin' in New York village another night made me waver. And I thought to myself, if Josiah knew jest how it was—the circumstances environin' us all round, and if he considered that my board bill would cost 3 dollars more if I staid another night, I felt that he would consent, though it seemed perilous, and almost hazardous in us. So I wavered, and wavered, Betsey see me waver, and took advantage of it, and urged me almost warmly.

But I didn't give my consent in a minute. I am one that calmly weighs any great subject or undertakin' in the ballances.

Says I' "Betsey have you considered the danger?" Says I, "The shore we was born on, may sometimes seem tame to us, but safety is there. Says I, "more freedom may be upon the deep waters, but it is a treacherous element. Says I, "I never tempted its perils in my life, only on a bridge."

"Nor I neither," says she. But she added in still more despairin' tones, "What do I care for danger? What if it is a treacherous element? What have I got to live for in this desert life?" "And then" says she, "the captain of a boat here, is mother's cousin, he would let us go cheap."

Says I in awful deep tones of principle. "*I* have got Josiah to live for—and the great cause of Right, and the children. And I feel for their sakes that I ought not to rush into danger." But agin I thought of my board bill, and agin I felt that Josiah would give his consent for me to take the voyage.

Betsey had been to the village with her father on the canal, and she knew the way, and suffice it to say, as the sun descended into his gory bed in the west, its last light shone onto Betsey and me, a settin' in the contracted cabin of the canal boat.

We were the only females on board, and if it hadn't been for Betsey's bein' his relation, we couldn't have embarked, for the bark was heavily laden. The evening after we embarked, the boat sailin' at the time under the pressure of 2 miles an hour, a storm began to come up, I didn't say nothin', but I wished I was a shore. The rain come down—the thunder roared in the distance—the wind howled at us, I felt sad. I thought of Josiah.

As the storm increased Betsey looked out of the window, and says she,

"Josiah Allen's wife we are surrounded by dangers, one of the horses has got the heaves, can you not heah him above the wild roah of the tempest? And one of them is balky, I know it." And liftin' her gloomy eyes to the ceilin' so I couldn't see much of 'em but the whites, says she, "Look at the stovepipe! see it sway in the storm, a little heavich blast will unhinge it. And what a night it would be for pirates to be abroad, and give chase to us." "But" she continued, "my soul is in unison with the wild fury of the elements. I feel like warbling one of the wild sea odes of old, and she begun to sing,

"My name is Robert Kidd,
 As I sailed, as I sailed.
 My name is Robert Kidd, as I sailed.

She sung it right through; I should say by my feelin's, it took her nigh on to an hour, though my sufferin's I know blinded me, and made my calculations of time less to be depended on than a clock. She sang it through once, and then she began it agin, she got as far the second time as this,

My name is Robert Kidd,
And so wickedly I did
As I sailed, as I sailed,
Oh! so wickedly I did
As I sailed.

The cabin was dark, only lit by one kerosene lamp, with a chimbly dark with the smoke of years. Her voice was awful; the tune was awful; I stood it as long as I could seemin'ly, and says I, in agitated tones,

"I wouldn't sing any more Betsey, if I was in your place."

Alas! better would it have been for my piece of mind, had I let her sing. For although she stopped the piece with a wild quaver that made me tremble, she spoke right up, and says she,

"My soul seems mountin' up and in sympathy with the scene. My spirit is soarin', and must have vent. Josiah Allen's wife have you any objections to my writin' a poem. I have got seven sheets of paper in my portmanty."

The spirit of my 4 fathers rose up in me and says I, firmly,

"When I come onto the deep, I come expectin' to face trouble—I am prepared for it," says I, "a few verses more or less haint a goin' to overthrow my principles."

She sot down by the table and began to take off her tow curls and frizzles, I should think by a careless estimate that there was a six quart pan full. And then she went to untwistin' her own hair, which was done up at the back side of her head in a little nubbin about as big as ½ a sweet walnut. Says she,

"I always let down my haih, and take out my teeth when I write poetry, I feel moah free and soahing in my mind." Says she in a sort of a apoligy way,

"Genious is full of excentricities, that seem strange to the world's people."

Says I, calmly "You can let down, and take out, all you want to, I can stand it."

But it was a fearful scene. It was a night never to be forgot while memory sets up on her high chair in my mind. Outside, the rain poured down, overhead on deck, the wind shrieked at the bags and boxes, threatenin' 'em with almost an instant destruction. The stove pipe that run up through the floor shook as if every blast would unjinte it, and then the thought would rise up, though I tried to put it out of my head, who would put it up again. One of the horses was balky, I knew, for I could hear the driver swear at him. And every time he swore, I thought of Josiah, and it kep him in my mind most all the time. Yes, the storm almost raved outside, and inside, a still more depressin' and fearful sight to me—Betsey Bobbet sot with her few locks streamin' down over her pale and holler cheeks, for her teeth was out, and she wrote rapidly, and I knew, jest as well as I know my name is Josiah Allen's wife, that I had got to hear 'em read. Oh! the anguish of that night! I thought of the happy people on shore, in thier safe and peaceful feather beds, and then on the treacherous element I was a ridin' on, and then I thought of Josiah. Sometimes mockin' fancy would so mock at me that I could almost fancy that I heard him snore. But no!

cold reality told me that it was only the heavey horse, or the wind a blowin' through the stove pipe, and then I would rouse up to the agonizin' thought that I was at sea, far, far from home and Josiah. And then a solemn voice would sometimes make itself heard in my sole, "Mebby you never will hear him snore agin." And then I would sithe heavily.

And the driver on the tow path would loudly curse that dangerous animal and the wind would howl 'round the boxes, and the stove pipe would rattle, and Betsey would write poetry rapidly, and I knew I had got to hear it. And so the tegus night wore away. Finally at $\frac{1}{2}$ past 2, wore out as I was with fateegue and wakefullness, Betsey ceased writin' and says she.

"It is done! I will read them to you."

I sithed so deeply that even Betsey almost trembled, and says she,

"Are you in pain, Josiah Allen's wife?"

Says I, "only in my mind."

"Wall" says she, "It is indeed a fearful time. But somehow my soul exults strangely in the perils environing us. I feel like courtin' and keepin' company with danger to night. I feel as if I could almost dare to mount that steed wildly careering along the tow path, if I only had a side saddle. I feel like rushin' into dangeh, I feel reckless to-night."

Here the driver swore fearfully, and still more apaulin' sight to me, Betsey opened her paper and commenced readin':

## BETSEY'S SEA POEM.

### STANZES, WRITTEN ON THE DEEP.

#### BY BETSEY BOBBET.

The ground seems hollow unto me;
Men's vests but mask deep perfidee;
My life has towered so hard and steep,
I seek the wild and raging deep.

Such knawing pains my soul doth rack,
That even the wild horse on the track
Doth madly prance, and snort and leap;
Welcome the horrors of the deep.

Oh, Jonesville! on that peaceful shoah,
Methinks I'll see thy towehs no moeh.
When morn wakes happy, thoughtless sheep
Betsey may slumbeh in the deep.

If far from thee my bones are doomed,
In these dark waves to be entoomed,
Mermaids I hope will o'er her weep,
Who drownded was, within the deep.

Dear Augur hopes in ruin lays;
My Ebineezah I could not raise;
Deah lost gazelles, I can but weep,
With gloomy eyes bent o'eh the deep.

One Slimpsey star, whose name is Simon,
Still twinkles faint, like a small sized diamond;
Oh, star of hope, I sithe, I weep,
Thou shinest so faint across the deep.

There was between 20 and 30 verses of 'em, but truly it is always the darkest jest before daylight, for as she was a readin' of 'em, I—a leanin' back in my chair—dropped off to sleep, and forgot my trouble. Betsey also went to sleep before she read the last of 'em. And when I waked up, the boat had stopped in front of our house, the wind had gone down, the sun was a shinin', and Josiah was comin' down to the bank. The danger was all past—Home and Josiah was mine agin. I grasped holt of his hand as he helped me get off, and in a voice tremulous with feelin's I could not control I said,

"I have got home Josiah! is breakfast ready?"

There was a tenderness in his tone, and a happy smile on his face that reminded me of the sweet days of our courtship, as he answered me in a tone almost husky with emotion.

"Yes Samantha, all but settin' the table."

AT HOME.

Says I, "I'm glad of it, for I'm dreadful hungry."

# OLD FRIENDS IN NEW GARMENTS.

IT was a lovely Monday forenoon some three or four weeks after my voyage. I was a sittin' near the open back door enjoyin' the pleasant prospect, and also washin' some new potatoes for dinner. Truly it was a fair scene. The feathered hens was a singin' in their innocent joy as they scratched the yieldin' turf after bugs and worms. Old "Hail the Day" was proudly struttin' round, standin' first on one foot and then on the other, and crowin' joyfully in his careless freedom and glee. The breezes blew sweetly from the west, and I thought with joy that my clothes on the clothes line would be ready to iron by the time I got dinner out of the way. The sun shone down out of a blue and cloudless sky, and I looked pensively at my green gages, and thought fondly how the sun was a ripenin' 'em. All nature was peaceful and serene, and my mind as I gently scraped the large fair potatoes, and thought how good they was goin' to be with the baked lamb I had got in the oven, was as peaceful and serene as the same. Suddenly I heard the gate click to and I saw old Mr. Bobbet comin' up to the house. He seemed dreadfully agitated, and I could hear him talkin' to himself. He came right into the door and took his hat off in one hand, holdin' his crooked cane in the the other and swung 'em both over his head to once, and says he,

"It's done! It's done!"

"What's done," says I droppin' my knife onto the floor.

"Betsey's gone!" shouted he, and he run out the door like a luny.

I was a most skairt to death, and remained motionless nigh onto a minute, when I heard Josiah comin' in. Little did I dream what a blow was comin' onto me. He come and stood right in front of me, and I thought at the time, he looked at me dreadful curious, but I kep on a scrapin' my potatoes, (I had got 'em most done.)

Finally all at once Josiah spoke up and says he,

"Betsey Bobbett is married."

I dropped the pan of potatoes right down onto the floor for I was as weak as a weak white cat. "Who! Josiah Allen! who! is the man?"

—"Simon Slimpsey," says he, "They was married last night—as I was comin' by the old cider mill——"

"I see all through it," says I mournfully. "He and seven or eight of his children have been sick, and Betsey would go and take care of 'em."

"Yes" says Josiah, "As I was comin' past the old cider mill——"

Says I with spirit, "It ought to be looked into, He was a helpless old man, and she has took the advantage of him." I went on warmly, for I thought of his gloomy fourbodin's, and I always felt for the oppressed and imposed upon. I had went on I presume as much as 2 minutes and a ½ when Josiah says he,

"I wouldn't take on so about it Samantha, anybody to hear you talk would think you was a perfect farrago."

Says I, "If I was a goin' to abuse my wife and call her names I would do it accordin' to grammar, you mean "virtigo" Josiah."

"Wall I said virtigo, didn't I?" Josiah never will own that he is in the wrong.

"And I didn't say you *was* a virtigo Samantha, only anybody would take you for a virtigo, that did'nt know you."

I remained almost lost in sad thoughts for pretty nigh ½ a minute, and then I says, in mournful tones,

"Have you heard any of the particulars Josiah? Have you seen any of the relatives? was the old man any more reconciled to the last?"

"Yes" says Josiah, "As I was comin' by the old cider mill—"

"Wall do for conscience sake *come* by the old cider

mill, and be done with it," says I, feelin' worried out in my mind and by the side of myself.

"How be I goin' to get by Samantha? you are so agravatin', you'll never let me finish a story peacible, and I should think it was about dinner time."

"So 'tis" says I, soothin'ly, hangin' on the teakettle, and puttin' the potatoes over the stove in the summer kitchen. For a long and arduous study of the seet has convinced me that good vittles are more healin' than oil to pour onto a mans lacerated feelin's. And the same deep study has warned me *never* to get mad at the same time Josiah does, on these 2 great philisofical laws, hangs all the harmony of married life. Then I stepped out onto the stoop agin, and says to him in calm, affectionate accents,

"What is it about the old cider mill, Josiah?"

"Nothin'" says he, "Only I met one of the first mourners—I mean one of old Slimpsey's sisters there, and she told me about it, she said that sense the Editer of the Auger was married, and sense Betsey had got back from New York she had acted like a wild critter. She seemed to think it was now or never. The awful doom of not bein' married at all, seemed to fall upon her, and craze her with wild horror. And findin' Slimpsey who was a weak sort of a man any way, and doubly weakened now by age and inflamatory rheumatism, she went and took care of him, and got the upper hand of him, made him a victim and married him, at his own house, Sunday night at half past seven."

I was so lost in sorrowful thought as Josiah continued the mournful tale, that Josiah says, in a soothin' tone,

"You ought to try to be reconciled to it Samantha, it seems to be the Lord's will that she should marry him."

"I don't believe in layin' every mean low lived thing to the Lord, Josiah, I lay this to Betsey Bobbet;" and I agin plunged down into gloomy thought, and was roused only by his concludin' words,

"Seems to me Samantha, you might have a few griddle cakes, the bread—I see this mornin'—was gettin' kinder dry."

"Mechanically I complied with his request, for my thoughts wasn't there, they was with the afflicted, and down trodden.

One week after this I was goin' up the post office steps, and I come face to face with Simon Slimpsey. He had grown 23 years older durin' the past week. But he is a shiftless, harmless critter hurtin' himself more'n any body else. He was naturally a small boned man. In the prime of his manhood he might have come up to Betsey's shoulders, but now withered by age and grief the highest hat was futile to bring him up much above her belt ribbon. He looked sad indeed, my heart bled for him. But with the instinctive delicacy inherient to my sect, I put on a jokeuler tone, and says I, as I shook hands with him,

"How do you do, Simon? I hain't seen you before, sense you was married, Simon Slimpsey."

He looked at me almost wildly in the face, and says he in a despairin' tone,

"I knew it would come to this, Miss Allen! I knew it. I told you how it would be, you know I did. She always said it was her spear to marry, I knew I should be the one, I always was the one."

"Don't she use you well, Simon Slimpsey?"

"She is pretty hard on me," says he. "I hain't had my way in anything sense the day she married me. She begun to 'hold my nose to the grindstone,' as the saying is, before we had been married 2 hours. And she hain't no housekeeper, nor cook, I have had to live on pancakes most of the time sense it took place, and they are tougher than leather; I have been most tempted to cut some out of my boot legs to see if they wouldn't be tenderer, but I never should hear the end of it, if I did. She jaws me awfully, and orders me round as if I was a dog, a yeller dog—" he added despairin'ly, " if I was a yeller dog, she couldn't seem to look down on me any more, and treat me any worse."

Says I, "I always did mistrust these wimmen that talk so much about not wantin' any rights, and clingin' and so forth. But," says I, not wantin' to run anybody to thier backs, " she thought it was her spear to marry."

"I told you," says he, in agonizin' tones, "I told

you that spear of hern would destroy me, and it has."

He looked so sorrowful that I says to him in still more jokenler tones than I had yet used, "Chirk up Simon Slimpsey, I wish you joy." I felt that he needed it indeed. He give me an awful look that was jest about half reproach, and half anguish, and I see a tear begin to flow. I turned away respectin' his feelin's. As he went down the steps slowly, I see him put his hands in his pockets, as if searchin' for his handkerchief, seemin'ly in vain. But he had on a long blue broadcloth swallow tailed coat that he was married in the first time long years ago, and as he went round the corner he took up the skirts of his coat and wiped his eyes. I said to myself with a deep sithe, "And this is woman's only spear." And the words awakened in my breast as many as 19 or 20 different emotions, and I dont know but more.

I murmured mewsin'ly to myself, "It seems to me, if I was a woman I should about as lives be a constable."

While I was still mewsin, Betsey, his wife tore down the street, in a distracted way, and paused before me.

"Have you seen my husband?" says she, "can you tell a distracted wife—have you seen her husband Simon Slimpsey?"

She looked wild, as if she feared a catastrophe, and she cried out, loosin' holt of her self control, in a firm constable like tone,

"He shall not escape me! I will telegraph to the next station house! I will have the creek dragged! the woods shall be scoured out! says she.

"Be calm, and compose yourself," says I frigidly, "Simon Simpson has gone up towards his house."

She heaved a deep sithe of content, and triumph agin brooded down upon her eyebrow as she follered on after him.

I hadn't no idee of callin' on her, I wouldn't, but the next day, Simon Slimpsey went by on his old white horse. It is a very dejected lookin' horse in the face, besides carryin' a couple of wash-boards in its sides, in the line of ribs. Thomas Jefferson says, "What gives it its mournful expression, it is mournin' for the companions of its youth." Says he, "you know Noah saved a pair of everything," and says he, "his poor companion passed away several thousand years ago." That boy worrys me, I don't know what he is comin' to. Slimpsey's old horse haint more'n 35 or 40 years old, I don't believe. They say Betsey is makin' a pale blue cambric ridin' dress, and is goin' to ride him a horse back this fall. It don't seem to me there would be much fun in it, he is so lame, besides havin' a habit of fallin' frequently with the blind staggers; howsomever its none of my business.

But as I was a sayin' I stood silently in the door, to see old Slimpsey go by a horseback, and I thought to myself as I pensively turned out my tea grounds,

(I was a gettin' dinner) how much—how much it looks like a night mare that has broke out of its lawful night pastures, and is runnin' away with a pale and harassed victim. So haggard and melancholy did they both look. And I sithed. I had'nt much more'n got through sithin', when he rode up, and says he,

"The seventh boy is worse, and the twin girls are took down with it, it would be a melankoly pleasure Miss Allen if you could go up." I went.

Betsey had got the most of 'em to sleep, and was settin' between a few cradles, and trundle beds, and high chairs all filled with measles, and a few mumps. Betsey's teeth was out, and her tow frizzles lay on the table with a lot of paper—so I mistrusted she had been writin' a poem. But she was now engaged in mendin' a pair of pantaloons, the 8th pair—she told me—she had mended that day, for Simon Slimpsy was a poor man, and couldn't afford to buy new ones. They was a hard and mournful lookin' pair, and says I to her—in a tone in which pity and contempt was blended about half and half—

"Betsey are you happy?"

"I am at rest," says she, "more at rest than I have been for years."

"Are you happy?" says I, lookin' keenly at her.

"I feel real dignified," says she, "There isn't no use in a woman trying to be dignified till she is married, for she can't. I have tried it and I know. I can truly say Josiah Allen's wife, that I never knew what dignity was, until one week ago last Sunday night at half past seven in the evenin'," says she, turnin' over the pantaloons, and attactin' a ghastly hole of about 7 by 9 dimensions in the left knee.

I sot silently in my chair like a statute, while she remarked thus, and as she paused, I says to her agin, fixing my mild but stern grey eyes upon her weary form, bendin' over the dilapitated folds of the 8th.

"Are you happy Betsey?"

"I have got something to lean on," says she.

I thought of the fragile form bendin' over the lean and haggard horse, and totterin' away, withered by age and grief, in the swallow tailed coat, and says I in a pityin' accent,

"Dont lean too hard Betsey."

"Why?" says she.

Says I, in a kind of a blind way, "You may be sorry if you do," and then I says to her in clear and piercin' accents these words,

"Do you love your husband Betsey?"

"I dont think love is necessary," says she, "I am married, which is enough to satisfy any woman who is more or less reasonable, that is the main and important thing, and as I have said, love and respect, and so forth are minors as—

"Miners!" says I in a tone of deep indignity, "Miners! Betsey Bobbet—"

"Mrs Betsey Bobbet Slimpsey," says she correctin' of me proudly, as she attacted another mournful lookin' hole as big as my two hands.

"Well! Betsey Slimpsey!" says I, beginnin' agin, and wavin' my right hand in a eloquent wave, "There hain't no more beautiful sight on earth than to see two human soles, out of pure love to each other, gently approachin' each other, as if they must. And at last all thier hopes and thoughts, and affections runnin' in together, so you can't seperate 'em nohow, jest like two drops of rain water, in a mornin' glory blow. And to see 'em nestlin' there, not carin' for nobody outside the blow, contented and bound up in each other, till the sun evaporates 'em, (as it were) and draws 'em up together into the heaven, not seperatin' of 'em up there—why such a marriage as that is a sight that does men and angels good to look at. But when a woman sells herself, swaps her purity, her self respect, her truth, and her sole, for barter of any kind, such as a house and lot, a few thousand dollars, the name of bein' married, a horse and buggy, some jewellry, and etcetery, and not only sells herself, but worse than the Turk wimmen goes round herself, huntin' up a buyer, crazy, wild eyed, afraid she won't find none—when she does find one, suppose she does have a minister for salesman, my contempt for that female is unmitigable."

Betsey still looked so wrapped up in dignity, as she bravely attacted the seat of another pair of trousers, that it fairly made me mad. Insted of that proud and triumphant mean I wanted her to look some stricken, and I resumed in a tone of indignaty, almost burnin' enough to set fire to her apron,

"Nor I don't want these wimmen that have sold themselves for a certificate with a man's name on it— I don't want to hear 'em talk about infamy; haint they infamous themselves? What have they done different from these other bad wimmen, only they have got a stiddy place, and a little better wages, such as respectability in the eyes of fools and etcetery. Do you suppose that a woman standin' up in front of a minister and tellin' a few pesky lies, such as, 'I promise to love a man I hate, and respect a man that hain't respectable, and honor and obey a man I calculate to make toe the mark'—do you suppose these few lies makes her any purer in the eyes of God, than if she had sold herself without tellin' 'em, as the other infamous wimmen did? Not any. Marriage is like baptism, as I have said more'n a hundred times, you have got to have the inward grace and the outward form to make it lawful and right. What good does the water do, if your sole haint baptised with the love of God? It haint no better than fallin' into the creek."

I paused, spotted in the face from conflictin' emotions, and Betsey begun in a haughty triumphant tone,

"Womans speak—"

Which words and tone combined with recollections of the aged sufferer in the blue swallow tailed coat, so worked on my indignation, that I walked out of the house without listenin' to another word, and put on my bunnet out in the door yard.

But I hollered back to her from the bars—for Josiah Allen's wife haint one to desert duty in any crisis—"that the four youngest boys ought to be sweat, and take some saffern tea, and I should give the five girls, and the twins, some catnip, and I'd let the rest of 'em be, till the docter come."

I haint seen Betsey since, for she is havin' a hard time of it. She has to work like a dog. For Simon Slimpsey bein' so poor, and not bein' no calculator, it makes it hard for 'em to get along. And the old man seems to have lost what little energy he had, since he was married, Betsey is so hard on him. He has the horrors awfully. Betsey takes in work, but they have a hard time to get along. Miss Gowdey says that Betsey told her that she didn't mind workin' so hard, but she did hate to give up writin' poetry, but she didn't get no time for it." So as is jenerally the case, a great good to the world has come out of her sufferin'.

I guess she haint wrote but one piece sence she was married and they was wrote I suppose the day I ketched her with her teeth out, for they come out in the next week's Gimlet, for just as quick as the Editor of the Anger was married, Betsey changed her politix and wrote agin as formally for the Gimlet.

The following are some of the verses she wrote:

## I AM MARRIED NOW.

### A Him of Victory.

#### BY MRS. BETSEY SLIMPSEY *knee* BOBBET.

Fate, I defy thee! I have vanquished thee, old maid.
Dost ask why thus, this proud triumphant brow?
I answer thee, old Fate, with loud and joyful burst
Of blissful laughteh, I am married now!

Once grief did rave about my lonely head;
Once I did droop, as droops a drooping willow bough;
Once I did tune my liah to doleful strains;
'Tis past! 'tis past my soul! I am married now!

Then, sneering, venomed darts pierced my lone, lone heart;
Then, mocking married fingers dragged me low,
But now I tune my liah to sweet extatic strains,
My teahs have all been shed, I am married now!

No gossip lean can wound me by her speech,
I, no humilitatin' neveh more shall know;
Sorrow, stand off! I am beyond thy ghastly reach,
For Mrs. Betsey Slimpsey (formerly Bobbet) is married now!

Oh, mournful past, when I in Ingun file
Climbed single life's, bleak, rocky, mounten's brow,
Blest lot! that unto wedlock's glorious glade
Hath led me. Betsey's married now!

Oh female hearts with anxious longings stirred,
Cry Ho! for wimmen's speah, and seal it with a vow,
Take Mrs. Betsey Bobbet Slimpsey's word
That thou shalt triumph! *I* am married now!

Yes, Betsey's married! sweet to meditate upon it,
To tune my happy liah with haughty, laughing brow
To these sweet, glorious words, the burden of my sonnet,
That Mrs. Betsey Bobbet Slimpsey's married now!

# HORACE AND JOSIAH.

WHEN the news come to me that Horace Greely was dead I almost cried. The tears did just run down my face like rain-water, I don't know when I have come nearer cryin' than I did then. And my first thought was, they have tried awful hard to keep him out of the White House, but he has got into one whiter than any they have got in Washington, D. C. And then my very next thought was, Josiah Allen's wife did you say anything to hurt that man's feelin's, when you was a tryin' to influence him on your tower?

I believe if folks would only realize how every harsh word, and cold look they stab lovin' hearts with, would just turn round like bayonets, and pierce their own heart in a time like this—they would be more careful how they handled 'em. But glad enough was I to think that I didn't say a hard word to him, but had freed my mind, and told him jest how good I thought he was, and how much he had done for the Black African, and the Human Race, before it was too late. Glad enough was I that I didn't wait till that noble heart was cold and lifeless, and couldn't be pained by unkindness, or made gladder by sympathy, before I gin him mine.

But in the time of trouble, the love that had been his best reward for all the successes of his hard workin' life, had gone from him. And I know jest how that great heart ached for that love and sympathy. I know jest how poor the praise of the world would have looked to him, if he couldn't have seen it a shinin' through them lovin' eyes—and how hard it was for him to bear its blame alone. Tired out, defeated the world called him, but he only had to fold his hands, and shet his eyes up and he was crowned with success in that world where He, who was once rejected by a majority, crowned with thorns of earthly defeat waits now to give the crown of Eternal Repose to all true souls, all the weary warriors on life's battle field who give their lives for the right. And it seemed so kinder beautiful too, to think that before she he loved so, hardly had time to feel strange in them "many mansions," he was with her agin, and they could keep house together all through Eternity.

Yet,—though as I say, I don't know when I have come so near cryin' as I did then—I said to myself as I wiped my eyes on my apron, I wouldn't call him back from that happy rest he had earnt so well if I could.

But there are other things that are worrysome to me, and make me a sight of trouble. It was a day or 2 after this, and I was settin' alone, for Josiah had gone to mill, and Thomas Jefferson and Maggy Snow and Tirzah Ann and Whitfield Minkley had gone a slay ridin',' (them two affairs is in a flourishin' condition and it is *very* aggreeable to Josiah and me, though I make no matches, nor break none—or that is, I don't make none, only by talkin' in a encouragin' manner, nor break none only with thoroughwert in a mild way.

I sot all alone, a cuttin' carpet rags, and a musin sadly. Victory in jail! And though I felt that she richly deserved it, and I should liked to have shut her up myself in our suller way, for darin' to slander Beecher, still to me who knows her sect so well, it seemed kinder hard that a woman should be where she couldn't go a visatin'. And then to think the good talkin' to, I give her when I was on my tower hadn't ammounted to nothin', seemin'ly. I wasn't sorry I had labored with her—not a mite, I had did my duty anyway. And I knew jest as well as I know that my name was formally Smith, that when anybody is a workin' in the Cause of Right, they hadn't ought to be discouraged if they didn't get their pay down, for you can't sow your seeds and pick your posy's the same day anyway. And I know that great idees was enough sight harder to get rooted and a growin' than the Century plant, and that takes a hundred years for it to blow out.

I know all this, but human nater gets kinder tired a waitin', and there seems no end to the snows that lay between us and that summer that all earnest souls are a workin' for. And then I want my sect to do right,—I want 'em to be real respectable, and I felt that take Victory all together she wasn't a orniment to it. I thought of my sect, and then I thought of Victory, and then I sithed. Beecher a bein' lied about, Tilton ditto and the same, for you see *I* don't nor won't believe what Victory says against 'em, although they don't come out and deny the truth of it, either of 'em, just to satisfy some folks who say that they ought to. Miss Anthony havin' a hard tussle of it at Rochester.

Whitfield Minkley had told me too that day that Miss Aster didn't keep tavern herself, and there I had had all my trouble about her for nothin', demeanin' myself by offerin' to wash dishes for—I know not who. And to think that Jonothan Beans'es ex-wife should have deceived me so, when I befriended her so much when she first went to grass. And then when I thought how all the good advice I had given Victory hadn't done her no good, and how Mr. Greely had died, before the seeds I sowed in his bosom on the great question of Wimmen's Rights had sprouted and brought forth fruit, when I see my tower had been in vain, say nothin' of the money it cost, oh! how holler the world looked to me, it almost seemed as if it would break in and let me through, rockin' chair and all.

As I sot there a mewsin' over it, and a cuttin' my rags, I almost made up my mind that I would have the dark stripe in my carpet black as a coal, the whole on it, a sort of mournin' stripe. But better feelin's got up inside of my mind, and I felt that I would put in my but'nut color rather than waste it.

Yet oh how holler and onstiddy everything looked to me; who could I trust, whose apron string could I cling to, without expectin' it would break off short with me? For pretty nigh 2 minutes and a half, I had the horrors almost as bad as Simon Slimpsey, (he has 'em now every day stiddy, Betsey is so hard on him), but oh how sweetly in that solemn time there came to me the thought of Josiah. Yes, on that worrysome time I can truly say that Josiah Allen was my theme, and I thought to myself, there may be handsomer men than he is, and men that weigh more by the steelyards, but there hain't one to be found that has heftier morals, or more well seasoned principles than he has. Yes, Josiah Allen was my theme, I felt that I could trust my Josiah. I guess I had got mewsin' agin on jails and wickedness, and so 4th, for all of a sudden the thought knocked aginst my heart,

"What if Josiah Allen should go to cuttin' up, and behavin'?"

I wouldn't let the thought in, I ordered it out. But it kep' a hangin' round,—

"What if your Josiah should go to cuttin' up?"

I argued with it; says I to myself, I guess I know Josiah Allen, a likelier man never trod shoe leather. I know him like a book.

But then think'es I—what strange critters men and wimmin be. Now you may live with one for years, and think you know every crook and turn in that critter's mind, jest like a book; when lo! and behold! all of a sudden a leaf will be turned over, that had been glued together by some circumstance or other, and there will be readin' that you never set eyes on before. Sometimes it is in an unknown tongue—sometimes it is good readin', and then again, it is bad. Oh how gloomy and depressted I was. But Josiah Allen's wife haint one to give up to the horrers without a tussle, and though inwardly so tosted about, I rose up and with a brow of calm, I sot my basket of carpet rags behind the door, and quietly put on the tea-kettle, for it was about time for Josiah to come.

Then I looked round to see if there was anything I could do to make it look more pleasant than it did for Josiah Allen when he came home cold and tired from the Jonesville mill. It never was my way to stand stun still in the middle of the floor and smile at him from half to three-quarters of an hour. Yet it was always my idee that if a woman can't make home the pleasantest spot in the world for her husband, she needn't complain if he won't stay there any more than he can help. I believe there wouldn't be so many men a meanderin' off nights into grog shops, and all sorts of wickedness, if they had a bright home and a cheerful companion to draw 'em back, (not but what men have to be corrected occasionally, I have to correct Josiah every little while.) But good land! It is all I can do to get Josiah Allen and Thomas Jefferson out of the house long enough to mop.

I looked round the room, as I said, but not a thing did I see that I could alter for the better; it was slick as a pin. The painted floor was a shinin' like yaller glass, (I had mopped jest before dinner.) The braided mats, mostly red and green, was a layin' smooth and clean in front of the looking-glass, and before the stove, and table. Two or three pictures, that Thomas Jefferson had framed, hung up aginst the wall, which was papered with a light colored buff ground work with a red rose on it. The lounge and two or three rockin' chairs was cushioned with handsome copper plate. And Tirzah Ann had got a hangin' basket of ivy on the west winder that made that winder look like summer. I'll bet her canary hangin' there in the thickest of the green leaves, thought it was summer, he sang like it. The stove hearth shone like a silver dollar, and there was a bright fire, and in a minute the teakettle began to sing most as loud as Whitey, that is her canary's name. (I mistrust she named it in that kinder underhanded way, after Whitfield Minkley—though I never let her know I mistrusted it, but I never could think of any other earthly reason why she should call it Whitey, for it is as yaller as any goslin' I ever laid eyes on.)

I felt that I couldn't alter a thing round the house for the better. But as I happened to glance up into the lookin'-glass, I see that although I looked well, my hair was slick and I had on a clean gingham dress, my brown and black plaid, still I felt that if I should pin on one of Tirzah Ann's bows that lay on the little shelf under the lookin'-glass I might look more cheerful and pleasant in the eyes of my companion Josiah. I haint made a practice of wearin' bows sense I jined the meetin'-house. And then agin I felt that I was too old to wear 'em. Not that I felt bad about growin' old. If it was best for us to have summer all the year round, I know we should have it. As I have said to Josiah

Allen more'n once when he got kinder down hearted, says I, Josiah Allen look up where the stars are shinin' and tell me if you think that with all them countless worlds, with all that wealth in His hands, and His lovin' heart, the Lord begruches anything that is for His children's good. No! I am willin' to take God's year as it comes, summer and winter.

And then do you s'pose I would if I could by turning my hand over, go back into my youth agin, and leave Josiah part way down hill alone? No! the sunshine and the mornin' are on the other side of the hill, and we are goin' down into the shadders, my pardner Josiah and me. But we will go like Mr. and Mrs. Joseph John, that Tirzah Ann sings about—

>  "Hand in hand we'll go
>  And we'll sleep together at the foot."

knowing that beyond them shadders is the sunshine of God's Great Mornin'.

As I said, I dont make a practice of wearin' bows, and this bein' fire red, I should have felt a awful backslidin' feelin' about wearin' it, if I hadn't felt that principle was upholdin' me.

Then I drawed out the table, and put on a clean white table-cloth, and begun to set it. I had some good bread and butter, I had baked that day, and my bread was white as snow, and light as day, some canned peaches, and some thin slices of ham as pink as a rose, and a strawberry pie,—one of my cans had bust that day, and I made 'em up into pies. And then I brought up some of my very best cake, such as I keep for company—fruit cake, and delicate cake. And then after I had put on a great piece of white honey in a glass dish, and some cheese that was like cream for richness, the table looked well.

I had got the table all set, and had jest opened the door to see if he was a comin', when lo! and behold! there he stood on the door-step—he had come and put his horses out before I see him. He looked awful depressted, and before he got the snow half offen his boots, says he:

"That new whip I bought the other day is gone Samantha. Some feller stole it while I was gettin' my grist ground."

Says I, "Josiah I have been a mewsin' on the onstiddiness, and wickedness of the world all day, and now that whip is gone. What is the world a comin' to, Josiah Allen?"

Josiah is a man that don't say much, but things wear on him. His face looked several inches longer than it usially did, and he answered in a awful depressted tone:

"I don't know, Samantha, but I do know, that I am as hungry as a bear."

"Wall," says I, soothingly, "I thought you would be, supper's all on the table."

He stepped in, and the very minute that man ketched sight of that cheerful room, and that supper table, that man smiled. And it wasn't a sickly, deathly smile either, it was a smile of deep inward joy and contentment. And says he in a sweet tone, "it seems to me you have got a awful good supper to-night, Semantha."

As I see that smile, and looked into that honest beamin' face, I jest turned out them gloomy forebodin's about him, out of my heart, the whole caboodle of 'em, and shet the door in their faces. But I controlled my voice, till it sounded like a perfect stranger to me, and says I :

"Don't I always get good suppers, Josiah Allen?"

"Yes," says he, "and good dinners and breakfess'es, too. I will say this for you, Samantha, there haint a better cook in Jonesville, than you be, nor a woman that makes a pleasanter home." And he went on placidly, as he stood there with his back to the fire a warmin' him, a lookin' serenely round that bright warm room, and ont' that supper table.

"There haint no place quite so good as home, is there, Samantha? haint supper about ready?"

Says I, firmly, "The Cause of Right, and the Good of the Human Race will ever be dear to the soul of her who who was formally Samantha Smith. But at the same time that don't hender me from thinkin' a sight of my home, and from gettin' good suppers. It

THE PLEASANT SUITE.

will be ready, Josiah, jest as quick as the tea is steeped, I didn't want to make it till you come, for bilein' jest spiles that last tea you got," and I went on in tones as firm as Plymouth Rock, yet as tender as a spring chicken.

"As I have said more'n a hundred times, if it is spelt right there haint another such a word as home in the English language. The French can't spell it at all, and in my opinion that is jest what makes 'em so light minded and onstiddy. If it is spelt wrong, as in the case of Bobbet and Slimpsey, it means the horrors, and the very worst kinds of discomfort and misery. In fact love is the only school-master, that can put out that word worth a cent. And if it is put out by him, and spelt, for instance, by a couple who have loved each other for goin' on fifteen years, with a firm and almost cast iron affection, why it stands for peace and rest and comfort, and is the plainest picture God has give us below, kinder as we put painted pictures in children's story books, of that great Home above, where the colors won't never rub off of the picture, and the peace and the rest are everlasting."

I had been real eloquent, I knew it, and Josiah knew it, for that man looked awful kinder earnest and serene like. He was silent for mebby half or three quarters of a minute, and then he said in calm, gentle tones:

"I guess I'll carry the grist up stairs before supper, Samantha, and have it done with."

There haint a lazy hair in that man's head, and for that matter there haint many of any kind, either smart or shiftless, he grows bald every day, not that I blame him for it.

He came down stairs, and we sot down to the table, happy as a king and queen, for all the old world was a caperin' and cuttin' up as if it would go crazy. The little blackslidin' feelin' about wearin' that fire red bow died away too, as ever and anon, and I don't know but oftener, I would look up and ketch the eye of my companion Josiah bent on me in a pleasant and sort of a admirin' way. That bow was becomin' to me I knew. For as Josiah passed me his cup for his second cup of tea, (no dishwatery stuff, I can tell you) he says:*

"I don't see what makes you look so young and handsome, to-night, Samantha, I believe I shall have to go to courtin' you over agin."

And I answered him in the same aggreable accents, "I don't know as the law could touch you for it Josiah if you did."

---

* See Frontispiece.

THE END.

www.ingramcontent.com/pod-product-compliance
Lightning Source LLC
Chambersburg PA
CBHW020535300426
44111CB00008B/668